SCIENCE FICTION

This is a volume in the
Arno Press collection

SCIENCE FICTION

ADVISORY EDITORS

R. Reginald

Douglas Menville

See last pages of this volume
for a complete list of titles

VISIONS

OF

TOMORROW

Six Journeys

from

Outer to Inner

Space

David Samuelson

ARNO PRESS

A New York Times Company

New York — 1975

Reprint Edition 1974 by Arno Press Inc.

Copyright © 1969 by David Norman Samuelson

Reprinted by permission of David Samuelson

SCIENCE FICTION
ISBN for complete set: 0-405-06270-2
See last pages of this volume for titles.

Publisher's Note: This book was
reprinted from the best available copy.

Manufactured in the United States of America

———◆———

Library of Congress Cataloging in Publication Data

Samuelson, David.
    Visions of tomorrow.

    Reprint of the author's thesis presented in 1969
to the University of Southern California under title:
Studies in the contemporary American and British
science fiction novel.
    Includes bibliographies.
    1. Science fiction, American--History and criticism.
2. Science fiction, English--History and criticism.
I. Title.
PS374.S35S2 1974   823'.0876   74-16519
ISBN 0-405-06334-2

FOREWORD

Completed in 1968, this work was the first large-scale critical study of post-World War II science fiction, and the first extended and detailed examination of individual science fiction novels. As a pioneer work, it presumably will be superseded, although it has not been in the almost six years that have passed. Although other critical volumes on science fiction have been published, they have been cursory surveys of briefly described trends and attitudes, or rearrangements of literary history as viewed from particular perspectives.[1] As such, they have repeated the same mistakes, in my estimation, as their predecessors, in oversimplifying science fiction as fantasy, myth, sociology, mass cultural phenomena, or the popularization of scientific ideas. An individual work of science fiction may of course be any or all of these, but it is only if we read it as literature, that we will find which of these categories are appropriate, let alone determine the work's success. And to study a verbal composition as literature means that we must pay attention to details, of character and convention, of style and symbolism, into which each of the other categories can be resolved.

Since so much of what is published as science fiction is little more than simple-minded fluff, sensational fantasy intended only for the lowest common denominators of mass market appeal, it may appear that I am overemphasizing the view of science fiction as literature. If "Literature" means only The Great Books, then of course I have, for no science fiction novel that I have read compares favorably with the classics on their own terms. But those terms, compelling though they may be for the vast majority of humanists, determined to preserve what is good of the past (and thus to serve both ends of a self-fulfilling prophecy of cultural continuity), are not the only terms to be applied to science fiction, since they largely ignore the other considerations mentioned above. I am not at all sure that I have found the right balance between intrinsic (literary) and extrinsic (extra-literary) concerns in my study, but I am quite certain that few other scholars have even tried.

Balance, however, is probably a key word for describing this book. In writing a dissertation, I had to keep in mind the varying kinds of expertise represented on my doctoral committee, as well as the committee members' relative lack of background in my subject. But with a general audience also in mind, I strove to avoid the deadening prose and preoccupation with esoteric trivia that are the bane of so many scholarly works, defining the negative sense of the word "academic." In shying away from the kind of adulation with which many science fiction fans approach their reading, I did not wish to sink into purely destructive attacks on the shallowness of ineptitude of journeyman writers. Nor, in trying to avoid the shallowness of a broad survey, did I want to get involved in a kind of critical overkill, by making too much of too little. The results may in fact be too safe, because I do not generalize enough for some readers, but this study does at least manage to avoid the timidity of the traditional bio-bibliographical essay.[2] Six novels are by no means a wide enough selection for any fully meaningful generalizations about science fiction as a whole, but neither would twelve be; with each expansion, there would have to be an enlarging of the book beyond reasonable bounds, a diminution of each work studied, or a still more uneasy compromise.

If I were to revise the book now, after more than five years of teaching, talking and writing about science fiction, I might well reduce the size of each critique, and make some other adjustments, too; indeed, in the case of the Clarke critique (chapter three), I have already done so.[3] I don't believe that I would change chapter one very much; as it stands, it provides the best brief introduction to the genre available anywhere. The part which bothers me the most is chapter two, with its insistence on seeing science (or technology) as the core of science fiction. Although this is true for much of science fiction, and a case can be made for most good science fiction that some science fictional idea is directly or indirectly involved, it would not be fair to say that all science fiction proceeds outward from such a core.[4] To be sure, I allow room in this discussion for the less "pure" varieties of the form, but I fail to indicate in what ways other kernels or nuggets could serve as starters for the eventual pearl. An examination of different kinds of science fiction, distinguished by their central purposes, and of various approaches to individual works of science fiction, is in order, as I suggest in chapter nine. Such a study will necessarily involve many works I have been unable to cover here, with a concentration less on single works, and more on elements of literature.[5]

The present volume might never have been contemplated, were it not for the example of Professor Thomas Dean Clareson's 1956 dissertation on science fiction at Penn State, and his unremitting efforts, through *Extrapolation,* the Modern Language Association seminar on science fiction, and the Science Fiction Research Association, to make the study of science fiction respectable. This work certainly would not have been completed without the aid of my wife, Marilee, and of Professor David H. Malone, my dissertation advisory at the University of Southern California, who took the time to become familiar with a subject with which he was none too comfortable, and to keep me within the bounds of scholarly acceptability. I also wish to take this opportunity to thank the other members of my committee, Professor Norma Lorre Goodrich and Professor Edward Phinney, for their tolerance, interest, and assistance.

Newport Beach, California
September 1, 1974

NOTES

[1] Brian W. Aldiss, *Billion Year Spree: The True History of Science Fiction* (Garden City: Doubleday, 1973); James E. Gunn, *Alternate Worlds* (due for publication 1974); David Ketterer, *New Worlds for Old: The Apocalyptic Imagination. Science Fiction, and American Literature* (Garden City: Doubleday Anchor, 1974); Alexei and Cory Panshin, *The World Beyond the Hill* (due for publication 1974; draft portions have been published in *Amazing Science Fiction);* Robert W. Philmus, *Into the Unknown; The Evolution of Science Fiction from Francis Godwin to H. G. Wells* (Berkeley and Los Angeles; University of California Press, 1970); Lois and Stephen Rose, *The Shattered Ring: Science Fiction and the Quest for Meaning* (Richmond, Virginia: John Knox, 1970); Donald A. Wollheim, *The Universe Makers: Science Fiction Today* (New York: Harper and Row, 1971). There are also handbooks of science fiction available, of varying quality, and any number of text anthologies for schools with a minimum of criticism. In addition, there are critical works by foreign authors which I have not yet been able to obtain for study, by Stanislaw Lem (Polish), Franz Rottensteiner (in English), Jacques Sadoul, Jacques Van Herp, and Pierre Versins (in French).

[2] Compare my "The Frontier Worlds of Robert A. Heinlein," in *The Worlds of Science Fiction,* ed. Thomas D. Clareson (due for publication by early 1975).

[3] "Clarke's *Childhood's End:* A Median Stage of Adolescence?" *Science Fiction Studies,* I:1 (Spring, 1973), 4-17.

[4] I have already recanted to some extent in my 1973 MLA talk, due for publication as "The Spinning Galaxy: A Shift in Perspective on Magazine Science Fiction," *Extrapolation* XVI:1 (December, 1974).

[5] See for example my essay on literary modernism in two novels not covered in this volume, "New Wave, Old Ocean; A Comparative Study of Novels by Brunner and Delany," *Extrapolation* XV:1 (December, 1973), 75-96. From another angle, I expect to publish early in 1975 a collection of essays emerging from the 1974 MLA seminar on science fiction, the topic of which is "Science Fiction and Future Studies: The Usefulness of Literature."

TABLE OF CONTENTS

INTRODUCTION

This study is primarily an attempt to place and evaluate six novels representative of American and British science fiction in the period following World War II. To understand the goals and achievements of these works, however, the reader must have some idea of what science fiction is and how it relates to other kinds of literature. The term "science fiction" is rather nebulous and the concepts for which it stands are somewhat controversial. Even the definition of the term is fairly elaborate, and the reader, in order to have a clear grasp of this definition, requires considerable background. Therefore, these six readings are preceded by two chapters of a more general nature.

Chapter I discusses how science fiction emerged from its historical antecedents, how it developed as a specialized category of popular literature, and how it has progressed, more or less in isolation, to a point where it appears ready to return to the main stream of literature.

Chapter II explores chiefly the ways in which science fiction differs from its historical antecedents and from other literature contemporary with it. The difference

1

is seen to be due largely to the fusing together of
science, fantasy, and the conventions of popular literature,
into a kind of science fictional cosmology. As a definition emerges from these considerations, it can be seen that
there is much in science fiction which alienates many
potential readers, which may blind them to individual
achievements in the genre, and which has set up obstacles
to their acceptance of its bid to rejoin the main stream.

With this information in hand, the reader can then
follow the argument of the succeeding chapters, III through
VIII, not only as it relates to a novel's literary worth,
but also as it relates to the novelist's achievement in the
genre, the conventions of which he has accepted. For each
book, the relation of the book to the author's other works
is taken into account, as is the relation between his use
of certain themes and techniques and the use made of them
by other writers. The primary purpose of each examination,
however, is an analysis and evaluation of one particular
novel, a close reading which involves matters of form,
style, imagery, symbolism, theme, and philosophical content
as they relate to the success of this particular book, not
merely to its representative quality.

Following these readings, Chapter IX then offers
some general inferences regarding the similarities and
dissimilarities found in these novels, along with some

comments concerning. their relative failure and success as science fiction and as literature, concluding with some brief remarks on the future of science fiction and of science fiction studies.

CHAPTER I

HISTORICAL OVERVIEW

As an historical category, science fiction is
generally taken to mean one of two things, a body of literature reflecting the impact of "science" on man, dating
back to the earliest examples of story-telling, or a
commercial publishing category aimed at a specialized
audience, dating back to the founding of the first American
science fiction magazine in 1926.

Students of literature seem to emphasize the continuity of the present with the past in science fiction.
Marjorie Nicholson and Roger Lancelyn Green, for example,
have written about the persistent motif of the voyage into
space, beginning their studies with Lucian and ending with
C. S. Lewis.[1] Numerous books have been written on the
history of the utopia, from Plato to the present day,
sometimes stressing the increasingly important role of
science in making these dreams and/or nightmares not only

---

[1]Marjorie Hope Nicolson, Voyages to the Moon
(New York, 1948); Roger Lancelyn Green, Into Other Worlds:
Space-Flight in Fiction, from Lucian to Lewis (London,
1958).

4

more realistic as literature but also possible in reality.[2]
Historians of the Gothic novel, of the supernatural and the
marvelous in literature, and of the relations between
science and literature have also contributed to our knowledge of science fiction before the twentieth century.[3] Few
of these books were written from the standpoint of science
fiction, of course, and in most of them the sense of continuity does not extend to the commercial specialty first
called "science fiction" in the 1930s.

Studies oriented more towards modern science fiction
also tend to cite historical antecedents. J. O. Bailey
begins the historical first half of his pioneering study
with a consideration of "scientific fiction before 1817,"
his earliest reference being to More's Utopia (1515-6).[4]
Sam Moskowitz, a long-time "fan" and amateur scholar of
science fiction, cites Plato and even Homer as significant

---

[2]See especially Nell Eurich, Science in Utopia:
A Mighty Design (Cambridge, Massachusetts, 1967); Richard
Gerber, Utopian Fantasy (London, 1955); Raymond Ruyer,
L'Utopie et les utopies (Paris, 1955).

[3]For an example of each, see: Montague Summers,
The Gothic Quest: A History of the Gothic Novel (London,
[1938]); Dorothy Scarborough, The Supernatural in Modern
English Fiction (New York and London, 1917); H[ubert]
Matthey, Essai sur le merveilleux danx la littérature
française depuis 1800 (diss. Lausanne, 1915); Robert Fath,
L'Influence de la science sur la littérature française dans
la seconde moitié 19ᵉ siécle (diss. Lausanne, 1901).

[4]J. O. Bailey, Pilgrims through Space and Time:
Trends and Patterns in Scientific and Utopian Fiction
(New York, 1947).

ancestors, although he begins his study proper with Cyrano de Bergerac.[5] The surveys by Kingsley Amis and the British astronomer Patrick A. Moore also give some cursory attention to the venerable ancestry of science fiction, more or less as a way of establishing its credentials.[6] One study, by the German scholar Martin Schwonke, rather thoroughly documents the continuity of utopian elements from Plato to the 1950s, including magazine science fiction, in its consideration of twentieth century literature.[7] Thomas Dean Clareson, now editor of the newsletter of the Conference on Science Fiction of the Modern Language Association, stresses in his study of American science fiction at the turn of this century the continuity of fantasy, and within fantasy of "extrapolation," a term in popular use within the science fiction community:

> Extrapolation from the known and accepted . . . is
> the basic method of science fiction. It is not of
> recent innovation. For as each field of science has
> developed and provided material provocative to the

---

[5]Sam Moskowitz, Explorers of the Infinite: Shapers of Science Fiction (Cleveland and New York, 1963).

[6]Kingsley Amis, New Maps of Hell: A Survey of Science Fiction (London, 1961); Patrick A. Moore, Science and Fiction (London, 1957).

[7]Martin Schwonke, Vom Staatsroman zur Science Fiction, in Göttinger Abhandlungen zur Soziologie, 2 (Stuttgart, 1957). Ruyer (above, note 2) also comments on the similarity and continuity between science fiction and utopia, but Schwonke's thesis is disputed by Hans-Jürgen Krysmanski, Die utopische Methode, in Dortmunder Schriften zur Sozialforschung, 21 (Köln and Opladen, 1963), pp. 89-91.

imagination, <u>writers</u> <u>have</u> <u>used</u> <u>that</u> <u>material</u> <u>in</u>
<u>their</u> <u>stories</u>. . . .

> If there is to be a logical pattern to the
> definition of science fiction so that its emergence
> and development can be studied, the basic premise
> must be that the genre may exist in any historical
> period if the stories to be so named use as a point
> of departure a fact or theory accepted as scientif-
> ically true, or possible, at the time of the story's
> composition.[8]

Given such a basic premise, one could so modify the meaning

of science as to make myths and folktales of ancient and

primitive peoples into examples of science fiction, illus-

trating man's recognition of nature and his first "fictions"

of order and system, as Anton Lampa suggested back in

1919.[9] But Clareson, despite the implications in his defi-

nition, maintains that science fiction really got its start

in the nineteenth century when, as others have indicated,

science and technology began to play a larger role in

Gothic and utopian fantasies and imaginary voyages.

"Science" has perhaps never been wholly absent from

the conception of utopia. Will Durant suggests that Plato

was dabbling with eugenics and psychoanalysis as well as

political science in the <u>Republic</u>, and the Greek philosopher

was obviously interested in showing the effect on man of a

-----

[8]Thomas Dean Clareson, "The Emergence of American
Science Fiction: 1880-1915," unpubl. diss. (Pennsylvania,
1956), pp. 12-13.

[9]Anton Lampa, <u>Das naturwissenschaftliche Märchen</u>
(Reichenburg, 1919).

"scientifically" organized society.[10] The Renaissance
utopias of More and Bacon, Andrae and Campanella all
describe technological innovations not yet a part of their
authors' societies, in addition to fictionalizing an ideal
state.[11] And it was in the eighteenth century that the
first anti-utopia, satirizing science (Swift's "Voyage to
Laputa," in Gulliver's Travels, 1726), and the first utopia
set in the future (Sebastian Mercier's L'An 2440, 1770)
appeared. But by the last half of the nineteenth century,
utopia was generally located in the future, to be brought
about by scientific thinking and with full utilization of
technological devices. And the possibility of man's being
dominated by the machine and by scientific order was
already seen as probable and frightening enough to provoke
other authors into writing anti-scientific utopias and
satires: Samuel Butler's Erewhon appeared in 1872, W. H.
Hudson's A Crystal Age in 1887, and William Morris' News
from Nowhere in 1890, and a large number of utopian and
anti-utopian novels seem to have been inspired by the need
to support or rebut Edward Bellamy's Looking Backward,
published in 1888.[12]

---

[10]Will Durant, The Story of Philosophy (New York,
1953), pp. 15-39.

[11]Bailey, pp. 24-26. Original works cited, unless
citation is quite specific, will be found below in
Bibliography A: Primary Works.

[12]Vernon Louis Parrington, Jr., American Dreams:
A Study of American Utopias, 2nd ed. (New York, 1964),

The Gothic novel might never have achieved its popularity around the turn of the nineteenth century if it had not been that reason and science had so exercised the belief in ghosts and other bogeymen from the minds of cultured Europeans that a tale of horror and the supernatural could entertain and titillate a large audience. But there are also more direct connections than that between the Gothic tradition and science fiction. Mary Shelley's Frankenstein (1817) is one of the last and best of the Gothic novels and it is also an early example of science fiction, a fable warning against the scientist's temptation to play God. Goethe's Faust (1808, 1832) inverts the moral of Frankenstein and of the original Faust story by awarding a place in Heaven to his hero who seems to stand for the questing spirit of science and modern man. Faust's "science," however, is largely the alchemy, magic, and spiritualism of the Middle Ages which played an important role in Gothic fiction. Medievalist trappings and an atmosphere of subdued horror, both creditable to the influence of the Gothic novel, sometimes outweigh the rationality associated with science in early American science fiction, such as Charles Brockden Brown's Wieland

---

pp. 77 ff. See also Sylvia E. Bowman et al., Edward Bellamy Abroad: An American Prophet's Influence (New York, 1962).

and occasional fantasies of Poe, Hawthorne, and Melville.[13]
The same is true in later novels on the borderline between
science fiction and fantasy, such as Villiers de l'Isle-
Adam's story of a female automaton, L'Eve future (1886);
Gustave Meyrink's revival of the medieval legend of an
artificial man, Der Golem (1915); The Created Legend (1906-
13), a trilogy by the Russian novelist Sologub which begins
in an atmosphere of terror and magic, continues through
various occult experiences, and concludes with a departure
from the earth by spaceship; and the science fiction tales
of the American Gothicist, H. P. Lovecraft, in the 1920s.

Science and the scientific attitude also found their
way into contemporary fiction in the nineteenth century.
Balzac, George Eliot Flaubert, Turgenev, and Zola all at
some point describe with admiration a medical doctor as the
epitome of the scientist, not as the bumbling fool so much
previous literature, probably copying from life, had made
physicians out to be.[14] Oliver Wendell Holmes wrote three
novels he called "medicated," which were dedicated to
replacing superstition with science in the consideration of

---

[13]For examples and commentary, but no thorough
study, see H. Bruce Franklin, Future Perfect: American
Science Fiction of the Nineteenth Century (New York, 1966).

[14]For a general discussion of science in nineteenth
century fiction, see Philo M. Buck, The World's Great Age
(New York, 1936), and Leo J. Henkin, Darwinism in the
English Novel 1860-1910 (New York, 1940).

mental aberrations.[15] Zola, especially, but other Natural-
ists as well, attempted to adopt the "experimental method"
for the novel, showing in fiction what a certain combination
of causes will produce in life.[16]

A seminal figure in nineteenth century science
fiction is Edgar Allan Poe. His adaptation of the ratioci-
native method of solving crimes in fiction, as in "The
Mystery of Marie Roget," "The Murders in the Rue Morgue,"
and "The Purloined Letter," has influenced science fiction's
handling of problem-solving, partly through its effect on
the modern detective story.[17] His practice and its actual
and supposed correspondence with his theory of composition
attracted the attention of the Brothers Goncourt, whose
reaction in 1856 was almost prophetic in terms of modern
science fiction:

> Reading Edgar Allan Poe is a revelation of something
> that criticism does not seem to suspect the existence
> of. Poe, a new literature, the literature of the
> twentieth century; the scientific miracle, the
> creation of fable by a+b; a literature at once

[15]Miriam R. Small, "Afterword" to the Signet
Classic edition of Elsie Venner (New York, 1961), pp. 359-
366.

[16]Emile Zola, The Experimental Novel and Other
Essays, trans. Belle M. Sherman (New York, 1893).

[17]Howard Haycraft, Murder for Pleasure: The Life
and Times of the Detective Story (New York and London,
1941), pp. 8-27; Régis Messac, Le "Detective Novel" et
l'influence de la pensée scientifique, Bibliothèque de la
Revue de Littérature Comparée, 59 (Paris, 1929), passim;
A[lma] E[lizabeth] Murch, The Development of the Detective
Novel (New York, 1958), pp. 67-83.

monomaniacal and mathematical. Imagination the
product of analysis; Zadig become an examining magis-
trate; Cyrano de Bergerac become a pupil of the
astronomer, Arago. Things here play a greater part
than beings. And love, love which Balzac had already
reduced to second place after money--love makes way
for other sources of interest. In a word, the novel
of the future, bound to concern itself more with the
story of what happens in the brain of humanity than
in its heart.[18]

The French scholar Hubert Matthey has credited Poe with the

invention not only of the deductive mystery, but also of

the "roman merveilleux-scientifique," seeing as his primary

contribution his artistic formula, his domestication of the

improbable by means of "cohesion" and "logic," as in "The

Facts in the Case of M. Valdemar," "A Tale of the Ragged

Mountains," and "Descent into the Maelstrom."[19] Poe also

revived the old convention of the marvelous journey, and

buttressed it with contemporary "scientific" theory in The

Narrative of Arthur Gordon Pym (1838), a book which caught

the eye of Jules Verne at the beginning of his career in

literature.[20] Verne eventually wrote a sequel to the

unfinished Pym, Le Sphinx des Glaces (1895), but he had

long since turned the voyage extraordinaire into a science

---

[18]Edmond and Jules de Goncourt, The Goncourt
Journals 1851-1870, ed. and trans. Lewis Galantière (Garden
City, 1958), p. 35.

[19]Matthey (above, note 3), pp. 236 ff.

[20]I. O. Evans, "Introduction," The Sphinx of the
Ice-Fields, trans. unknown, in Edgar Allan Poe and Jules
Verne, The Mystery of Arthur Gordon Pym, ed. Basil Ashmore
(London, 1964), pp. 81-83.

fiction formula, filling his narratives with scientific, quasi-scientific, and pseudo-scientific data and descriptions of the moon, under the sea, the center of the earth, and other places to which he took his adventurous heroes and readers.

Besides popularizing the scientist-adventurer and taking his readers off to unexplored locales, Verne also discovered, or was discovered by, a somewhat specialized audience who would buy every book he wrote. He summed up, not only for children, but also for adults in the nineteenth century, the romance of science and technology, as Kenneth Allott has shown.[21] And it may be, as Mark Hillegas suggests, that Verne's "greatest contribution was to establish in the public consciousness science fiction as a distinct mode of writing."[22] Others were not slow to attempt to reach those same readers. Jean-Jacques Bridenne counts at least eighteen French novelists, from the last quarter of the nineteenth century through the first quarter of the twentieth, as pupils, disciples, or imitators of Verne.[23] In the United States, a number of dime novels, individually and in series, began propagandizing for new

---

[21]Kenneth Allott, Jules Verne (London, 1940).

[22]Mark R. Hillegas, The Future as Nightmare: H. G. Wells and the Anti-Utopians (New York, 1967), p. 11.

[23]Jean-Jacques Bridenne, La Littérature française d'imagination scientifique (Dassonville, 1951), pp. 138 ff.

kinds of adventure set in motion by marvelous discoveries
and machines.[24] Popular magazines, too, in America and
England around the turn of the century, were already featur-
ing as a fairly common commodity stories recognizable as
science fiction, including the early works of H. G. Wells.[25]

Wells had some of the ideal characteristics for a
writer of science fiction: a strong presentiment of the
vastness of space and time, a prolific imagination attuned
to the future and to the possibilities of science and technology, a background in literature as well as in science, a
genuine feeling for style and narrative construction. But
he also had a need to be regarded as a significant social
prophet (a need fulfilled in the first quarter of the
twentieth century), which resulted in his turning from
imaginative fiction to essays thinly disguised as fiction
and books of a clearly expository nature.[26] Although he
may never have been an optimist regarding the future of
mankind, the popularity of his apparent optimism and easy
acceptance of the machine, as Mark Hillegas has shown, seems
to have been partly responsible for the pessimistic anti-
utopias of this century (which, compounding the irony, have

---

[24]Moskowitz, Explorers (above, note 5), pp. 106-127.

[25]Sam Moskowitz, "Introduction: A History of
Science Fiction in the Popular Magazines, 1891-1911,"
Science Fiction by Gaslight (Cleveland and New York, 1968),
pp. 15-50.

[26]W. Warren Wagar, H. G. Wells and the World State
(New Haven, 1961), passim.

attacked Wells with his own images and forms).[27] The total impact of Wells on Western civilization, and on the reaction of the intellectual community against utopia, as against science and technology in general, has yet to be measured, but his influence was considerable on the future development of what is now known as science fiction. As Hillegas notes in passing, and Moskowitz in more detail, Wells supplied writers in the pulp magazines of the Twenties and after with a large reservoir of ideas and themes.[28] But he also contributed, however indirectly and unintentionally, to the intellectual disrepute of those same ideas and themes which resulted in their being restricted primarily to that same literary "ghetto" for over thirty years.

Writers as capable as Verne (if not equal to Wells) had written "scientific romances," "utopian novels," and "cosmic fantasies" in the decades preceding World War I: Kurd Lasswitz, Paul Scheerbart, and Bernhard Kellermann in Germany; J. H. Rosny ainé in France; Mark Twain, Jack London, and Edward Bellamy in the United States; Arthur Conan Doyle in England; Fyodor Sologub and Valeriy Briussov in Russia. After the war, however, literary men, if they concerned themselves at all with the future and with Wellsian projections, tended to be quite dogmatically anti-utopian and anti-scientific. Zamiatin's We, Huxley's Brave

---

[27]Hillegas, passim.
[28]Hillegas, p. 12; Moskowitz, Explorers, pp. 128-141.

New World, and Orwell's <u>1984</u> are the most famous examples
of this tendency, but essentially anti-utopian and/or anti-
scientific romances were also written during the first half
of the twentieth century by such authors as E. M. Forster
(as early as 1909), C. S. Lewis, Evelyn Waugh, Percy
Wyndham Lewis, Robert Graves, André Maurois, Franz Werfel,
Alexander Döblin, Ernst Jünger, Alexey Tolstoi, Mikhail
Bulgakov, and Karel Capek.

Although Bernard Shaw published <u>Back to Methusaleh</u>
in 1921 and the fictionalized essays in projection of
W. Olaf Stapledon, as significant a source for pulp writers
as Wells's books, appeared in the Thirties and Forties,
fictional speculation on science and the future was generally limited to the realm of popular literature.[29] In
Germany, for example, a number of "utopisch-phantastische"
novels were written before World War II, generally for a
specialized audience, some of which (preceding the Nazi
era) were even reprinted in the early American science
fiction magazines.[30] After Hitler gained power, such

---

[29]For information on Stapledon, see <u>Explorers</u>, pp.
261-277; in addition, Gerber (above, note 2) treats
Stapledon, Shaw, and Wells as major figures in modern
"utopian fantasy."

[30]Hans Dominik, Otto Willi Gail, Otfried von
Hanstein, Thea von Harbou, and Kurt Siodmak are among the
writers of this period listed in an error-filled German
bibliography, Heinz Bingenheimer, <u>Transgalaxis Katalog der
deutschsprachigen-utopisch-phantastischen Literatur 1460-
1960</u> (Friedrichsdorf, 1960).

fiction was apparently tailored to meet the government's
propaganda needs, as it apparently was also in the Soviet
Union during the Thirties and Forties.[31] The predominant
field of activity, however, was the United States,
especially after 1926, when Hugo Gernsback founded the first
pulp magazine specializing in what he called "scientifiction."[32] Gernsback's venture had a good deal of competition: Argosy, All-Story, Weird Tales, and Gernsback's own
Science and Invention were also publishing stories adver-
tised as "different" or "impossible," and tales of "pseudo-
science" or "super-science." In addition, the new Amazing
Stories does not seem to have been inundated with original
manuscripts, since the first issues consisted largely of
reprints from the works of Verne and Wells.[33] The demand
became great enough, however, that other specialized
magazines soon followed, and the field became stable enough
for one generic term to win precedence ("scientific fiction"

[31]According to conversations with Siegfried Raguse,
fan and bibliophile, in West Berlin (March-May, 1955), East
German science fiction is following a similar pattern today.
See also Peter Yershov, Science Fiction and Utopian Fantasy
in Soviet Literature (New York, 1954). A general discussion
of some German science fiction can be found in Fred S.
Topik, "Utopische Gedanken in modernen deutschen Romanen
1930 bis 1951," unpubl. diss. (Southern California, 1956).

[32]Explorers, pp. 225-242.

[33]In addition, Gernsback's later science fiction
magazines also carried, by choice or necessity, stories and
novels by Gail, von Hanstein (above, note 30), and other
German authors. See Donald Byrne Day, Index to the Science
Fiction Magazines 1926-1950 (Portland, Oregon, 1952).

yielded to "science fiction" in the Thirties).[34] Most of
these magazines (one hundred seventy-one titles, up to
1961) were quite short-lived, but two are still published
today. Amazing Stories has survived a number of name
changes and lapses in publication, and now appears
bi-monthly. Astounding Stories (now Analog Science Fiction-
Science Fact) has not missed a month since October, 1933
(having begun in January, 1930).[35]

The longevity of these two periodicals and the
proliferation of others are an indication, not of a large,
popular following for science fiction in this country, but
of a relatively small readership, more or less homogeneous
in taste, and somewhat dedicated, or even addicted, to this
shared interest. Since the Twenties, at least, these
readers have tended to congregate, identifying themselves
as science fiction "fans," and to correspond with their
favorite writers and magazine editors, keeping the latter
informed of their customers' reactions.[36] The genuine

[34]Explorers, pp. 313-333.

[35]Sources for publishing data include: Day Index;
Erwin S. Strauss, The MIT Science Fiction Society's Index to
the S-F Magazines, 1951-1965 (Cambridge, Massachusetts,
1966); annual supplements (1966, 1967) to the MIT Index,
published by the New England Science Fiction Association
(Cambridge, Massachusetts, 1967, 1968); Bradford M. Day,
The Complete Checklist of Science-Fiction Magazines
(Woodhaven, New York, 1961); and personal collections.

[36]Sam Moskowitz, The Immortal Storm: A History of
Science Fiction Fandom (Atlanta, 1954); see also Robert
Bloch, The Eighth Stage of Fandom: Selections from 25
Years of Fan Writing, ed. Earl Kemp (Chicago, 1962).

science fiction fans, the dedicated readers and collectors, who write letters to the editor, join fan clubs, hold and attend conventions, compose and publish their own amateur journals ("fanzines"), and even become professional science fiction writers, editors, critics, and publishers are a relatively small group. Yet it is largely these fans who supported the science fiction enterprise through the Thirties and Forties, who made American science fiction into a tight-knit community or literary "movement," and who, by their votes for annual awards (named "Hugo," in honor of Gernsback), still exert some influence over the magazines and paperbacks which are at the center of science fiction even now.[37] And it is at least partly through their missionary activities that fan clubs and fanzines have been started in other countries, that American-type science fiction is published in several languages, and that the term "science fiction" has been adopted outside of English-speaking countries.[38] American provincialism may

---

[37]A very brief sketch of the history of the "Hugo" is given in The Hugo Winners, ed. Isaac Asimov (New York, 1962). The book's appendix lists the winners in all categories from 1953 through 1961. Subsequent winners are identified yearly by P. Schuyler Miller in his book review column in Analog (January, 1963; December, 1963; January, 1965; February, 1966; January, 1967; March, 1968). Proceedings of the World Science Fiction Conventions of 1962 (Chicago) and 1963 (Washington) are available from Advent: Publishers, a science fiction publishing house in Chicago.

[38]Explorers, p. 331; correspondence with Pierre Versins (fan and bibliophile, Lausanne) and Jürgen vom Scheidt (fan, critic, and author, München) 1963-1965; conversations with Siegfried Raguse (above, note 31) and with

be held partially responsible for the fact that the annual
World Science Fiction Convention has only twice been held
outside of the United States (both times in England, where
readers were attracted early to American science fiction,
probably due to linguistic ties and their own utopian tradition).[39] But the main reason would seem to be American
predominance in "fandom" as well as in the writing of
science fiction.

It is the literature of this American-based "movement" which I wish to focus on, largely because it is here
that the lines of development are most obvious, that the
concept of "pure" science fiction has been developed and
to some extent maintained, and that the struggles between
"science" and "literature," can be seen most clearly.

The earliest days of American science fiction have
been documented to some extent by H. Bruce Franklin, Thomas

Forrest J. Ackermann (writer, editor, publisher, agent,
promoter and "professional" fan, Los Angeles) 1963-1966.
Use of the term "science fiction" has been noted in
Schwonke and Krysmanski (above, note 7); see also Hubertus
Schulte Herbrüggen, Utopie und Anti-Utopie: Von der Struk-
turanalyse zur Strukturtypologie, in Beitrage zur Englischen
Philologie, 43 (Bochum-Langendreer, 1960), p. 10; Pierre de
Boisdeffre, Une Histoire vivante de la littérature
d'aujourd'hui (1938-1958) (Paris, 1958), pp. 437-442; and
Jacques Bergier, "La science-fiction," Histoire des Littéra-
tures, ed. Raymond Queneau, in Encyclopédie de la Pléiade,
III (Paris, 1958). "Fiction scientifique" is used for Ray
Bradbury and others in R.-M. Albérès, Histoire du roman
moderne (Paris, 1962), pp. 397-402.

[39]There has been talk, however, for several years,
about holding the convention in Germany, and Heidelberg
seems likely for 1970, according to Frederick Pohl's
editorial, IF (December, 1968), p. 4.

Dean Clareson, J. O. Bailey, and Sam Moskowitz.[40] Only the
latter two extended their studies into the period dominated
by the magazines, but that period also has been summarized
briefly in a number of short articles and books.[41] In
general, there seems to be agreement that magazine science
fiction has seen three relatively distinct stages, variously
named but more or less coincident with the emphases and
prejudices of three important editors, Gernsback, John W.
Campbell, Jr., and "Anthony Boucher" (William Anthony Parker
White).

The first period, sometimes known as the era of
"physical" science fiction, was in part a continuation of
the turn-of-the-century emphasis on tales of terror and
episodic "he-man" adventure. Edgar Rice Burroughs' first
adventure of John Carter on Mars appeared in 1912, shortly
before the arrival of Tarzan.[42] The exotic fantasies of
H. P. Lovecraft and A. Merritt, blending Gothic horror and
sometimes scientific theory, were first published in 1917.[43]
But under the influence of Gernsback, first at Modern
Electrics (where his own novel, Ralph 124C 41+, appeared

---

[40]All cited above: Franklin, note 13; Clareson,
note 8; Bailey, note 4; Moskowitz, note 5.

[41]Sam Moskowitz, Seekers of Tomorrow: Masters of
Modern Science Fiction (Cleveland and New York, 1966).

[42]Explorers, pp. 172-188.

[43]Explorers, pp. 189-207, 243-260.

serially in 1911), then at _Amazing_, later at a number of other magazines of popular science and "scientifiction," more emphasis came to be placed on physical science and less on physical adventure and horror.[44] Although Ray Cummings' adventure stories (the first of which, _The Girl in the Golden Atom_, was published in 1919) generally involved only a single scientific (or quasi-scientific) premise, and Otis Adalbert Kline's swashbuckling heroes of space and the jungle (in stories published in 1929 and after) were no more versed in science than Tarzan or John Carter, a number of authors seem to have shifted their attention away from the mere "extraordinary journey."[45] The noted mathematician Eric Temple Bell, whose science fiction began appearing in 1924 under the name of "John Taine," varied the formula in that he used eccentric scientists as heroes, who uncover and attempt to explain mysterious phenomena in distant lands on Earth. A leaden style and a sophomoric sense of humor mar both these earlier books and his later, more mature, more intellectual novels such as _Seeds of Life_ (1931, about an accidental superman) and _Before the Dawn_ (1934, about the reconstruction, by

---

[44]_Explorers_, pp. 225-242; Isaac Asimov, "Social Science Fiction," in _Modern Science Fiction: Its Meaning and its Future_, ed. Reginald Bretnor (New York, 1953), pp. 168-171. On Gernsback, see also P. O'Neil, "Barnum of the Space Age," _Life_, July 26, 1963, pp. 62-64.

[45]_Explorers_, pp. 185-187, 196.

means of an ingenious time-photographing device, of the prehistoric life of the dinosaurs).[46] But the dominant variation of science fiction in the late Twenties and early Thirties was a form called "space opera."

Space opera (so named by analogy with "horse opera," or popular fiction about the American Old West) could be described as situating against a galactic background the traditional forms of the "war story," "spy story," "historical novel," and "western," singly or in combination, but it was also more than that, for, in order to write at all convincingly of the future, an author had to make some kind of projections regarding science and technology. These stories, novels, and series, sometimes extending to a considerable length, still featured adventure-seeking heroes who were powerful and pure (even chaste), but much of their power was becoming "brain power," as indicated by their ability to invent fantastic machines on the spur of the moment (machines which worked immediately and infallibly, and invariably saved the day). And the merely linear strings of adventures, on the model of Verne and Burroughs, gave way to panoramic intrigues, involving rulers and races of many different worlds and multi-world

---

[46]For a very short biographical sketch, see "Editor's Preface" to John Taine, "Writing a Science Novel," in Of Worlds Beyond: The Science of Science Fiction Writing, ed. Lloyd Arthur Eschbach (Reading, Pennsylvania, 1947; reprinted Chicago, 1964), pp. 21-22.

alliances, which usually were resolved only by three-
dimensional (and four-dimensional) space battles of "epic"
scope.[47] E. E. ("Doc") Smith, whose "Skylark" and "Lensman"
series (four and six volumes, respectively, in recent paperback reprints) stretch from 1928 to his death in 1965,
rarely deviated from this pattern.[48] Some of his contemporaries, however, were more flexible and capable of development. Edmond ("World Saver") Hamilton, whose stories were
first published in 1926, was known in the Forties almost
exclusively as the author of the violent juvenile adventure
series, Captain Future, but he adapted to later forms of
science fiction as well.[49] Jack Williamson began with a
combination of space opera and the exotic horror associated
with A. Merritt, but he soon mastered the sociological
extrapolation typical of the next era; his novel The
Humanoids (1948, about the insidious implications of a
"race" of humanoid robots devoted to protecting man from
all harm) was one of the first books of American science
fiction translated into French and German after World War
II.[50] Campbell, whose fiction appeared almost entirely in

---

[47]Asimov, pp. 169-171; Basil Davenport, Inquiry
into Science Fiction (New York, London, and Toronto, 1955),
pp. 17-30.

[48]Moskowitz, Seekers (above, note 41), pp. 9-26.

[49]Seekers, pp. 66-83.

[50]Seekers, pp. 84-100; the early date of the translation of The Humanoids is mentioned in correspondence with

the Thirties, became better known as an editor.

Astounding Stories (founded January, 1930) became
Astounding Science Fiction as of March, 1938, and changed
again in the Sixties to Analog (Science Fact and Fiction,
later Science Fact--Science Fiction, now Science Fiction--
Science Fact). Throughout all these changes, and in fact
from the October issue of 1937, its editor has been John W.
Campbell, Jr., who for more than a decade was practically
the literary dictator of science fiction, and who still
exerts considerable influence in a market no longer totally
dependent on the pulp magazines. From the first, Campbell
emphasized the need for sound application of scientific
theory, consideration of its likely impact on society, and
a sense of organizing thought or philosophy, within the
framework of "a good yarn," i.e., an interesting, even
exciting story. He has paid well for stories meeting his
qualifications, has given encouragement and editorial advice
to writers he thought promising, and has even given away
story ideas by the handful at periodic conferences with his
writers.[51]

Campbell also has campaigned in writing for the kind
of science fiction he wanted to see. His monthly editorials

Pierre Versins and Jürgen vom Scheidt (above, note 38) and
is supported by Bingenheimer (above, note 30).

[51]Explorers, pp. 336-343; Asimov, pp. 171-177;
Seekers, pp. 27-46. See also Roul Tunley, "Unbelievable
But True," Saturday Evening Post, October 8, 1960, pp. 90-
92.

frequently contain scientific or quasi-scientific hypotheses
which may serve as ideas for stories, when he is not lashing
out at complacent Establishment attitudes toward science and
research, art and literature, national and international
politics.[52] In articles for more general publications, he
usually defends his conception of science fiction and/or
challenges others to master it.[53] At his most belligerent,
Campbell has even denied that science fiction is literature,
at least in the sense that the latter, he believes, is concerned mainly with human character and the "eternal"
verities: "where classical values hold that human nature is
enduring, unchanging, and uniform, science-fiction holds
that it is mutable, complex, and differentiated. . . ."
The main function for science fiction, he asserts in the
same article, is prophecy, a role for which scientists (and
science-fiction writers) are well-qualified because they are
"Universe-Directed," motivated mainly by a search for truth
in the physical universe, but a role which, translated into
literature, leaves scant room for matters of opinion and

---

[52]See John W. Campbell, Collected Editorials from
"Analog," ed. Harry Harrison (Garden City, 1966).

[53]John W. Campbell, Jr., "The Place of Science
Fiction," in Bretnor (above, note 44); "Science Fact and
Science Fiction," Writer, August, 1964, pp. 26-27; "The
Science of Science-Fiction," The Atlantic Monthly, May,
1948, pp. 97-98; "The Science of Science Fiction Writing,"
in Eschbach (above, note 46); "The Value of Science
Fiction," in Science Marches On, ed. James Stokley (New
York, 1951).

other factors in human character: "The scientist will
appear from the viewpoint of someone who considers opinion
the dominant force in reality [Campbell's favorite "straw
man"]--rigid, cold-blooded, emotionless, and authoritarian-
dogmatic. He isn't; the Universe is, and he's acting simply
as the messenger of the Universe."[54]

This controversial article represented an extreme
position even for Campbell; in the fiction he publishes, he
does not encourage characterization which is either totally
wooden ("rigid, cold-blooded, emotionless, and authoritar-
ian-dogmatic") or so "mutable, complex, and differentiated"
as to be unrecognizable from contemporary life or from
traditional pulp fiction. Indeed, the concern for social
extrapolation almost made it necessary for writers in
Astounding to create some kind of human norm in character,
by which to measure the effects of their projections.
Although some of these writers developed something in the
way of a distinct literary style, most of their work had
other characteristics in common, too; it generally was
written with a matter-of-fact tone, a veneer of superficial
realism, and a stress on ideas and their potential, i.e.,
in the Campbell manner.

Isaac Asimov, Hal Clement, L. Sprague de Camp,

---

[54]John W. Campbell, Jr., "Science-Fiction and the
Opinion of the Universe," Saturday Review, May 12, 1956,
p. 10.

Lester del Rey, Robert Heinlein, Eric Frank Russell,
Theodore Sturgeon, and A. E. Van Vogt were either first
published, or quickly discovered and developed in Campbell's
Astounding. In addition, writers who were already fairly
well established managed to adapt themselves to Campbell's
demands, among them Murray Leinster (first published in
1919), Clifford Simak (1933), C. L. Moore (1933), and Henry
Kuttner (1936).[55] Together with Campbell, they produced the
shift to what Moskowitz calls "modern" science fiction, and
Asimov, I believe more aptly, calls "social" science
fiction. And it was their stories, especially in the many
anthologies that followed World War II, which won for pulp
science fiction its first critical and popular attention.

In 1945, there were eight science fiction magazines
in the United States; in 1952, there were over thirty.[56] As
of 1948, fifteen anthologies of what was more or less
science fiction had been published; as of 1951, the total
was thirty-eight, a number which was doubled in the next
two years; in 1954 alone, thirty anthologies were

---

[55]Moskowitz, Seekers (above, note 41) has chapters
on all of these but one: Asimov, pp. 249-265; de Camp,
pp. 151-166; del Rey, pp. 167-186; Heinlein, pp. 187-212;
Russell, pp. 133-150; Sturgeon, pp. 229-248; Van Vogt,
pp. 213-228; Leinster, pp. 47-65; Simak, pp. 266-282; Moore,
pp. 303-318; Kuttner, pp. 319-334. Clement receives brief
notice, pp. 415-416.

[56]Anthony Boucher, "The Publishing of Science
Fiction," in Bretnor (above, note 44), p. 33; see also
"Science Fiction Rockets into Big Time," Business Week,
October 20, 1951, pp. 82-84, 89.

published.[57] Until 1946, what science fiction appeared in books was almost always printed by fans in semi-professional publishing houses.[58] By 1950, with a number of major publishers competing, the number of new books in a year had reached sixty, an average maintained throughout the following decade.[59] As of 1951-52, a hard-cover book by one author could be counted on to sell from 5,000 to 10,000 copies, an anthology might sell 30,000, and a paperback could expect sales of from 200,000 to 1,000,000 copies.[60] The increasing impact of science fiction could be seen in other areas, too. Articles popularizing, explaining, and criticizing science fiction appeared more often in general and literary periodicals.[61] Mass-circulation magazines

---

[57]Statistics compiled from W. R. Cole, A Checklist of Science Fiction Anthologies ([New York], 1964).

[58]Boucher, pp. 37-38; see also Algis Budrys, "Galaxy Bookshelf," Galaxy, October, 1965, pp. 142-150.

[59]Boucher, pp. 36-39. See also the annual summaries of the year's books in The Magazine of Fantasy and Science Fiction (F&SF) by Boucher and co-editor J. Francis McComas, Winter-Spring, 1950; April, 1951; April, 1952; March, 1953; March, 1954; and by Boucher alone, March, 1955; March, 1956; March, 1957; March, 1958. See also J. Francis McComas, "The Spaceman's Little Nova," New York Times Book Review, November 20, 1955, p. 53, and Judith Merril, "The Year's S-F: A Summary," The Year's Best S-F, 5th annual edition (New York, 1961), p. 314.

[60]Boucher, in Bretnor, pp. 37-38; Business Week (above, note 56).

[61]By my count, five articles were published between 1936 and 1945, nine more appeared from 1946 through 1950, followed by four in 1951, eight in 1952, and twenty-one in 1953. Some, but not all, of these articles are listed below in Bibliography B: Secondary Works.

began to publish science fiction, including stories by such
acknowledged American pulp writers as Ray Bradbury, Robert
A. Heinlein, and Murray Leinster, and their British counterparts, John Christopher, Arthur C. Clarke, and John
Wyndham.[62] Science fiction also began to show up in films
(frequently and significantly transformed into horror
movies) and on television (which it first entered in the
guise of such children's adventure programs as Captain
Video, Space Patrol, and Tom Corbett, Space Cadet).[63]

This economic boom in science fiction was due mainly
to factors other than good writing. In the aftermath of a
war unprecedented in size and scope, and in its emphasis on
technology (climaxed by the harnessing of atomic energy, an
achievement long anticipated by science fiction fans), some
of the reasons for the surge in popularity of pulp science
fiction surely included its reputation for technological
prediction, its promise of exploring the dreams and nightmares made possible by science, and its essentially escapist
appeal.

The first of these, the reputation for prediction,

---

[62]Boucher, in Bretnor, pp. 33-34. Moskowitz,
Seekers includes similar references, and chapters on
Bradbury, pp. 352-373; Clarke, pp. 374-391; and Wyndham,
pp. 118-132.

[63]Don Fabun, "Science Fiction in Motion Pictures,
Radio, and Television," in Bretnor, pp. 43-70. See also
Jacques Siclier, Images de la Science Fiction (Paris, 1958),
and Paul S. Nathan, "Books into Films," Publisher's Weekly,
June 18, 1949, p. 2463.

was largely undeserved. Most predictions in science fiction are wrong, and the more detailed and remote they are, the more wrong guesses result. The relatively few predictions in science fiction that succeed, usually do so because of luck or because the writer is already familiar with research leading almost inevitably to the result he (along with the researcher) expects.[64] Actually, prediction in science fiction is primarily a matter of literary convention; each story generally assumes certain future possibilities proposed by other stories already existent, then introduces one or more variations more or less logically extrapolated from either the present or this conventional future, variations which are highly improbable as actual predictions.

The other two reasons offered above for science fiction's surge in popularity tend to cancel each other out, as far as most readers are concerned. A person who wants his reading matter to explore social problems of the present and their likely results and possible solutions in the future will recognize that science and technology may cause, and solve, some of these problems, but he will probably not be very interested in stories of fantasy and unlikely adventure, set in a distant time or place. On the other

---

[64]Robert A. Heinlein, "Science Fiction: Its Nature, Faults, and Virtues," in Basil Davenport et al., The Science Fiction Novel: Imagination and Social Criticism, 2nd ed. (Chicago, 1964), pp. 30-40. See also G. Harry Stine, "Science Fiction is Too Conservative," Analog, May, 1961, pp. 83-99.

hand, someone looking for instant gratification of his desires is also unlikely to appreciate fiction that continually involves him in solving problems, some of which are uncomfortably close to the problems he is trying to forget.

The remaining newcomers, presumably tolerant toward both fantasy and the solving of problems, may be divided into three general groupings, which are not mutually exclusive: fans, browsers, and critics. The lack of any large numerical gain in fans may be indicated by the gradual decline of the pulp magazines: in 1953, forty-three magazines published at least one issue each, and of those forty-three, seven survived through 1967, some in a perpetually shaky financial situation, seldom if ever with a circulation (including foreign editions) that ever surpassed 150,000.[65] The fact that a large number of people learned to read some science fiction, however, is indicated by the paperback market and the proliferation of science fiction outside the pulps. The number of volumes published averaged around sixty through most of the Fifties, then took a

---

[65]Data on number of magazines compiled from Day Index, MIT Index, NESFA supplements (above, note 36). Circulation figures of 125,000 for Galaxy (plus eight foreign editions) and 135,000 for Astounding (in American and English editions) are cited without documentation by Amis (above, note 6), p. 57, and a circulation for Astounding of 150,000 is claimed by Campbell, in Bretnor, p. 21, but publishers' legal statements for the years 1960-1968 show the following circulation figures rounded off to the nearest thousand: Analog (Astounding) climbed steadily from 74,000 to 102,000; Galaxy fell from 92,000 to 75,000; F&SF had a low of 48,000 (1960), a high of 57,000 (1961), and an average of 53,000.

large jump to about 100 in 1960 and 1961, and most of these were paperbacks.[66] Twenty-five or more paperback lines now feature something called science fiction, including pulp serials from the Twenties and Thirties, stories and novelettes puffed up or pasted together, "quickies" by middlebrow writers of contemporary fiction, and a few novels and collections of stories of some quality by writers in and out of the science fiction community.[67] Outside the pulp magazines' immediate sphere of influence, according to Judith Merril, in her fifth annual Best S-F anthology, the number of science fiction stories in general and literary periodicals increased from about 50 in 1955 to over 200 in 1959.[68] And films and television have seen some notable achievements, along with a number of disasters, in their continued attempts to adapt science fiction to media of mass entertainment.[69]

---

[66]Anthony Boucher, "S-F Books--1960," The Year's Best S-F, ed. Judith Merril, 6th annual edition (New York, 1962), p. 378.

[67]Paperback books from more than twenty American publishers are listed in the catalogs of F&SF Book Co. of Staten Island, New York. Catalogs from Fantast (Medway) Ltd., in Wisbech, England, identify five and sometimes more independent British paperback publishers.

[68]Merril (above, note 59), p. 314.

[69]"Hugo" winners have included the film Dr. Strangelove (1965 dramatic award), the television series The Twilight Zone (1960-1962), and the episode "The Menagerie" from the television series Star Trek (1967). See also Susan Sontag, "Imagination of Disaster," Against Interpretation (New York, 1966), for an unfavorable critical appraisal of science fiction in the movies.

Criticism came from both inside and outside the
science fiction community, and in numerous forms. Essays of
many kinds (articles, chapters, symposia, books, doctoral
dissertations) also appeared mainly after 1950, most of them
polemical or didactic. Adherents of science fiction have
gone so far as to say that it is the only kind of literature
that matters today, sometimes supporting their argument by
the circular reasoning that science fiction alone takes into
account the effect of science and technology on man's
present and past, and especially on his future.[70] Its
detractors have responded with half-truths, based partly on
an insufficient or indiscriminate sampling, to the effect
that the science in science fiction is negligible and often
bogus, that the fiction is composed mainly of passé conventions, warmed-over mythology, stylistic clichés, and inept
writing in general, and that the whole is supported by a
shallow and pretentious philosophy.[71] At various times,

---

[70]This argument is usually proposed in conversation,
but modified forms of it can be found in Heinlein (above,
note 64), pp. 53 ff., and in Edmund Crispin's introduction
to his anthology Best SF Three: Science Fiction Stories
(London, 1958), pp. 9-13.

[71]See, for example, the following essays: John
Lear, "Let's Put Some Science into Science-Fiction," Popular
Science Monthly, August, 1954, pp. 135-137, 244-248; Arthur
Koestler, "The Boredom of Fantasy," Trail of the Dinosaur
(New York, 1955); Siegfried Mandel and Peter Fingesten, "The
Myth of Science Fiction," Saturday Review, August 27, 1955,
pp. 7-8, 24-25, 28; Joseph Kostolefsky, "Science, Yes--
Fiction, Maybe," Antioch Review, June, 1953, pp. 236-240;
Thomas P. McDonnell, "The Cult of Science Fiction," Catholic
World, October, 1953, pp. 15-18.

science fiction has been hailed as a powerful agent of
social criticism, damned as dangerous escapism, hailed as
big business, belittled as childishness, and even admired
as a minor kind of poetry.[72]

The net result of most of this writing could be
summed up in three brief statements: (1) we don't know
exactly what science fiction is, but (2) not everyone likes
it, and (3) there is probably room for improvement. Fortu-
nately, some bibliographical and historical research has
been done, making it possible, if not to define science
fiction, at least to point to what it has been and has
included, and some theorizing has been done with the aid of
a dispassionate examination of more than a handful of
convenient examples, so that we know something about the
peculiar situation of science fiction that gives rise to
the second statement above. As for the third, a number of
people tried to do something about it.

Four new pulp magazines, started between 1946 and
1952, are still in business. To some extent their survival
is due to the demands of their editors for more or less

---

[72]See, for example, the following essays: L. W.
Michaelson, "Science Fiction, Censorship, and Pie-in-the-
Sky," Western Humanities Review, XIII, 4 (Autumn, 1959),
409-413; Bruno Bettelheim, The Informed Heart (Glencoe,
Illinois, 1960), pp. 52-63; H. W. Häusermann, "Science
Fiction, A New Kind of Mass Literature," Levende Talen
(Brussels), CLXXXI (1955), 394-405; Angelica Gibbs, "Onward
and Upward with the Arts: Inertrum, Neutronium, Chromaloy,
P-P-P-Proot!" The New Yorker, February 13, 1943, pp. 42-53;
C. S. Lewis, "On Stories" (1947), Of Other Worlds (New York,
1966).

polished writing and for an emphasis on psychological
themes, character, and personal involvement sufficient to
characterize the period since 1950 as the era of "psychological" science fiction. The Magazine of Fantasy and
Science Fiction (F&SF) was founded in 1949 (the first issue
was titled The Magazine of Fantasy) and emphasized from the
start a sense of style and fictional technique even at the
expense of story and scientific content. A year later,
Galaxy Science Fiction (now Galaxy Magazine) released its
first issue, stressing sociological (and psychological)
extrapolation, social criticism, and satire in a well-made
frame. In 1952, IF, Worlds of Science Fiction made its
first appearance, specializing in the kind of technological-
sociological extrapolation which made Astounding famous, but
edited more strictly for story values. Meanwhile, Campbell
had become more and more interested in fiction which dealt
with "psionics" (or para-psychological engineering) and with
probable inventions and developments on earth and in space
in the very near future (treated almost as documentary).
The other new magazine, New Worlds, was British; founded in
1946, it survived competition with the higher-paying
American magazines and their British editions, and became in
the Sixties the leader in the kind of subtle and intricate
literary puzzles and exercises in symbolism, full of
personal involvement, which Judith Merril sees as the new
"SF" (speculative fantasy) that is breaking down the

barriers between science fiction and literature in
general.[73]

In 1953, the first "Hugos" were awarded, at the
Eleventh World Science Fiction Convention in Philadelphia;
the tradition has continued since 1955, indicating the
desire of the fans to award, and therefore encourage,
quality in science fiction.[74] In the pulps and fanzines of
the Fifties, book review columns became a commonplace.[75]
Although many reviews were little more than shopping lists,
those written by Damon Knight and James Blish frequently
indulged in genuine criticism, a practice revived in the
Sixties by Judith Merril and Algis Budrys.[76] In addition,
a number of anthologies began to appear, claiming to be
representative of the best science fiction written, or at
least the best of the year, each accompanied by an introduction which not only summed up the contents, but also

[73]Judith Merril, "What Do You Mean--Science?/
Fiction?" Extrapolation, VII (May, 1966), 30-46, VIII
(December, 1966), 2-19, and The Year's Best S-F, 7th-11th
Annual Editions (New York, 1962-66). Publication data
from indexes listed above (notes 33 and 35).

[74]See note 37, above.

[75]Budrys (above, note 58), p. 143.

[76]Damon Knight, In Search of Wonder: Essays on
Modern Science Fiction, rev. ed. (Chicago, 1967); William
Atheling, Jr. [James Blish], The Issue at Hand: Studies in
Contemporary Magazine Science Fiction, ed. James Blish
(Chicago, 1964); Judith Merril, book reviews, F&SF, monthly
(with a few exceptions) since March, 1965; Algis Budrys,
book reviews, Galaxy, every issue since February, 1965.

pointed the way toward what the editor viewed as improvement.[77]

All the scourging and awards, encouragement and
exhortation in the world, of course, would be merely so
much more in the way of wasted words if the writers themselves did not take seriously the need to better themselves
in the eyes of the outside world and of the increasingly
aware fans. And all the attempts at improvement, no matter
how well motivated and grounded in the study of classics
and contemporaries, would also be worthless if the writers
were unable to write any better, or their material were
intractable to any other treatment than that which was
visible in the past. The motivation was there, in the mood
of the community (the desire for respectability), and in
the need to compete, in both the pulps and the general
magazines, with writers more polished, if less trained in
science fiction, than those inside the community.[78] The

[77]For example: The Year's Best Science Fiction
Stories, ed. Everett Bleiler and T. E. Dikty (New York,
1949-1954); S-F: The Year's Greatest Science-Fiction and
Fantasy, changed in 1960 to The Year's Best S-F, ed. Judith
Merril (New York, since 1956); Best SF: Science Fiction
Stories to Best SF Five: Science Fiction Stories, ed.
Edmund Crispin (London, 1954, 1956, 1968, 1961, 1964).

[78]Stories by writers outside the science fiction
community can frequently be found in F&SF, in regard to
which see James Yaffe, "The Modern Trend Toward Meaningful
Martians," Saturday Review, April 23, 1960, p. 22. See
also The "Post" Reader of Fantasy and Science Fiction
(Garden City, 1964) and The "Playboy" Book of Science
Fiction and Fantasy (Chicago, 1966).

ability was there: Asimov, Clarke, Sturgeon, Alfred Bester, Hal Clement, Frederick Pohl and C. M. Kornbluth, and John Wyndham, all of whom had written science fiction since the late Thirties or early Forties, wrote their best books in the Fifties. And the material was not inflexible, as was shown not only by such outsiders as Bernard Wolfe, Kurt Vonnegut, Jr., William Golding, and Anthony Burgess, but also by the new writers inside the science fiction community. In the Fifties, such new writers included James Blish, Algis Budrys, Philip K. Dick, Philip José Farmer, Walter M. Miller, Jr., and Edgar Pangborn, each of whom developed his own style and subject matter largely on his own, with the concept of science fiction as literature at least in sight. In the Sixties, important new writers include three Americans, Samuel Delany, Roger Zelazny, and Cordwainer Smith, and two Britons, Brian Aldiss and J. G. Ballard, each of whom seems to be at least partly convinced, not only that science fiction can be, but that it is, literature.

As long ago as 1953, Reginald Bretnor, in his pioneering symposium on science fiction, predicted the return of science fiction to literary status: "Eventually, we will again have an integrated literature. It will owe much, artistically, to non-science fiction. But its dominant attitudes and purposes, regardless of whether it happens to be dealing with the past, 'the present,' or the future--will have evolved from those of modern science fiction."[79] The major contribution of science fiction to this integrated literature, he felt, would be that attitude which most distinguished science fiction from other forms of writing, an "awareness of the importance of the scientific method as a human function and of the human potentialities inherent in its exercise," an awareness which at best revealed itself "not only in plot and circumstance, but also through the thoughts and motivations of the characters," and which at least took the form of an awareness of "certain potential products of the scientific method."[80] Warning that this integrated literature would not be science fiction as it was and had been, Bretnor also cautioned against any immediate expectations of the millennium. The problem, as he saw it, was one of cultural lag: most people were not yet willing even to accept science, let alone science fiction.[81]

Some of Bretnor's predictions, regarding the early stages of the transition, seem to have come true. Critical and scholarly interest in science fiction has increased, although it still seems largely apologetic in tone. The market for science fiction in general did expand, although

---

[79]Reginald Bretnor, "The Future of Science Fiction," in Modern Science Fiction (see above, note 44), p. 292.

[80]Bretnor, p. 273.

[81]Bretnor, passim.

the fortunes of the pulps have fluctuated. The use of
science fictional themes in serious short stories has also
grown, unless Judith Merril's annual survey anthologies
represent merely a broadening or adulteration of the term
"SF" as some of her critics charge.[82] In addition, there
are other indications that the cultural lag between scientific and public knowledge may be decreasing. Books and
articles, magazines and magazine sections presenting science
for the layman seem to have increased in number, especially
since the first artificial satellite, Sputnik, was put into
orbit in 1957; as Martin Green noted in 1965, however, in a
book about one literary man's crash program of education in
the sciences, many of these books and articles are next to
useless in narrowing the gap between the "two cultures" of
the sciences and the humanities.[83] Jacques Barzun, in a
survey of contemporary art, finds a great deal of utilization of the scientific method, as well as of products of
technology, but both, he maintains, are being used by the
artist in an attempt to escape from a world made untenable
for him by these same agents, science and technology.[84] In

---

[82]See, for example, Algis Budrys' reviews of
Merril's ninth and tenth annual volumes, Galaxy, April,
1965, and August, 1966.

[83]Martin Green, Science and the Shabby Curate of
Poetry (New York, 1965).

[84]Jacques Barzun, Classic, Romantic and Modern, rev.
ed. (Garden City, 1961), pp. 140-146.

business and industry, in government, and in everyday life,
people are becoming more aware, not only of new technological developments, but also of the need for planning and
projecting developments into the future. Such books as
Designing the Future, On Thermonuclear War, Thinking the
Unthinkable, The Dynamics of Change, The Year 2000, and
Toward the Year 2018 are undoubtedly making more people
aware of Bretnor's second stage of science fictional thinking, i.e., an awareness of the scientific method not only
in terms of its products, but also in terms of its role in
"circumstance and plot."[85] From this point it may be
possible for some readers to progress to the third stage of
awareness, wherein the "human function" of the scientific
method and "the human potentialities inherent in its
exercise" can be seen to play a role in "the thoughts and
motivations of [fictional] characters."

Bretnor's major prediction, however, that we will
have an integrated literature, has not yet been realized.
A large number of writers outside the movement have written

---

[85]Robert W. Prehoda, Designing the Future: The
Role of Technological Forecasting (Philadelphia, 1967);
Herman Kahn, On Thermonuclear War (Princeton, 1961); Herman
Kahn, Thinking About the Unthinkable (New York, 1962); Don
Fabun, The Dynamics of Change (Englewood Cliffs, New Jersey,
1967); Herman Kahn and Anthony J. Wiener, The Year 2000:
A Framework for Speculation on the Next Thirty-Three Years
(New York, 1967); Toward the Year 2018, ed. Foreign Policy
Association (New York, 1968). For a brief, general essay
on such predicting, see Daniel Bell's introduction to the
Kahn and Wiener volume, pp. xxi-xxviii.

novels, plays, and stories to some extent science fictional
since 1950, but many of these are no better written than
their pulp counterparts, and few of them show any awareness
of science beyond Bretnor's first level.[86] A few science
fiction writers may have received some critical attention
outside the pulp field, but rarely in regard to the science
fictional nature of their works.[87] Then, too, the phrase
"science fiction" is probably familiar to most people today,
but those to whom it signifies horror movies or such
juvenalia as the television series Lost in Space, and those
to whom it means predictions that "science is catching up
to," like heart transplants and moon rockets, no doubt
vastly outnumber the relative few who can relate it to the
scientific method at all.[88]

---

[86]Among these writers, books by whom are cited
below in Bibliography A (see above, note 11), are the
following: Martin Caidin, Nigel Dennis, David Ely, Howard
Fast, Pat Frank, Diana and Meir Gillon, John Hersey, Shirley
Jackson, John D. MacDonald, Warren Miller, Ayn Rand, Nevil
Shute, George R. Stewart, Gore Vidal, Leonard Wibberly, and
Angus Wilson.

[87]Ray Bradbury, for example, is sometimes singled
out for attention because he is not strictly science
fictional in his writing. Reviews of A Canticle for
Leibowitz by Walter M. Miller, Jr., tended to downgrade its
science fiction content (see below, Chapter V).

[88]See, for example, "Outpaced by Space," Time,
January 14, 1963, pp. 71-72, and "Overtaking the Future,"
Newsweek, October 8, 1962, p. 104. The assumptions in these
articles are refuted to some extent in Isaac Asimov, "Fact
Catches Up with Fiction," New York Times Magazine, November
19, 1961, pp. 34, 39, 42, 44.

But ignorance of science is not the only reason offered for disliking science fiction, and it is highly improbable that the general and literary publics have failed to appreciate science fiction merely because they have never been fully exposed to it. The adverse criticism science fiction has received often is based on at least some reading of stories and novels by authors featured frequently in the pulp magazines, and this criticism tends to center on four general features which seem to be basic to the genre, at least as it presently exists. These central issues, fantasy, science, pulp qualities, and homogeneity, will be examined in more depth in Chapter II.

CHAPTER II

THEORETICAL OVERVIEW

The historical antecedents claimed for modern
science fiction, such as the fantastic journey, the utopian
blueprint, the marvelous discovery, the gods and devils of
mythology, the elves and witches and such of fairy tales,
the horrors of Gothic and dystopian romance, all share
certain characteristics with science fiction, and in fact,
versions of all of these antecedents exist in some form
today in the general area referred to as science fiction.
Since they existed before science fiction, and can exist
without science or the scientific mentality, such motifs
obviously do not define science fiction, however inter-
twined with it they may have become, and however significant
such connections may seem.

Insofar as it has a distinct character, science
fiction depends far more on its connections with science
than with such more or less accidental features, which
point to its similarities with other literature rather than
to its individuality. For it is modern science which is at
the root of the difference between Plato's Republic or

45

More's Utopia and Wells's A Modern Utopia or B. F. Skinner's
Walden Two, between a trip to the moon in Lucian's time and
one in our own, between the devil-figures of the magician
and the scientist, between the titillating horrors of
Lewis' The Monk and the prophetic horrors of Orwell's 1984.
Although a given science fiction writer may know little more
about science than a tribal storyteller knows about his
shaman's secret lore, the conventions which make up science
fiction have been developed from certain assumptions about
the role of science, pure and applied, in the history,
prehistory, and future history of man and the universe.
And despite the myriad variations and manipulations, modifi-
cations and distortions to which these conventions can be
and have been subjected in fiction, a scientific conception
of the world is basic to the conventions themselves.

Regardless of the religious, philosophical, or
political beliefs of any given scientist as a man, he
assumes as a scientist certain axioms about the nature of
the phenomena with which he is dealing, and about certain
goals toward which his activity is directed. He may believe
in some degree of free will, but he must assume that the
causes and conditions of events can be determined with a
high degree of probability. He may believe in certain human
values, in normative behavior, in moral and ethical abso-
lutes, but he must strive to prevent them from interfering
with an objective interpretation of things. He may believe

in a Higher Being and a Higher Truth, but as a scientist he must assume that truth reveals itself in ways which can be repeatedly sensed and measured by men and their mechanical extensions. And no matter what purpose his work may ultimately serve, he must first strive to predict the fulfillment of his hypotheses, to control the succession of events in terms of the fewest possible variables, and to comprehend the phenomena before him intellectually, in terms of how things work.

Given these assumptions, which may loosely be called determinism, relativism, and empiricism, and these goals, which we may term prediction, control, and comprehension, science and scientists have been quite successful in narrowing the odds that man must face in his confrontation with his environment in its physical, social, and even psychological manifestations.[1] Contemplating their success, one could easily take the short step necessary to formulate a belief that the scientific view is the only effective and

---

[1]This theory of the basic goals and assumptions of science, proposed by Professor Robert Friedrichs in his course, "Introduction to Cultural Anthropology," Drew University, Fall, 1958, I can find no fault with, after considerable readings in the history and philosophy of science, other than that problem which Friedrichs himself admitted: few scientists or philosophers, since the early twentieth century, would state the case so baldly, since we now know the principles of determinism, relativism, and empiricism have no absolute validity. But people, even scientists, do tend to depend on oversimplifications such as these when they are not constrained to think, speak, or write with the utmost precision.

useful way of describing the universe and all that goes on
in it; untempered by other considerations, the scientific
world view can lead to a regard for science as a most
unscientific absolute.[2]

Such a scientistic hypothesis, and the assumptions
and goals leading up to it, I submit, lie at the core of
science fiction, and are at least partly responsible for
many features, perpetuated and even approved of in science
fiction circles, which literary critics and other readers
who are not afficionados of the genre find inexplicable,
distasteful, or even reprehensible. To show how scientism
affects the literature, let us imagine an ideal type which
we shall call pure science fiction, many of whose features
we can see in science fiction as it exists.

Pure science fiction can be expected to deal largely
with things, facts, statistics, machines, measurable quanti-
ties and forces, evidence of the senses, and interpretations
of phenomena derived mainly from mechanistic thinking. In
such a context, human values should be viewed primarily as
isolated phenomena, variations on which may be approved or
censured only on pragmatic grounds, such as whether the
species or society survives, whether the force or machine
works, whether the system functions smoothly and perpetuates

---

[2]See, for example, F. A. Hayek, The Counter-
Revolution of Science: Studies in the Abuse of Reason
(Glencoe, Illinois, 1952), and Scientism and Values, ed.
Helmut Schoeck and James W. Wiggins (Princeton, 1960).

itself. From this pragmatic viewpoint, the encouragement of
scientific investigation and technological innovation can
almost always be justified in terms of its survival value.

As the scientist attempts to predict the results of
an experiment, the writer of pure science fiction should try
to predict the outcome of certain forces at work in the
contemporary world. Not strictly predictive, the process
of imagining more or less probable worlds of the future is
usually called extrapolation, a term which signifies a
logical, and sometimes a chronological, extension of mathematical curves and trends of change and development. In
theory, extrapolation may range either forward or backward
in time, using as its base a setting in past, present, or
future, or even a kind of never-never land outside of time;
usually, the basic setting can be expected to be in the
present and the projection into the future.[3]

Such a projection should, ideally, avoid the moral
directives associated with prophecy, merely indicating the
more or less probable result of the dynamics contained in a
given set of circumstances. Consistent with Zola's theory
of the "experimental novel," the writer of pure science
fiction should attempt to control only the beginning of his
story, selecting a setting, a cast of characters, and a

---

[3]But not all stories set in the future should be
called science fiction. See I. F. Clarke, The Tale of the
Future: From the Beginning to the Present Day (London,
1961).

limited number of trends or ideas operating upon them,
letting the outcome emerge as if by itself. Presumably the
result of such a procedure would be an objective description
of what might happen in one possible future, leaving up to
the reader the question of morality or desirability and the
decision as to whether man should attempt to exert control
over the forces leading toward that future.[4]

Although the given circumstances of the present and
the forces leading toward the imagined future may show
themselves in plot, setting, or explanations, or in various
conventions adopted by the author from other science fiction
stories, the extrapolative process itself is essentially
aliterary. It takes place most often before the act of
writing, often in minds other than the author's. Its truest
form of expression is the mathematical equation, whose
meaning for man is usually more intellectual than artistic.
In literature, extrapolation is most at home in a relatively
technical essay, working out a prediction as logically as
possible from a carefully described set of original conditions. In style as in form such an essay should be
aliterary, i.e., its language should be scientific rather
than poetic, calling no attention to itself or to its
author, its aim should be communication of concepts more
than of a sense of style, and its major goal should be to

---

[4]See Basil Davenport, Inquiry into Science Fiction
(New York, London, and Toronto, 1955), pp. 31-44.

elicit from the reader a response which stresses intellectual comprehension more than it does sensual or emotional
experience.[5]

If pure science fiction is indeed scientistic in
origin, extrapolative in intent, and essayistic in form, we
can expect certain aliterary or even anti-literary tendencies in the imaginative literature (fiction, drama, poetry)
derived from that ideal. Things will be more important than
people; the brain will predominate over the heart; ideas,
more than experience, will be basic to setting, character,
and plot. These three principles, which the Goncourt
Brothers found in Poe, many readers have found objectionable
in nineteenth-century Naturalism.[6] There, as in science
fiction, scientistic tendencies were at work, and the
results in many cases included a flat, unembellished style,
a theoretical plan of structure and message, an analytical,
sometimes simplistic treatment of behavior, motivation, and
ideas, and an amoral lack of involvement. If a few authors,

---

[5]The relationship of science fiction to the "speculative essay" is also noted in Robert A. Heinlein, "Science
Fiction: Its nature, Faults, and Virtues," in Basil
Davenport et al., The Science Fiction Novel: Imagination
and Social Criticism, 2nd ed. (Chicago, 1964), p. 58.

[6]The Goncourts' observation is quoted above, pp. 11-
12. On naturalism, see, for example: Ferdinand Brunetiére,
Le Roman naturaliste, rev. ed. (Paris, 1892), passim;
P. Martino, Le Naturalism français (1870-1895) (Paris,
1923), especially pp. 1-6, 189-206, 214-217; Aloys Rob.
Schlismann, Beiträge zur Geschichte und Kritik des Naturalismus (Kiel and Leipzig, 1903), especially pp. 63-74.

notably Zola, managed to transcend these limitations., it was largely through a plethora of details taken from actual life situations, with which the reader could immediately identify, and a strong sense of unscientific personal involvement transmitted to the reader by means of a good command of fictional techniques. Where the source of the story is essentially speculation rather than direct observation, however, such details, as well as the main body of the work, must be made up, and personal involvement will probably stand out as a strong element of didacticism.

Of the three major elements mentioned above, setting, character, and plot, the first is the most easily derived from logic and confidently explained by essay. An alien planet can be deduced physically from natural laws governing astronomical bodies, then its physical characteristics can be used in determining certain ecological patterns, and these in turn may suggest possible human responses, both individual and social.[7] If the place is the Earth and the time is the future, the science fiction writer, like the Hudson Institute researchers who contributed to The Year 2000: A Framework for Speculation, can deduce a "Standard World" and "Canonical Variations,"

---

[7]See, for example, the author's account of the planning of Mission of Gravity: Hal Clement, "Whirligig World," Astounding, June, 1953, pp. 102-114. At the 1964 World Science Fiction Convention, Oakland, California, Frank Herbert gave a talk of a similar nature, regarding the working out of background for his novel, Dune.

choosing one of these or a modification based on further
extension of some independent variable, in order to arrive
at his social setting.[8]   In any case, he is likely to base
his extrapolation on changes or variations in civilization
as a whole, the most important of which will be not changes
in individual people but changes in the level of science and
technology.[9]

Individuals need not be considered in making the
transition from the real world contemporaneous with the
writing to the fictional world in which the story takes
place, but they are necessary for the story which is to
unfold in that fictional world. Determined for the author
partly by his setting, partly by their role in illustrating
the forces he wishes to show at work in that setting, and
partly by his lack of concern for individuals to begin with,
they are quite likely to be character types rather than
three-dimensional figures, such as we are supposed to expect

---

[8]Herman Kahn and Anthony J. Wiener, The Year 2000:
A Framework for Speculation on the Next Thirty-three Years
(New York, 1967).

[9]"With a few exceptions, notably Chapter 8, I am
limiting myself to a single aspect of the future--its technology, not the society that will be based upon it. This
is not such a limitation as it may seem for science will
dominate the future even more than it dominates the present.
Moreover, it is only in this field that prediction is at all
possible; there are some general laws governing scientific
extrapolation, as there are not (pace Marx) in the case of
politics or economics." Arthur C. Clarke, Profiles of the
Future: An Inquiry into the Limits of the Possible
(New York, Toronto, and London, 1965), p. xi.

from great literature. The protagonist should be a man of
science, who is the first to understand the problem, and
who solves it, if it can be solved, partly by means of logic
and planning, partly by means of manipulation of technology
and people. If the problem cannot be solved, he should be
the first to realize it and to recommend and plan escape,
retrenchment, or whatever can be done to alleviate whatever
adverse effects are likely. Since his predominant quality
is intelligence, his antagonist should be stupid, or at
least unreached by reason, and therefore more of an obstacle
than a villain. Such antagonists might include the mindless
powers of nature, extraterrestrial beings with whom no
agreement can be reached, and representatives of human
groups prevented from independent thought by inertia,
entrenched interests, or sheer bull-headedness (e.g., military men, bureaucrats, profiteers, do-gooders). An innocent
outsider is also useful, either as narrator or as foil, if
the author does not wish to address explanatory essays
directly to the reader, but other characters may well be
superfluous in pure science fiction, doubling or reinforcing
one of the three principals, or introducing interests and
considerations not germane to the central problem.[10]

---

[10]In a sociological survey of random stories listed
in the Day Index, scientists were found to be the most
frequent group whose members were cast as heroes, but scientists were also the most common villains (along with
businessmen, politicians, and the military). See Walter
Hirsch, "American Science Fiction, 1926-1950: A Content
Analysis," unpubl. diss. (Northwestern, 1957).

As the characters are somewhat determined by other
considerations, such as setting, theme, and plot, so the
plot of a science fiction novel, that is, the particular
twists and turns of causally related events which make up
the narrative, is also not a completely independent variable. The plot is most commonly one in which "action"
predominates, which, as Norman Friedman points out, is only
to be expected in popular literature:

> We rarely, if ever, become involved here in any
> serious moral or intellectual issue; nor does the
> outcome have any far-reaching consequences for the
> fortune, character, or thought of the protagonist,
> leaving him free to start all over again, it may
> be, in a sequel; and the pleasures we experience
> are almost wholly those of suspense, expectation,
> and surprise, the plot being organized around a
> basic puzzle and solution cycle. There is a gang-
> ster to track down, a murderer to discover and
> apprehend, a treasure to be gotten, or a planet to
> be reached. Examples of this type are most
> frequently found in those classes of fiction
> called adventure, detective, western, and science-
> fiction stories.[11]

Action, or simple interest in what happens next, is not the
sole intent of the science fiction writer--in fact, all
fourteen of Friedman's variations of plots of fortune,
character, and thought can be and have been used in science
fiction--but a "puzzle and solution cycle" is part of the
scientistic metaphysic.[12] As the writer of mystery stories

---

[11]Norman Friedman, "Forms of the Plot," in The
Theory of the Novel, ed. Philip Stevick (New York, 1967),
p. 158.

[12]The fourteen categories, according to grouping,
are: action, pathetic, tragic, punitive, sentimental,
admiration (plots of fortune); maturing, reform, testing,

traditionally invites his reader to "play the game" along
with the detective, so the science fiction writer frequently
plants clues for the dénouement of his book by means of
establishing the lines of extrapolation leading up to and
operating within his fictional setting.[13] In both cases,
the solution to the problem brings with it a sense of
vicarious achievement for the reader, but the kind of
achievement varies significantly, the one being introverted,
the other extroverted. In the mystery story, the murderer
is a kind of scapegoat, the identification of whom, Auden
has suggested, lets the reader indulge his fantasy of "being
restored to the Garden of Eden, to a state of innocence."[14]
In the science fiction story, innocence seems to be assumed
from the first, the victory over nature or unreason is a
temporary thing, reversible by time, and the fundamental
achievement is a hard-won beachhead in the territory of the
real enemy, the unknown.

This simplicity of design represents an ideal infrequently, if ever, achieved; when pure science fiction, in
essay form, is converted to imaginative literature, it

degradation (plots of character); education, revelation,
affective, disillusionment (plots of thought). Friedman,
pp. 154-165.

[13]See Howard Haycraft, Murder for Pleasure: The
Life and Times of the Detective Story (New York and London,
1941), pp. 223-258.

[14]W. H. Auden, "The Guilty Vicarage," The Dyer's
Hand (New York, 1962), p. 158.

becomes subject to the whims of the artist and the rules of
the literary form. Plot, character, setting, theme, structure, or some other aspect of literature may become more
important than extrapolation; science and scientism may
become no more important than any other human institutions
or ideas, and may even take on negative values.[15] Only
where there is a concerted effort to approach, or stay close
to the ideals of pure science fiction, can we expect those
ideals to remain fairly close to the surface. Such an
effort has been exerted in the American pulp science fiction
magazines for over forty years.

The proprietary interest evinced by science fiction
fans may thus have preserved the scientistic qualities
enumerated above. It has certainly contributed to the
identification of science fiction with such features of
popular literature as fantasy, the characteristic style of
the pulps, and an essential homogeneity of form as well as
of purpose. Yet each of these is closely bound up with the
pure form of science fiction as well, as should become
clearer as we proceed.

The relationship of fantasy to science fiction is a
complex one, even if only because the word "fantasy" (like
the phrase "science fiction") means different things to

---

[15]Not everyone in the science fiction community
would agree that science fiction can attack science and
remain science fiction. See, for example, Heinleim (above,
note 5), pp. 59-60.

different people. In a psychological sense, popular literature, including science fiction, can easily be regarded as
escapist fantasy.[16] In a literary sense, we can see that
science fiction is a particular kind of such writings as are
called fantasies.[17] Yet within the science fiction community, and to some extent outside it, an attempt is also made
to distinguish clearly between science fiction and fantasy,
as representative of the possible and impossible, respectively.[18] And all three of these interpretations are

---

[16]Friedman, p. 158; Leslie A. Fiedler, Love and
Death in the American Novel (Cleveland and New York, 1962),
pp. 472-480. See also Mass Culture: The Popular Arts in
America, ed. Bernard Rosenberg and David Manning White
(Glencoe, Illinois, 1957), and Robert C. O'Hara, Media for
the Millions: The Process of Mass Communication (New York,
1962). For a psychoanalytic treatment of all literature as
fantasy, see Norman N. Holland, The Dynamics of Literary
Response (New York, 1968).

[17]"Most simply, science fiction may be considered
that continuing, recognizable genre within the broad scope
of fantasy which attempts to present the impact of the
mechanistic and allied sciences upon the imagination of
man." Thomas Dean Clareson, "The Emergence of American
Science Fiction: 1880-1915: A Study of the Impact of
Science upon American Romanticism," unpubl. diss.
(Pennsylvania, 1956). "Science fiction is a branch of
fantasy identifiable by the fact that it eases the 'willing
suspension of disbelief' on the part of its readers by
utilizing an atmosphere of scientific credibility for its
imaginative speculations in physical science, space, time,
social science, and philosophy." Sam Moskowitz, Explorers
of the Infinite: Shapers of Science Fiction (Cleveland and
New York, 1963), p. 11.

[18]The line between science fiction and fantasy
fluctuates, of course, depending on what a person regards as
possible, as indicated in L. Sprague de Camp, Science-
Fiction Handbook: The Writing of Imaginative Fiction
(New York, 1953), pp. 20-22.

applicable to our discussion.

In the first place, the basic plot of popular
fiction, a variation on the ancient motif of the quest,
supplies the reader with, as Friedman says, "suspense,
expectation, and surprise," and with a sense of vicarious
adventure and achievement.[19] Identifying with the hero, he
too becomes heroic in this fantasy world, able to do extraordinary things, able to forget the major and minor frustrations of daily life. This is what C. S. Lewis calls
"Normal Castle-building" of the "Egoistic" type, and it is
what most popular literature involves the reader in, pander-
ing perhaps to the wishes he already has, and about which he
will do nothing if his daydream world is satisfactory
enough.[20] But the specifically science fictional variety of
the quest involves a distinct sort of hero, a man of
science, with whom not everyone can identify; like a detective, he uses reason to solve problems, like a cowboy, he
may use technology as a weapon, but his education involves
detailed knowledge of the physical and social environment,
which is brought to bear on that which is unknown, not only
to the characters in the book, but also to the reader, the
author, and man in general. Thus the escape of science
fiction may be into a larger reality, as it is into the

---

[19]Friedman, p. 158.

[20]C. S. Lewis, An Experiment in Criticism
(Cambridge, England, 1965), p. 52.

possibilities of the future.[21]

In terms of literary form and style, Herbert Read's description of fantasy is instructive as it relates to science fiction. Defining fantasy as a product of deliberate, rational speculation, he finds in it an extraversion of feelings, a concern with objects, an apparent arbitrariness of order, and an expository rather than a narrative style.[22] Read goes on from there to criticize H. G. Wells for not quite reaching a state of pure fantasy: "He errs, as in The Time Machine, by imparting to his fantasies a pseudo-scientific logicality; it is as though having conceived one arbitrary fantasy he were compelled by the habits of his scientific training to work out the consequences of this fantasy. Real fantasy is bolder than this; it dispenses with all logic and habit and relies on the force of wonder alone."[23] Wells's error, of course, is quite deliberate; he is writing science fiction, for which that "one arbitrary fantasy" supplies a framework to be filled in by imagination, a faculty which Read finds to be introverted, sensuous, symbolic, and narrative, in opposition to fantasy.[24]

---

[21]A similar inference is drawn in Isaac Asimov, "Escape into Reality," Is Anyone There? (Garden City, 1967), pp. 283-290.

[22]Herbert Read, English Prose Style (Boston, 1952), pp. 125-127.

[23]Read, pp. 133-134.

[24]Read, pp. 125-127.

That "one arbitrary fantasy" to which Read refers
has been formulated into a rule by some science fiction
writers: Jack Williamson and Fletcher Pratt, for example,
have each stated that a science fiction story can have only
one such unexplained principle or assumption.[25] Many
writers and critics have accepted this dictum implicitly,
as is shown by the frequent reference to "what if?" as a
guiding principle of science fiction, and indeed it is
suggestive of the underlying difference between science
fiction and outright fantasy as Read has defined it.[26] But
it is a dictum honored more in the breach than in the
observance. Many stories which are ostensibly science
fiction can be found to have numerous fantasies, the explanation for which is either nonexistent or unconvincing.
And in an example of pure science fiction, we should expect
to find nothing which cannot be rationalized in terms of
extrapolation from contemporary reality.

Even assuming, however, that every departure from
the ordinary and present-day which made its appearance in a
work of science fiction were explained in a manner satisfactory to every reader (an impossible task, the attempted

---

[25] Jack Williamson, "The Logic of Fantasy," in Of
Worlds Beyond: The Science of Science Fiction Writing, ed.
Lloyd Arthur Eschbach (Reading, Pennsylvania, 1947;
reprinted Chicago, 1964), pp. 39 ff.; Fletcher Pratt,
"Introduction" to his anthology, World of Wonder (New York,
1951), pp. 20-21.

[26] C. Robert Morse, "The Game of If," National
Review, May 3, 1958, pp. 427-428; and many other essays.

fulfillment of which would certainly be unreadable), we would still not have freed ourselves unequivocally from the taint of fantasy. Extrapolation, itself, is a kind of fantasy, although disciplined by a mathematical or quasi-mathematical sense of order. The further away you extrapolate from the point of origin, and the more details you try to extrapolate for your fictional world, the less probable your prediction becomes, and the more you are likely to rely on sources other than analysis and calculation.[27] One of these alternative sources is the unconscious. Another is the body of motifs and conventions already in existence in science fiction or science fictional speculation.

One result of the unconscious being loosed in a science fictional work is that desires and fears which have no necessary connection with what is objectively real or probable may become determining factors in the story and in its effect on the reader. If they are kept generally under control, the work may be utopian or dystopian, at least in terms of the author's attitude toward his narrative, often in terms of the overall structure of his imaginary world.[28]

---

[27]For further discussion, see Year 2000 (above, note 7), pp. 34-39.

[28]The principles of utopia and dystopia as literary forms, and their similarities, are most thoroughly examined in Hubertus Schulte Herbrüggen, Utopie and Anti-Utopie: Von der Strukturanalyse zur Strukturtypologie, in Beiträge zur Englischen Philologie, 43 (Bochum-Langendreer, 1960).

Without some kind of tight rational control, however, science fiction can deteriorate into what Leslie Fiedler sees it as to begin with, terror fiction: "Its writers propagate, for instance, non-Aristotelian logic, engram psychology, interracial (even interplanetary) tolerance, and, of course, the general cause of science. Yet simultaneously, they pander to fantasies of flight, dreams of omnipotence--and, not least of all, the shameful pleasure of imagining the stench of burning bodies, the acrid dust of crumbling cities, the desolation of the man lost in space, the anguish of the oppressed in totalitarian utopias as yet unborn."[29] It may be that an attempt to avoid such an accusation is partly responsible for the notable lack of emotion in science fiction, especially in its characters.

In its purest form, the product of the unconscious tends toward the archetypes of myth, which, as Northrop Frye has suggested, can be seen to form a coherent pattern of imagery (at least in Western civilization). Viewed favorably, in terms of human desire, this pattern approximates an apocalyptic world, similar to the heaven of religion; viewed negatively, as rejected by desire, it becomes a demonic world, similar to hell. Both worlds are essentially static, but they exert an influence over the kind of fictional worlds in which men act and narrative takes place. Less

---

[29]Fiedler (above, note 15), p. 479. Similar charges of fear-peddling and general pessimism are fairly common in other essays.

rigidly metaphorical, these worlds involve progressive rationalization of the mythic imagery, as they tend toward realism. Thus we arrive at a fictional world of romance, in which the central plot-form is the quest, in which protagonist and antagonist tend to be respectively good and bad, innocent and guilty, natural and unnatural, hero and villain, and in which the supernatural (apocalyptic and demonic) is never very far away.[30] With some modification, this could be the fictional world of science fiction, as in fact Frye himself suggests at another point: "Science fiction frequently tries to imagine what life would be like on a plane as far above us as we are above savagery; its setting is often of a kind that appears to us as technologically miraculous. It is thus a mode of romance with a strong inherent tendency to myth."[31]

Like Frye's fictional worlds, the world of science fiction is a system of conventions and motifs agreed upon by a number of writers and readers. Although at bottom it is founded on natural law and the goals and assumptions of science, it is for the most part a set of fictional constructs consciously fabricated, and subjected to scrutiny and modification before becoming a part of this modern

---

[30]Northrop Frye, Anatomy of Criticism (Princeton, 1957), pp. 131-239. For an introduction to the modern form of the prose romance, see Robert Scholes, The Fabulators (New York, 1967).

[31]Frye, p. 49.

cosmology (Frye suggests a similar process, poetic rather
than scientific, was responsible for the medieval cosmology).[32] It is a new cosmology, which does not have the
accumulated resonances for the general reader that we associate with that old picture of the universe, although for
science fiction fans the resonances are strong enough for
the writer not to have to explain everything he introduces,
for him to assume knowledge of conflicting interpretations
of a science fictional projection, and for him to evoke and
invite comparisons of his work with others of a similar
nature or on a similar theme. It is a somewhat inconstant
cosmology, too, which may be disconcerting to some readers:
it has many levels and layers, in space and in time; it
allows for differing and even conflicting projections into
the same time and place; even its foundations are subject to
change, as scientists (and science fiction writers) adjust
the reigning theories and "laws" from time to time, and as
various projections come true in reality (differing greatly
in detail from many, if not all, predictions) or are ruled
out by actual happenings contradictory to them.

In addition to being a handy compendium of fantastic
motifs, conventions, and ideas, the science fictional
cosmology is also a genuine object of belief (which perhaps
strengthens the claims both of those who see it as myth and

---

[32]Frye, pp. 160-161.

those who see it as delusion).[33] Obviously, for the sake of
the story, writer and reader agree to suspend disbelief.
But there is also a genuine communal acceptance of some of
the basic principles making up the cosmology, regardless of
quibbling over details. Thus travel to the stars, the
existence of intelligent life elsewhere in the universe, and
the desire of man to increase his knowledge and power are
rather firm articles of faith; slightly less firm is the
belief in the possibilities of robots, artificial life,
man's achieving some control over his combative instincts;
somewhat shaky beliefs, but acceptable conventions include
immortality, matter transmission, and the various kinds of
phenomena called "parapsychological."[34] For the most part
this communal acceptance is rather on the level of what
Tolkien calls "literary belief," the acceptance of things

---

[33]"As a type [science fiction] conforms to the
expression of a myth. This myth, not yet in wide acceptance
among the population at large, is that the mind of man is
capable of solving all problems directed to it by the exercise of logical thinking and through the logical disciplines
of orthodox science." Don Fabun, "Science Fiction in Motion
Pictures, Radio, and Television," in Modern Science Fiction:
Its Meaning and Its Future, ed. Reginald Bretnor (New York,
1953), pp. 46-47. See also Siegfried Mandel and Peter
Fingesten, "The Myth of Science Fiction," Saturday Review,
August 27, 1955, pp. 7-8, 24-25, 28, and Ednita P. Bernabev,
"Science Fiction: A New Mythos," Psychoanalytic Quarterly,
XXVI, 4 (1957), 527-535.

[34]See the expository treatment given these and other
motifs in Clarke (above, note 8).

as real within the fictional or Secondary World.[35] But the science fiction community also has its lunatic fringe, who regard this Secondary World as better or realer than the Primary World and seek to live within this new framework.[36]

Such a communal acceptance, for all of its unfortunate by-products, may well have been necessary for science fiction to maintain its identity in the twentieth century. The general public and the main stream of literature certainly don't seem to have had any interest in promulgating science or propagandizing for the future in the Twenties and Thirties, and even since World War II, the acceptance of science fiction and its way of thinking has not been overwhelming. But whether the public's rejection caused the descent into subliterature or vice versa, by the time of World War I, fictional considerations of science and its possibilities could be found almost only in literary dystopias, warning of science's dangers, or in dime novels, exploiting science for sensationalism.

At first glance, the conventions of dystopia, like those of utopia, might seem rather well suited to the aims of pure science fiction. The emphases on theory and logical

---

[35] J. R. R. Tolkien, "On Fairy-Stories," Tree and Leaf (London, 1964), pp. 36-37.

[36] Case studies may be found in Martin Gardner, Fads and Fallacies in the Name of Science, rev. ed. (New York, 1957), and Robert Lindner, "The Jet-Propelled Couch," The Fifty-Minute Hour: A Collection of True Psychoanalytic Tales (New York, 1961).

construction, on settings and customs more than on individual people, on rational and generalized behavior in preference to personal and emotional idiosyncrasies, the relative
unimportance placed on developed characters, on plot and
action, on things as they are now, both positive and
negative utopias hold in common with science fiction.[37] In
addition, writers of utopias and dystopias have often placed
their imaginary worlds in the future, have stressed their
realizability, and have admitted the importance of science.
But the stress on value judgments for or against these
imaginary worlds, the predominance of desire over likelihood, and the importance of rigid, authoritarian, unchanging
"perfection," such as would allow no scientific innovations
and admit of no problems to solve, are uncongenial to pure
science fiction.[38] And the demand made by the traditional
utopian and dystopia on the reader, for intelligence,
perspective, a taste for social criticism and satire, and
the patience to endure lengthy and complex description and
exhortation, was not likely to attract a communal response,
whereas pulp fiction could, and did.

---

[37]See Herbrüggen (above, note 27).

[38]This is not meant to imply that dystopian science
fiction cannot or does not exist. The contrary has been
established quite clearly in Kingsley Amis, New Maps of
Hell: A Survey of Science Fiction (London, 1961), and in
Mark R. Hillegas, The Future as Nightmare: H. G. Wells and
the Anti-Utopians (New York, 1967). I merely wish to point
out the "impurity" of the form.

The average reader of <u>Astounding Science Fiction</u>,
according to the most recent poll conducted by John W.
Campbell, Jr., in 1957-58, is "about thirty years old, male,
a college graduate in one of the engineering sciences . . .
who's been reading <u>Astounding</u> since his Sophomore year in
college. . . ."[39] Fifty per cent identified their college
major as engineering or physical science; including biology,
medicine, mathematics, psychology, and social science, about
83 per cent could be called scientifically oriented. Fifty-
seven per cent had graduated from college, and an additional
16 per cent had gone beyond high school in their education;
over 80 per cent had read <u>Astounding</u> five years or more,
over 54 per cent more than ten years, over 33 per cent more
than fifteen years.[40] Although Campbell's poll, and
Campbell's magazine, may not be fully representative of the
science fiction community, Isaac Asimov, in a 1963 article,
cited personal experience to support Campbell's findings of
a connection between science and science fiction, and his
suggestion that reading science fiction begins in

---

[39][John W. Campbell, Jr.], "Portrait of You,"
<u>Astounding</u>, May, 1958, p. 135. The poll, such as Campbell
has conducted before, was first announced in the June, 1957
issue, p. 138. The accuracy of the poll is open to question, since it was totally voluntary in nature (the questions and their categorized answers were given in a coupon
printed in the magazine). The reliability of inferences
from the data is also questionable, since the total number
of respondents was not given.

[40]"Portrait," pp. 135-136.

adolescence.[41] These factors suggest the necessity, in
keeping the science fiction community together, of satisfying the adolescent's thirst for adventure as well as the
scientist's interest in speculation. Other factors, such as
educational background and length of readership, suggest an
audience of some sophistication, at least as far as science
and science fiction are concerned, if not in literature and
the humanities as a whole.

If, then, science fiction is mainly "a relaxation
literature for the amusement of technically minded people,"
as Campbell states elsewhere, we can expect it to use
fictional techniques aimed more at keeping the story going
than at providing new kinds of artistic insight.[42] Not a
popular medium in the sense of having a vast, general audience, the pulp magazines are nevertheless dependent on, and
responsive to a mass public of a specialized kind. In order
to maintain that readership, they must merchandise a product
which is fairly stable not only in its outlook, but also in

[41]Isaac Asimov, "The Sword of Achilles," Is Anyone
There? (Garden City, 1967), p. 300.

[42]John W. Campbell, Jr., "The Value of Science
Fiction," in Science Marches On, ed. James Stokley (New
York, 1951), p. 445. Science fiction as a whole is almost
untouched by the "experiments" in form and technique which
fiction has seen in the twentieth century. But then science
fiction writers would generally fit the category of "contemporaries" rather than that of "moderns" in Stephen Spender,
The Struggle of the Modern (Berkeley and Los Angeles, 1965),
pp. 71-78.

its form.[43] In order to preserve this stability, popular
literature frequently resorts to formulas, stereotypes,
oversimplifications, and a general conformism; such conventions and prejudices can be found in science fiction,
although they may not fully agree with those of the general
public.[44] Hypothetical futures can easily become escapist
wonderlands, problem-solving stories become exercises in
consistently victorious adventure, and the scientist-hero
becomes an always resourceful superman, vague enough for the
adolescent in all of us to identify with and specific enough
to award the scientist or technician special recognition.
The adventure might not be as likely as the setting, the
temporary ego-gratification might not help the reader understand the real world and his society, and the afficionado
might find rather rare a really new idea that was titillating in its freshness and exciting in terms of the vistas
and perspectives it opened up. But by not taking science
fiction seriously as literature, people could read it as
entertainment; the short episodes, sketchy motivation,

---

[43]"This [statement by Vladimir Nabokov regarding the
advisability of the artist's ignoring his audience] is not
an extreme point of view; we have all encountered it. But
if this is art, if this is literature, science fiction could
afford to be literature . . . [sic] for its very essence is
communication of a variety of ideas to a variety of people.
And it has to lure them into coming to listen." P. Schuyler
Miller, "The Reference Library," Analog, February, 1964,
p. 92.

[44]Contrast O'Hara (above, note 15) and Hirsch
(above, note 9).

skimpy characterization, simplistic explanations, and flat cliché-ridden language in description and dialogue would make none of literature's "unreasonable" demands on the reader's full attention, and the content, mainly projections of science and technology into man's future, could be given a fairly wide circulation.

Whether or not a communal relationship between readers, writers, and editors actually was necessary for the preservation of science fiction, a fusion of science fictional ideas and pulp literary format did take place, and a highly specialized market of commercial fiction has kept its product within reasonable proximity of the ideals of pure science fiction. There is a definite family resemblance between the magazines (and their contents) of the Twenties and early Thirties and those of today, the late Sixties. This is due in large part to the continued regard for the principles we have just examined: the shared assumptions of science and conventions of science fiction which make up the modern cosmology; the shared desire for adventure, fantasy, and knowledge about the unknown which motivates the stories; and the shared techniques and conventions of pulp fiction which dominate the medium of popular communication. These similarities and their differences from the accepted norms of great literature are so pronounced that critics may well feel themselves justified in assuming an overall homogeneity throughout pulp science fiction, whereby an observation based on a few examples will hold true for the entire field.[45]

The homogeneity of science fiction, however, is more apparent to the outside observer than it is to the habitual reader, for all that the latter gravitates toward his favorite reading because it is in fact of a certain kind. Within this general sameness there is a good deal of variety, some of which has already been suggested, by the chronological division of "physical," "social," and "psychological" science fiction, and by the fact that the five leading pulp magazines today each tend to specialize in a different approach to science fiction.[46] A tolerance for diversity in the science fiction community is indicated by a number of other signs as well. Within the pages of these magazines, controversy is not avoided, but welcomed; practically any and all of the accepted conventions of science fiction mentioned above are fair game for attack, including the desire for adventure and wonder and the literary form and style, and not only in letters and editorials, but in the fiction itself as well. The critical literature, produced from within the community, never shied away from controversy in the fanzines, and does not now that it has attained book

---

[45]Many critical articles on science fiction seem to be based on just such a "select" sampling. Their contradictory conclusions suggest the inadequacy of the selections.

[46]See above, Chapter I, pp. 21-37.

publication either.[47] And the "Hugo" awards, given annually
at the World Science Fiction Convention since 1953 (except-
ing 1954), also indicate an allowance for variety. In
fifteen years, each of the five leading magazines (Analog,
F&SF, Galaxy, IF, New Worlds) has received at least one
"Hugo."[48] Winning novels have included the literarily
sensitive and the science fictionally conventional.[49] In
some cases, awards have been given despite widespread
reservations about the author's philosophy.[50]

Variations in quality are also noticeable, and
almost every regular reader of science fiction must have
his list of the best writers and books in the field.
P. Schuyler Miller, whose book review column has appeared
in Astounding/Analog since October, 1951, has invited

---

[47]See especially Damon Knight, In Search of Wonder:
Essays on Modern Science Fiction, rev. ed. (Chicago, 1967),
and William Atheling, Jr. [James Blish], The Issue at Hand:
Studies in Contemporary Magazine Science Fiction, ed. James
Blish (Chicago, 1964).

[48]According to sources given above (Chapter I, note
37), Astounding/Analog has six wins (1955, 1956, 1961, 1962,
1964, 1965) and two ties (1953, 1957); F&SF has four wins
(1958, 1959, 1960, 1963); IF has three wins (1966, 1967,
1968); Galaxy (1953) and New Worlds (1957) each tied once.

[49]Examples of each include, respectively, A Canticle
for Leibowitz by Walter M. Miller, Jr., winner of the 1961
award, and Way Station by Clifford Simak, winner of the 1964
award.

[50]Two of Robert A. Heinlein's four awards for best
novel were for controversial books: Starship Troopers,
winner of the 1960 award, and Stranger in a Strange Land,
winner of the 1962 award.

reader response three times (1952, 1956, 1966) in order to compile consensus lists of the (28, 26, and 27, respectively) "best" books in science fiction.[51] For the 1961 Modern Language Association Conference on Science Fiction, Mark Hillegas proposed a list, agreed upon by members of the Conference, of 108 books of at least historical interest, dating back to 1607 A.D.[52] Of the more recent entries in the MLA list, twelve titles agree with both Miller's 1956 and 1966 lists, and another nine agree with either the 1956 or the 1966 list (which were cut off arbitrarily at a certain standing in terms of total votes received for a particular book).[53] The MLA list included three of the seven "Hugo" winners up to that time, and the 1966 Analog

---

[51]P. Schuyler Miller, "The Reference Library," Astounding, January, 1953; Astounding, October, 1956; Analog, November, 1966.

[52]Mark R. Hillegas, "A Draft of the Science-Fiction Canon to be proposed at the 1961 MLA Conference on Science Fiction," Extrapolation, III (December, 1961), 26-30.

[53]One of the twelve is an anthology, Adventures in Time and Space, ed. Raymond J. Healy and J. Francis McComas (1946). The other eleven follow in alphabetical order by author: Isaac Asimov, Foundation (1952) and I, Robot (1951); Alfred Bester, The Demolished Man (1953); Ray Bradbury, The Martian Chronicles (1950); Arthur C. Clarke, Childhood's End (1953); Hal Clement, Mission of Gravity (1953); Robert A. Heinlein, The Man Who Sold the Moon (1950); Frederik Pohl and C. M. Kornbluth, The Space Merchants (1953); Theodore Sturgeon, More Than Human (1953); A. E. Van Vogt, Slan (1940) and The World of Null-A (1945). Three volumes listed by both Hillegas and Miller 1966 were not published in time for Miller 1956: Isaac Asimov, The Caves of Steel (1954); Walter M. Miller, Jr., A Canticle for Leibowitz (1959); John Wyndham, Re-Birth (1955).

list included six of the fourteen novels awarded a "Hugo"
up to that time.[54] Thus it can be seen that there is some
general agreement about what the best works of science
fiction are.[55]

There is, however, a considerable amount of dispute
about what makes a work of science fiction good. What might
amount to literary excellence in the eyes of many discerning
readers--a sense of style, a feeling for language, intelligent dialogue, emotional conviction, human characters
involved in honest interpersonal relationships, a wealth of
detail enforcing a sense of reality--many science fiction
fans find unnecessary, disconcerting, even a kind of camou-
flage for an author's having nothing to say. What they
seem to want first is that which only science fiction has
to offer (novelty, suggestive speculation, scientific accuracy), secondly that which it has in common with other kinds
of popular literature (adventure, excitement, entertainment,

---

[54]Hillegas: Bester, W. Miller (above, note 52),
and James Blish, A Case of Conscience (1958). Miller 1966:
Bester, W. Miller (above, note 52), two books by Heinlein
(above, note 49), Simak (above, note 48), and Frank Herbert,
Dune (1965).

[55]Miller's 1952 poll, based on only 41 ballots,
appeared before many of the best books on the other compila-
tions; five of its titles agree with Miller 1956 and 1966;
nine of the 1952 titles agree with Hillegas. A small poll
of British readers, conducted by a Scottish science fiction
magazine, Nebula, in February, 1959, correlates with others
as follows: Miller 1956, 11; Miller 1966, 11; Hillegas, 9;
Miller 1956 and 1966, 9; Miller 1956 and 1966 and Hillegas,
7. The Nebula poll was reported by Miller in Astounding,
October, 1959.

in a word, "story-telling"), and next, whatever craftsmanship is needed to cement the two into a workable construction.[56] Both groups of readers, I suspect, are in favor of
intellectual honesty, philosophical significance, and
aesthetic integrity, but they mean rather different things
by those phrases.

Thus, as in recent years, the marriage between
science fiction and mainstream literature has come to seem
more and more imminent, there has been some controversy
over the likely watering down of the science fictional
ideal.[57] Ironically, the very success of pulp science
fiction brought in enough competition to endanger financially the independent existence of the pulp base of
operations. The spread of science fiction into other
communications and entertainment media and the conversion of
science fictions into historical actualities has opened up,
in turn, a wider audience and more lucrative, less specialized markets for something _called_ science fiction. But

---

[56]Thus the three most popular authors in Miller's
1966 poll (measured by a separate vote and tabulation), the
only ones named by over half of the 441 respondents, were
Asimov (80.4 per cent), Heinlein (80.0 per cent), and Clarke
(66.9 per cent), the works of whom fit the latter description well, but not the former. _Analog_, November, 1966.

[57]Knight (above, note 46), pp. 277-283 and passim;
Algis Budrys, "Galaxy Bookshelf," _Galaxy_ (since February,
1965), especially August, 1966, December, 1966, and October,
1968. Others regret the passing of the "Golden Age" of the
Thirties; see especially Moskowitz (above, note 16), pp.
347-350, and Alva Rogers, _A Requiem for "Astounding"_
(Chicago, 1964).

reaching a more generalized audience could result in a loss of contact with science and extrapolation, since the general public (and the literary critics) will frequently accept as science fiction anything making use of a single device, convention, or gimmick borrowed from or resembling science fiction in its pure state.

Thus the theoretical modification we considered to be begun with the adaptation of pure science fiction to imaginative literature, and continued with the adaptation to the pulp fiction magazines, leads further to still another attenuation of the science fictional base, so that at least two definitions are necessary for dealing with science fiction as a literary form or genre. Historically, we have seen it as a general tendency in literature through the ages, and as an essentially commercial product of popular magazines catering to a specialized taste. Fundamentally, we have seen it as fictionalized scientific speculation, each extrapolation or projection being itself an individual "science fiction." Formally, then, we can build on that foundation to construct a definition applicable to that work which most closely approximates the ideal: imaginative literature based on extrapolation from contemporary reality, consistent with contemporary scientific assumptions and theory. In such a formulation, "imaginative literature" means stories, plays, and poems concerned with hypothetical settings, events, and/or characters, "extrapolation" means

logical and chronological extension, and the "scientific
assumptions and theory" tend toward the "scientistic" postu-
lates described above. A more general definition, inclusive
rather than exclusive, can be formed by expanding this one
with additional qualifiers (in parentheses): imaginative
literature based (at least in part) on extrapolation from
present (past, future, or un-) reality, consistent with
scientific (quasi-scientific, para-scientific, or pseudo-
scientific) assumptions and theory of the present (past, or
future, in this or a hypothetical parallel dimension or
"time-track").

The latter definition, allowing for the inclusion of
almost any sort of utopia, marvelous journey, or detailed
and consistent fantasy, seems to be the one in general use
today, both inside and outside the science fiction community. Inside, despite the theoretical allegiance to science
(or perhaps because of the security of that allegiance),
there is a good deal of experimentation being undertaken as
if to see how far the definition can be extended. Outside,
where there is no apparent concern for science fictional
purity, the guardians of public taste emphasize and encourage literary form, style, and technique, even at the expense
of specifically science fictional values.

The problem is not so much that the critics would
like to clean up the more subliterary features of science
fiction, as that they may not distinguish between those

features and the more or less defining characteristics of
the genre. Even if a critic does not have a definite philosophical bias against science, technology, and scientism as
potential or actual oppressors of the human spirit, he may,
by asking that science fiction become more literary, be
asking that it stop being science fiction. If a writer
becomes too subjectively involved with his characters, making them more specific, individual, emotionally motivated,
i.e. human, stressing felt life over theory, he is saying in
effect that man, not science, is the measure. If he puts
more stress on aesthetic construction of stories and
sentences, he may be accepting the implicit dicta that a
love of words is more important than a love of ideas, that
experimentation is permissible with literary form but not
with people and concepts, and that literary belief (a product of literary technique) is more significant than actual
belief in the possibility that a prediction or projection
might come true.

It may be that a compromise will be reached, whereby
neither literary nor science fictional considerations must
be slighted, along the lines of the "integrated" literature
forecast by Bretnor, but it should be a true compromise,
involving not only the appreciation of literary technique
and values by readers, writers, and critics presently inside
the science fiction community, but also the scientific

education of readers, writers, and critics outside.[58]
Although the genius who can make great literature out of
science fiction cannot be planned for, the outsider can
learn to accept science fiction conventions, and the insider
can learn to accept an optimum level of literacy. To some
extent, both have already done so since 1945 and, if Judith
Merril can be believed, the rapprochement is almost upon
us.[59] The evidence is fairly skimpy, however, and mostly
concentrated in the shorter forms of prose fiction, where a
single science fiction can support a story, or a fantasy
can be given a semi-scientific twist (as Ray Bradbury
discovered even before 1945).[60] The real test, I believe,
is in the novel, where people and life, as well as ideas
and technology, must be dealt with, and there the compromise
is not yet a reality.

A number of respectable novels, however, or books of
novel length, honest and intelligent, solid and craftsman-
like, have emerged from the pulp field since World War II.

---

[58]Reginald Bretnor, "The Future of Science Fiction,"
in Bretnor (above, note 32), pp. 265-294.

[59]Judith Merril, "What Do You Mean--Science?/
Fiction?" Extrapolation, VII (May, 1966), 30-46, VIII
(December, 1966), 2-19; The Year's Best S-F, 7th-11th Annual
Editions (New York, 1962-66); book reviews, F&SF, monthly
(with a few exceptions) since March, 1965.

[60]Sam Moskowitz, Seekers of Tomorrow: Masters of
Modern Science Fiction (Cleveland and New York, 1966),
pp. 355-363.

Of these I have chosen six, as relatively representative of
what has been written over the last twenty years, to subject
to close, critical examination. They are: Childhood's End
(1953) by Arthur C. Clarke; The Caves of Steel (1953) by
Isaac Asimov; More than Human (1953) by Theodore Sturgeon;
A Canticle for Leibowitz (1959) by Walter M. Miller, Jr.;
Rogue Moon (1960) by Algis Budrys; and The Crystal World
(1966) by J. G. Ballard. Three of these authors (Clarke,
Asimov, Sturgeon) began writing science fiction in the late
Thirties and early Forties, in the age of "social" science
fiction, two (Miller, Budrys) began in the Fifties, when the
pulp writers began to be noticed outside the science fiction
community, and one (Ballard) began in the Sixties, writing
mainly for New Worlds which stressed "psychological" science
fiction. The ratio of British to American writers is one to
two (Clarke and Ballard are British), somewhat higher than
the actual ratio in the magazines; two of the six writers
(Sturgeon, Ballard) are noted more for fantasy than
"possible" science fiction, also a somewhat higher percent-
age than actually obtains in the field. Each of the books
studied has at its base at least one major theme or motif
which the others do not, and which is fairly commonly used
in science fiction; each is written in a form and with a
style which, although distinctive enough to identify the
author, have also been used or approximated by other pulp
writers. From a thematic, formal, and stylistic analysis of

these six books, then, it should be possible to show both the underlying similarities which make them science fiction, and the level of artistic achievement which has been reached by certain individuals, and thus by the field in general.

CHAPTER III

ARTHUR C. CLARKE: <u>CHILDHOOD'S END</u>

Accepting UNESCO's Kalinga Prize for the popularization of science in 1962, Arthur C. Clarke, author of more
than thirty books of science fiction and non-fiction,
eulogized science fiction in his acceptance speech, as the
following excerpts show:

> I would claim that the percentage of competent writ-
> ing in the science fiction field is probably higher
> than in any other. This is because much of it is a
> labour of love, written by enthusiasts who have
> considerable scientific knowledge and who are them-
> selves practicing scientists. . . .
>
> Though it often serves to impart information, I
> think its chief value is <u>inspirational</u>. . . .
>
> In spreading the ideas of spaceflight [sic],
> science fiction has undoubtedly helped to change the
> world. More generally, it helps us to face the
> strange realities of the universe in which we
> live. . . .
>
> Anyone who reads this form of literature quickly
> realizes the absurdity of man's present tribal divi-
> sions. Science fiction encourages the cosmic view-
> point; perhaps this is why it is not popular among
> those literary pundits who have never quite accepted
> the Copernican revolution, nor grown used to the
> fact [sic] that man may not be the highest form of
> life in the universe. . . .
>
> It is, pre-eminently, the literature of change--
> and change is the only thing of which we can be
> certain today. . . .

> Science fiction . . . assumes that the future
> will be profoundly different from the past--though
> it does not, as is often imagined, attempt to
> predict that future in detail. . . .
>
> But by mapping out possible futures, as well as
> a good many impossible ones, the science fiction
> writer can do a great service to the community.
> He encourages in his readers flexibility of mind,
> readiness to accept and even welcome changes--in one
> word, adaptability.[1]

Although he purports to be describing science

fiction in general, and he follows the affirmative arguments

generally accepted within the science fiction community, his

comments have particular relevance to his own work. An

"enthusiast" of science fiction since at age ten he discov-

ered Amazing Stories, Clarke himself has "considerable

scientific knowledge" and apparently writes science fiction

as "a labour of love" since there is more money in writing

popular science. A radar instructor with the Royal Air

Force in World War II, he holds a Bachelor of Science degree

from the University of London (1948), has been chairman of

the British Interplanetary Society, and has done a great

deal of oceanographic research in and around Ceylon, his

adopted homeland.[2]

---

[1]Arthur C. Clarke, "Kalinga Award Speech," Voices
from the Sky: Previews of the Coming Space Age (New York,
1967), pp. 139-143.

[2]For biographical data on Clarke, see Godfrey Smith,
"Astounding Story: About a Science Fiction Writer," New
York Times Magazine, March 6, 1966, pp. 28, 75-77, and
sketches in Contemporary Authors, IV (1963), and Current
Biography, October, 1966.

In both his fiction and his non-fiction, Clarke brings his readers face to face with "the strange realities of the universe in which we live," with particular emphasis on space, time, and the sea. His short stories include the whimsical fantasy of Tales from the White Hart (1957) as well as the straight science fiction collected in Expedition to Earth (1953), Reach for Tomorrow (1956), The Other Side of the Sky (1958), and Tales from Ten Worlds (1962). His novels of the near future are soberly speculative, The Deep Range (1957) and Dolphin Island (1963) dealing with life in the sea, the others with the exploration of space. From the first moon-rocket described in Prelude to Space (1951), through the space stations of Islands in the Sky (1953), to the moon in A Fall of Moondust (1961), to Mars in The Sands of Mars (1951), and to the near planets in general in Earthlight (1951, expanded 1955), he guides us through man's expansion of his technological progress and territorial domain.

In three other novels, however, Clarke is less soberly scientific, more concerned with eschatological fantasy, as he considers possible destinies for man, the prediction of which can hardly be dated, although they can be seen as logical extensions of certain lines of thought. The first, Against the Fall of Night (1948, revised as The City and the Stars, 1956), is a tale of the far future on Earth, in which an adolescent succeeds in reawakening the

static civilization of an "immortal" city. The technology
is conceivable, the psychology is romantically childish, and
the style and tone, especially in the revised version, are
far more periodic and mellifluous, poetic and dreamlike,
than his usual modified journalese. The latest, 2001:
A Space Odyssey (1968), expanded from a short story into a
novel and a working script for the film of the same name,
carries man's space exploration out to Saturn (Jupiter in
the film). Concerned ostensibly with man's outward urge
and his contact with monuments of intelligent, extra-
terrestrial life forms, the book (like the movie) ends on a
note of intense introspection. The third, Childhood's End
(1953), is usually regarded as his greatest achievement in
science fiction.

Immediately upon publication, Childhood's End
received praise both inside and outside the science fiction
community. James J. Rollo wrote in The Atlantic Monthly
that the book was a "stimulating . . . novel of ideas . . .
crisply written . . . far from frivolous."[3] William Du Bois
in the New York Times called it "a first-rate tour de force
that is well worth the attention of every thoughtful citizen
in this age of anxiety."[4] Basil Davenport's enthusiasm
prompted this statement in the New York Times Book Review:

---

[3]Review by James J. Rollo, The Atlantic Monthly,
November 1953, p. 112.

[4]Review by William Du Bois, New York Times, August
27, 1953, p. 23.

"In 'Childhood's End' [sic] Arthur C. Clarke joins Olaf
Stapledon, C. S. Lewis, and probably one should add H. G.
Wells, in the very small group of writers who have used
science fiction as the vehicle of philosophical ideas--not
merely about the nature of future society, but ideas about
the End of Man."[5] Soon after its publication, Childhood's
End was cited by such critics as J. Donald Adams and Gilbert
Highet as an example of the best that science fiction had to
offer, a best good enough to make them recant earlier
derogatory statements about science fiction in general.[6]
Less surprised, perhaps, most science fiction reviewers
found it "impressive" and "ambitious" but cripplingly
disjointed.[7] Damon Knight wrote that it typified Clarke's
virtues and flaws as a writer, and he excused some of the
latter on the basis of the chronicle form, in which Time,
rather than human beings, is rightfully the protagonist.[8]

---

[5]Review by Basil Davenport, New York Times Book
Review, August 23, 1953, p. 19.

[6]J. Donald Adams, "Speaking of Books," New York
Times Book Review, July 12, 1953, p. 2, and September 13,
1953, p. 2. Gilbert Highet, "From World to World," People,
Places, and Books (New York, 1953), pp. 130-137, and
"Perchance to Dream," A Clerk of Oxenford (New York, 1954),
pp. 3-10.

[7]Reviews by Groff Conklin, Galaxy, March, 1954, pp.
118-119, H. H. Holmes [William Anthony White, editor of F&SF
as "Anthony Boucher"], New York Herald-Tribune Book Review,
August 22, 1953, p. 9, and P. Schuyler Miller, Astounding,
February, 1954, pp. 51-52.

[8]Damon Knight, In Search of Wonder: Essays on
Modern Science Fiction, 2nd ed. (Chicago, 1967), pp. 187-
188.

The passage of time, I suspect, has proven the more reserved opinions right. Childhood's End is an ambitious effort, better than people outside the science fiction community thought the pulp field capable of producing, but it is also an abortive effort, an impressive failure the flaws of which are indicative of the problems frequently present in science fiction as literature.

A novel of 75,000 words, Childhood's End portrays a series of fictional events taking place during the next 150 years and culminating in the metamorphosis of man into a composite entity incomprehensible to the rational mind.[9]   In three titled sections, roughly equal in length, Clarke attempts to balance panoramic scope and human involvement by means of alternating portions of generalized chronicle with a loose series of episodes involving the reactions of a half-dozen persons to the changes occurring around them. Much of the narrative involves the relationships between these humans and the extra-terrestrial beings who exercise a benevolent dictatorship on Earth in order to see that the metamorphosis is not prevented from taking place.

Following a brief prologue placing the aliens' arrival on the eve of man's first moon-rocket, Part One, "Earth and the Over-Lords," recounts the establishment of

---

[9]Arthur C. Clarke, Childhood's End (1953), in Across the Sea of Stars (New York, 1959), pp. 249-434.   Page numbers in the text will refer to this edition.

peace on Earth during the aliens' first fifty years of rule.
A slightly revised version of the novelette "Guardian
Angel," this section focuses on the relationship between
Stormgren, Secretary-General of the United Nations, and
Karellen, the Overlords' Supervisor for Earth, and consists
mainly of two melodramatic episodes, Stormgren's abduction
by gangsters and his attempt to discover what Karellen looks
like.[10]

Part Two, "Earth and the Overlords," begins with the
descent of Karellen to Earth, and the revelation, after
fifty years of rule, that the Overlords literally look like
the Devil. In the Golden Age that they have instituted,
life has become a bit static, as we see from the description
of a rather dull party which serves mainly to foreshadow
coming events and to introduce us to the characters whose
part in these events will be described. The remainder of
the section follows Jan Rodricks through the steps of an
elaborate subterfuge by means of which he manages to stow
away on a starship bound for the Overlords' home planet.
Part Two closes with Karellen's announcement of Rodricks'
accomplishment and the regretful proclamation that "the
stars are not for Man" (p. 362).

---

[10]Reference to this novelette is made in Knight,
p. 187, and Sam Moskowitz, Seekers of Tomorrow: Masters of
Modern Science Fiction (New York, 1966), p. 386, and it is
identified by the Day Index as having appeared in Famous
Fantastic Mysteries, April, 1950, and in New Worlds, Winter,
1950, but I have not been able to locate a copy of either
magazine.

Part Three, "The Last Generation," begins with
George and Jean Greggson, at a "utopian" artists' colony,
where their children become the first to show the signs of
those "extra-sensory" powers which the Overlords know to be
the first stage of metamorphosis. The Overlords, who now
reveal their real mission, take all the children to a single
place where they can grow, together, in their own way, while
the adults seek to accept their own obsolescence. When Jan
Rodricks returns, having seen some of the wonders of the
Universe, he finds himself the last man living, able to do
no more than observe the end of the world, and report it to
Karellen, who has already left on another mission. The
children depart, the Earth disintegrates, and Karellen is
last seen meditating on his race's solemn loneliness.
Giants of individual will and intellect, they are trapped in
an evolutionary cul de sac; never to share in or even to
understand the "Overmind" of which the children have become
a part, the Overlords can merely observe its ways and do its
bidding.

From the moon-bound rockets of the Prologue to the
last stage of the metamorphosis of man, familiar science
fictional motifs guide us gradually, if jerkily, from
predictable technological advances to prophetic eschatological fantasy. Besides futuristic hardware, we are shown
three rational utopian societies and occasional glimpses of
mysterious extra-sensory powers. Dwarfing these

conceptions, however, and reducing them practically to the status of leitmotifs, is the theme of alien contact, expanded to include something close enough to being infinite, eternal, and unknowable that it could be called God. Yet even this being, the Overmind, is rationalized, and assumed to be subject to natural laws, however difficult, even impossible, it may be for the individual intellect, using science as a tool, ever to know those laws.

Compared with other novels by Clarke, Childhood's End somewhat de-emphasizes technology; there is nothing like the sober detail of his near future settings or the imaginative reach of The City and the Stars, although we are presented with two cultural stages technologically advanced over our own. The first, achieved by man as of about 2050 A.D., is said to consist mainly in "a completely reliable oral contraceptive . . . an equally infallible method . . . of identifying the father of any child . . . [and] the perfection of air transport" (p. 307). Other advances, varying in seriousness and significance, include a mechanized ouija board, a complete catalogue of the stars, "telecaster" newspapers, elaborate undersea laboratories, plastic "taxidermy," and central community kitchens offering five-minute service to any home. Far more advanced is the technology of the Overlords; their gadgets include non-injurious pain projectors, three-dimensional image projectors, cameraless television capable of penetrating the past as well as

distances in the present, interstellar spaceships, and
vehicles which can move swiftly without the feeling of
acceleration. The extent of the Overlords' power is further
indicated by the fact that they have completely transformed
the atmosphere and gravity of their adopted home planet.
These advances may seem far removed from present-day experience, but they are not incomprehensible as possible developments from the thinking processes encouraged by "scientific"
Western Civilization, and all of them have been hypothesized
as human achievements by Clarke's predecessors and contemporaries in pulp science fiction. In this book, none of these
developments is treated in any detail, and together they
amount to no more than a suggestive sketch, serving as the
merest foundation for the hypotheses built up from and
around them.

Technology alone does not create the utopian social
organizations described in Childhood's End, although without
it they might not exist. The law and order established by
the Overlords' effective use of technology, and the freedom
of movement and sexuality made possible by human inventions,
are necessary for the establishment of "the Golden Age" on a
worldwide scale. The elimination of real suffering and
anguish, however, seems to require at least a reduction in
excitement and other sought-after emotions. Combined with
the sense of inferiority engendered by the very existence of
the supremely rational and apparently unemotional Overlords,

these changes seem to result in a condition of generalized
anxiety, mild resentment, and bored lethargy, at least in
the characters we meet. One effort to overcome these negative reactions is the establishment of an artists' colony,
with the traditionally utopian locale of an island, called
New Athens, but here too Clarke displays his ambivalence
towards utopia. Although the Overlords encourage the
colony's activities, even making occasional visits, only a
vague sense of civic pride can make any of the colonists
regard this attention as praise, for none of them seems to
be able to create anything of real value. Whether Clarke
could imagine something in the way of "predictable" great
art is irrelevant, since the artists' failure, due perhaps
to too much ease and to a sense of futility, serves to
underscore the utopian community's insignificance in the
larger context; from the Overlords' standpoint, New Athens
is a gathering-point for the most gifted children, an
arrangement convenient for the aliens' observation of the
early stages of the metamorphosis. Besides being unimportant, Clarke suggests, utopia is unreachable; just as
technology, even effectively used, does not make everyone
happy on Earth, so it is also insufficient for the supremely
rational and scientific Overlords. What glimpses we are
given of their society indicate a sense of placid orderli-
ness, presumably more pleasant to them than to the fright-
ened observer, Jan, and their long lives and abilities may

tend to excite our envy. But the Overlords in turn envy man and the other species which can commune with and become part of the Overmind; indeed, a large part of the melancholy mood Clarke associates with the Overlords seems due to their longing for such a loss of individuality, amid certain knowledge that they can never achieve it.

Clarke's ambivalence towards utopia, however, does not make <u>Childhood's End</u> a dystopia, as Mark Hillegas claims.[11] Utopia and dystopia alike require strong value judgments as to the desirability of certain social institutions, and Clarke deliberately bypasses all such judgments except one. His commitment to scientific thought and technological advance is visible throughout the novel. On the social level, he suggests, in traditional science fictional fashion, the indifference of technological progress to man's use of it for good or bad. On the level of speculative biology, his hypothesis of a predestined metamorphosis of the human race reminds us of the indifference of nature to man's approval or disapproval of her workings, and of the concern of science for those processes alone, not for their value. On the symbolic level, to be sure, indifference is replaced by anticipation; the coming of this "heavenly" destiny parallels the soul's return to God, and the

---

[11]Mark R. Hillegas, "Dystopian Science Fiction: New Index to the Human Situation," <u>New Mexico Quarterly</u>, XXXI, 3 (Autumn, 1961), 238-249, revised for <u>The Future as Nightmare: H. G. Wells and the Anti-Utopians</u> (New York, 1967).

acceptance of this fate parallels utopianism, not dystopianism, on the level of earthly accomplishment. Even on this level, however, the commitment to science and rationality is not completely abandoned, for these "human" activities will be carried on by the Overlords, and Clarke seems more in sympathy with them than with their superior, the Overmind.

The idea that man "may not be the highest form of life in the Universe" is hardly original with Clarke; alien beings have roamed the pages of science fiction at least since Wells. Clarke's biggest debt, in this respect, is to Olaf Stapledon, whose catalogue-like novels have served many writers as references. Stapledon's Last and First Men (1930) chronicles several metamorphoses in the future history of man and his Star Maker (1937) is essentially a dream-journey through the universe, conducted for the narrator by a "being" similar to Clarke's Overmind. Where Stapledon catalogues interminably, however, making no concessions to artistic form, Clarke has tried to isolate a few Stapledonian concepts, to make them meaningful on a simple, human level, and to make a rounded story out of the whole.

The affinity of science fiction with what Northrop Frye calls the apocalyptic and demonic imagery of mythology is quite explicit in Childhood's End.[12] Utopian fiction

[12]Northrop Frye, Anatomy of Criticism (Princeton, 1957), pp. 141-150.

frequently makes use of analogies with the Heaven of Chris-
tianity (despite the fact that the basic utopian premise of
the perfectibility of man is a Christian heresy), and the
similarities between dystopia and Hell are seldom ignored.
In science fiction, even with the most scrupulous attempts
at neutrality, any institution the reader favors in an
imaginary society is likely to evoke comparisons with utopia
and Heaven, any bad one with dystopia and Hell. In similar
fashion, any superior aliens will probably evoke reminiscences of supernatural beings, benevolence being attributed
to gods, malevolence to devils (or evil gods). This situation is complicated by the traditional association in
Western literature of science, scientists, and "forbidden"
knowledge with the supernatural representatives of evil, and
by the reversal of values frequently seen since the Romantic
period, whereby the writer opts for the position and direction of the Evil One in preference to the "oppressive" God
of Judeo-Christian tradition.[13] It seems to me that Clarke
deliberately chooses devil-figures as spokesmen for scientific thought in order to establish an increasing tension

---

[13]The idea of knowledge as a debasing force goes
back at least to the legends of Pandora and the Garden of
Eden; the Faust legend and its predecessors are examined
in E[liza] M[arian] Butler, The Myth of the Magus (Cambridge
and New York, 1948) and in Charles Dédeyan, Le Thème de
Faust dans la littérature européene, 4 vols. (Paris, 1954-
1962). The Romantic inversion of the respective values of
God and Satan is seen in Blake, Byron, Lermontov, and many
others, a recent example being J. B., by Archibald MacLeish.

between conflicting emotions as the climax of the novel approaches. Despite the overwhelming superiority of the Overmind, over man and Overlord alike, Clarke knows that he can rely on the science fiction reader's sympathy for the "losing" forces of rationality.

The few human characters with whom we have any chance to identify all side with the rational "scientific" kind of thought which Clarke, like many science fiction writers, seems to regard as man's greatest achievement. Stormgren resists the fear of some people that the as yet unseen Overlords may be that hoariest of science fiction clichés, B.E.M.'s (Bug-Eyed Monsters, whose intelligence is practically nil, sometimes despite their technological achievements, and who existed in early pulp science fiction primarily in order to kidnap luscious maidens for sinister purposes, only to be foiled by the hero in the nick of time). Reflecting on Karellen's refusal to show himself, Stormgren muses on the absurdity of man's superstitions, illustrating the more recent science fictional position regarding intelligent extra-terrestrial life forms, as he observes that, no matter how alien the form of life, "the mind, not the body, was all that mattered" (p. 268). George Greggson is a little less sure of himself but, when his son Jeff begins to have strange dreams, apparently of distant worlds, George confides in the Overlord Rashaverak, "I've never believed in the supernatural; I'm no scientist, but I think there's a rational explanation for everything," to which Rashaverak replies, "There is" (p. 395). Jan Rodricks, during his stay on the Overlords' planet, also retains his faith in reason, although he may not find it capable of controlling his emotions in the face of the unknown. As Clarke puts it: "Even Jan, for all his curiosity and scientific detachment, sometimes found himself on the verge of unreasoning terror. The absence of a single familiar reference point can be utterly unnerving even to the coolest and clearest minds" (p. 413). The application of science, i.e. technology, is represented by two helpers, Duval, who fashions the spy apparatus which Stormgren uses in his attempt to uncover Karellen's secret, and Sullivan, who builds the plastic model of a whale and giant squid in combat which, as a museum shipment, enables Rodricks to stow away on the starship. Each is seen only in relation to his own research and to the craftsmanship which helps others undertake their own "research."

The supreme representatives of reason, and of science, are the Overlords, who are thinkers and observers, and also in their role of guardians, manipulators and experimenters. Their espousal of the cause of scientific knowledge is open to some suspicion, however. They admit that they cannot comprehend the Overmind and that certain areas of intuitive knowledge and certain mental faculties are closed to them. They are repeatedly deceptive about

themselves, first about their appearance, thereafter about
their purpose in coming to Earth. First they say that they
have come to prevent man's self-destruction, and that man
is doomed never to reach the stars. Later they proclaim
they were sent to do the bidding of the Overmind, to
oversee man's metamorphosis, and, admittedly, to engage in
scientific observation of that transformation for themselves. Meanwhile, one man does reach the stars, returning
home to find that homo sapiens is no more and that the
children of man, although no longer recognizably human, will
indeed reach, and perhaps inherit, the stars. Only toward
the end do the Overlords admit that their name, made up by
their human "subjects," is an ironic one, in view of their
own "subject" circumstances. Until then, they are perfectly
content with the title, even reinforcing it at first with
the false image of fifty ships covering the globe when
there was only one, then with the demands that only one man
treat with them and that he be compelled to "ascend" in
their vehicle to the real ship hovering over New York.

It may be that their duplicity is necessary, that
man can only be given closer approximations to the truth as
he becomes ready for them. Approximations are also the
ways in which science and reason deal with the world outside the inquiring mind. However it could also be true
that even the closest approximation given by the Overlords
is far from the truth, perhaps because of the Overlords'

own inability to comprehend, perhaps because of further
deliberate fabrication. Their model or analogy in Earth's
folklore is called the "Father of Lies" and they certainly
resemble him in other ways. At Karellen's first appearance,
he is described in terms of his resemblance to Satan: "the
leathery wings, the little horns, the barbed tail--all were
there" (p. 303). He offsets his appearance by the dramatic
device, in emulation or parody presumably of Christ's
command to his disciples to "suffer little children to come
unto me," of making his entrance "with a human child resting
trustfully on either arm" (p. 303). The Overlords' names,
Karellen, Rashaverak, Thantalteresco, Vindarten, if they are
not traditional, seem to have been chosen for their somewhat
"devilish" sound.[14] Even their home planet suggests to Jan
the image of Hell: the light from its sun is red, the
natives fly through the dense atmosphere, their architecture
seems to him dystopianly functional and unornamented. If
Jan were better versed in literature, he might recognize
the parallel with Milton's _Paradise Lost_ in the fact that

---

[14]Rossell Hope Robbins, The Encyclopedia of Witch-
craft and Demonology (New York, 1959) gives the following
names as those of medieval demons: Ancitif, Arfaxat,
Asmodeus, Astaroth, Balberith, Beelzebub, Belias, Belphegor,
Calconix, Carnivean, Carreau, Consaque, Gressil, Grongate,
Iuvart, Leviathan, Lucifer, Mammon, Oeillet, Olivier,
Phaëton, Rosier, Satan, Sonneillon, Verrier, Verrine.
Bernard J. Bamberger, Fallen Angels (Philadelphia, 1952)
includes the following as names of demons or fallen angels:
Appolyon, Asbeel, Azazel, Jekon, Kafkefoni, Kasbiel,
Kasdaye, Kastimon, Lilith, Malchira, Metanbuchus, Samael,
Semjaza, Ben Temalyon, Uzzael.

this is not the world on which they had "evolved," but one which they have "conquered."

In stark contrast to the anthropomorphism of the Overlords, visible not only in their form but also in their thinking processes, in their technology, and in their desire to communicate, to sympathize, to be liked, is the totally alien quality apparently exhibited by the Overmind, which plays the role of God to the Overlords' Satan. In itself and through its creatures (Earth's children) the Overmind evokes images of unlimited power for unknowable purposes. To the human observer, Jan Rodricks, it appears in the guise of a "living volcano" on the Overlords' planet; the Overmind's power is also visible in the action of the children of Earth, who convert their planet to energy in order to propel themselves to an unknown destination. In both cases, the visible manifestation seems to be a side-effect, insignificant to the purposes of the "being." The Overlords appear to understand something of its behavior and composition, from having observed before the process of metamorphosis, as is indicated by the following speech of Karellen: "We believe--it is only a theory--that the Overmind is trying to grow, to extend its powers and its awareness of the universe. By now it must be the sum of many races, and long ago it left the tyranny of matter behind. It is conscious of intelligence, everywhere. When it knew that you were almost ready, it sent us here to do its bidding, to prepare

you for the transformation that is now at hand" (p. 404).
The change always begins with a child, spreading like
"crystals round the first nucleus in a saturated solution"
(p. 405). Eventually, the children will become united in a
single entity, unreachable by any communication understood
by Man or Overlord, unfathomable by any individual, rational
mind. This is the extent of the Overlords' knowledge, and
it may not be reliable; the metaphor of crystallization can
hardly be adequate to describe the transformed state. All
they can really know, when the Overmind contacts them, is
that it wants them to serve as "midwives" at another "birth"
(p. 398). And they go, like angels at God's bidding, but
"fallen angels," incapable of sharing in the deity's glory.

On the surface, the Overlords' inability (and ours)
to understand the Overmind is merely a sign of its strangeness and vastness, which may some day become comprehensible
to reason and science, but underneath, we feel the tug of
the irrational. This must be a symbol of the "being"
variously known as God, the Oversoul, the Great Spirit, and
other names, and the children's metamorphosis neatly
parallels Nirvana, the loss of self, or the awakening of
"cosmic consciousness" of which the mystics have so often
spoken. It is therefore fitting that the Overmind be no
more describable than it is, that it be known only through
its works, through unintentional side-effects of its works
at that. And the confidence of any man or Overlord in

isolation, that he will come to understand this being, rings as hollow as the boasts of Milton's Satan. Thus the interplay between the Overlords and the Overmind, explained with tantalizing incompleteness to Jan on his return from the stars, is a reworking of the old "morality play" situation of the Devil trying to steal away from God the souls of men. Here the Devil appears to be a devoted servant following out God's orders, but the Overlords never stop trying to bring Him down to their level, and they manage to convince the reason-loving men of the story that, just as our science has told us, everything has a natural explanation. Those men are doomed, of course, while their children ("the children of man") are saved, so the real stage of Clarke's morality play is the mind of the reader, who can be expected to take the side of reason, science, the West, and the Devil, with just the slightest anxiety over his choice.

The universe may be comprehensible to reason, as the Overlords assert, but even on the rational surface of the story, the Overmind and the metamorphosis cannot be grasped in terms of science as we know it. The existence of aliens and of "mental" phenomena beyond the reach of our five senses and their mechanical extensions may be posited, but neither has ever been verified by science, which can only deal with empirical data. Science fiction is not limited to verified fact, but it does usually make an attempt to domesticate the unknown in terms of sensory observation or at least in terms of some tentative theory not too openly contradictory of known natural law. Clarke, however, has considerably stretched these limitations.

His mechanical wonders and quasi-utopian communities do not stretch credibility to any great extent; although they are neither thoroughly explained nor convincingly shown in action, they are familiar conventions, plausible enough developments from our present state of technology. His aliens, too, although they are neither predictable nor controllable by man, are acceptable as science fictions. The Overlords are obviously there, present to the senses, and more or less understandable to human psychology. Through them we are given the theory which almost makes acceptable the concept of the Overmind. For both beings, however, this science fictional domestication is undercut by the literary domestication, i.e., it isn't reasonable that strange life forms should be so similar to long-established figures of human mythology. The real affront to credibility, however, comes from Clarke's apparent stand on e.s.p.

Contradicting himself in the space of two paragraphs, Karellen declares first that "there are powers of the mind, and powers beyond the mind, which your science could never have brought within its framework without shattering it entirely," then that the Overlords had been sent to Earth largely to stop scientists from investigating parapsychology, which they were doing presumably with some chance of success (p. 403). Using this fictional elimination of productive research as an excuse, Clarke has Karellen, who can only know "extra-sensory powers" from the outside, explain them in traditional "spiritualist" terms: these powers are genuine, man has labelled but not fully verified them in the past, and they have some mysterious connection with the powers and workings of the Overmind. Where Clarke shows us these powers in action, he is similarly vague: the children's dreams, their telekinetic powers, their united participation in a kind of "cosmic dance" are all credited to their mystical contact with the Overmind, while Jean Greggson's telepathic experience with an Overlord at the party in Part Two was accomplished by means of a ouija board and explained by the fact that she is a "sensitive," i.e. a potential spiritualist medium. Perhaps, if we can accept at face value the concept of the Overmind, we should not cavil at a little spiritualism, although it does seem a bit unfair to explain one "impossibility" (e.s.p.) by another (the Overmind), which in turn can only be partially comprehended by means of still another (the Overlords).[15] Even if we accept all of these

---

[15]It may be, of course, that Clarke does not regard e.s.p. as an impossibility, at least in the context of this book, although he evinces some skepticism in Profiles of the Future: An Inquiry into the Limits of the Possible (New York, Toronto, and London, 1965), pp. 20, 197-198. The

improbabilities as part of the context of the story, we may
balk with Knight at Clarke's rewriting history in order to
take another para-psychological excursion.[16] Despite the
existence of scholarship indicating a medieval European
origin for Satan as we now know him, out of bits and pieces
of pagan mythology, Clarke insists that the Devil is part of
the mythology of all peoples and has been for thousands of
years, because of a racial memory (or "premonition") of the
future.[17]

Not only does a gaffe of this magnitude, if it is
recognized as an error, tend to upset all but the most
hypnotic suspension of disbelief at the moment, but the
doubt that it raises as to the reliability of the narrator
also tends to undermine the credibility of the entire
narrative. Thus, the author may defeat even our tentative
acceptance for the duration of the novel, not only of e.s.p.
and of the Overmind's existence beyond the grasp of science,

---

problem would then be one of presentation, and spiritualism
seems a poor source of imagery, if credibility is desired.

[16]Knight, p. 188.

[17]Although demons of various kinds may have existed
in man's imagination for as long as he had one, the particular shape of the medieval Devil which Clarke has chosen for
his Overlords does seem to be an amalgamation peculiar to
the late Middle Ages. See Ernest Jones, Nightmare, Witches,
and Devils (New York, 1931), pp. 154-159. See also:
Bamberger (above, note 14), pp. 208-232; Pennethorne Hughes,
Witchcraft (Baltimore, 1967), pp. 104-115; and especially
Maurice Garçon and Jean Vinchon, The Devil: An Historical,
Critical and Medical Study, trans. Stephen Haden Guest
(London, 1929), passim.

but even of the powers of reason and the validity of
science, themselves. It may well be that Clarke wants us to
question the omniscience of science--Karellen's speech on
mental powers denigrates human science as a panacea--and
even to question the questioner--Karellen's lies and inadequacies suggest that--but undermining the veracity of the
narrator is a dangerous game to play when the reader already
knows that the subject matter is a tenuously anchored
fantasy.

Why does Clarke even attempt this explanation of
mythology? Why, in a science-fiction novel, does he fill
several pages with a spiritualistic séance? Neither was
necessary to the theme it would appear, or to the book as a
whole. The Overlords' parallel with the Christian Devil
could have been left unexplained, without impairing them as
alien beings or as literary symbols; the explanation given
is worse than none at all. The séance functions peripherally to show the similarity between human and Overlord
minds, and to foreshadow the role of Jean Greggson's children as first contacts with the Overmind. It also serves to
point up man's boredom with the Golden Age and the ridicu-
lous ends which his technology can be made to serve, namely
the production of mechanized ouija boards, but Rupert Boyce,
whom the party characterizes, is an unimportant figure, and
the success of the séance undercuts the satire. The least
important purpose the séance serves is to provide Jan

Rodricks with the catalogue number of the Overlords' home
star; his visit to the museum to consult the catalogue is
equally irrelevant to his stowing away on the starship,
which will go where it will, with or without his knowledge
of his destination. The problem, apparent here on the
science fictional level, is essentially a literary one:
Clarke is not fully in control of his materials, i.e. he
has attempted more than he is capable of fulfilling.

The "cosmic viewpoint" which Clarke praised in his
Kalinga Prize acceptance speech is common in science
fiction, as is its negative corollary, inattention to
details. Besides leading writers into multi-volumed "future
histories," the cosmic viewpoint encourages close attention
in smaller works only to the major outlines and the background.[18] The characters are frequently left to fend for
themselves, as it were, in a jungle of disorderly plots,
melodramatic incidents, and haphazard image-patterns, which
are symptomatic of an unbalanced narrative technique.
Unity, if there is any in such a composition, frequently is
maintained only by an uninspired consistency of style and
tone, and by the momentum built up in the unwary reader by

[18]A similar criticism may be found in Alfred Bester,
"Science Fiction and the Renaissance Man," in Basil
Davenport et al., The Science Fiction Novel: Imagination
and Social Criticism (Chicago, 1964), p. 115. Two recent
"future histories" that are quite well known are now each
collected in one volume: Isaac Asimov, The Foundation
Trilogy (Garden City, [1966]); Robert A. Heinlein, The Past
Through Tomorrow (New York, 1967).

the breakneck pace of events. Childhood's End, like many
books inferior to it, suffers from just such a dispropor-
tionate emphasis on the large, "significant" effects, at the
expense of the parts of which they are composed.

Structurally, this failing is visible in several
ways. The three titled sections are not balanced units,
except in length. Part One is unified by the person of
Stormgren and his relationship with the invisible Karellen
on one side and the entire human race on the other. It is
separated from Part Two by time as well as by characters,
Karellen alone carrying over from Part One. Parts Two and
Three share the same characters, working out two separate
story lines, and the same time period, although a large gap
opens in the middle of Part Three. Each succession of
actions ("plot" seems an inappropriate word) is broken down
into almost random fragments of panoramic chronicle, desul-
tory conversation, poorly motivated melodrama, and tentative
internal monologue. Part of the problem with form may have
to do with the fact that the book "just growed" from the
novelette that was originally Part One, but this fact is
symptomatic of Clarke's inability to conceive of his subject
in satisfactory fictional terms.

It is as if Clarke had written several stories of
varying length and intensity, which he then attempted to
interweave with each other and with connective tissue
supplied by an outline-summary of history. The point-of-

view is uniformly third-person-omniscient, yet the narrative
duties seem split between an awe-struck, would-be historian
and a disinterested story-teller, who lacks any sense of
drama. The historian at least is interested in his theme,
and so impressed with its magnitude that he feels called
upon to match it with his own attempts at grandeur, including panoramic, wide-angle photographs and impressive-
sounding, if vague and unsupported, generalizations and
miscellaneous _sententiae_. By contrast, the story-teller
seems somewhat detached, giving us "slices of life"--
political negotiating sessions, a party, a visit to a
library, a press conference, a group meeting, a counseling
session, a sightseeing trip--without revealing the principles on which he bases his selections. The individual
episodes stubbornly resist integration with the whole, yet
they are also unable to stand up as independent units,
partly because they are meant as "illustrations," partly
because they are insignificant in themselves.

Clarke's attempt is clearly intended to counterpoint the great, slow movement toward metamorphosis with
the everyday activities that people, ignorant of their
contribution to the whole, carry on independently, the kind
of activities he usually treats in his less ambitious
fiction of the near and "predictable" future. In such a
setting, what plot there is provides a mere peg on which to
hang the background. In such a context, where the

background is stable, detailed, and relatively familiar, a
bit of melodrama may add a little spice to the narrative,
and the withholding of necessary information may be justified as a means of making the situation come to life. But
where the background is continually shifting over a large
span of time and space, and where the context involves the
larger mysteries of life, of existence, and of divinity,
such "stagey" effects as the kidnaping of Stormgren, the
Overlords' gradual self-unveiling, the explanation of one
mystery in terms of another, are not only unnecessary but
also annoying and self-defeating because of their irrelevance. Instead of irrelevant episodes of mystery and
melodrama, Childhood's End might well have benefitted from
a series of actions dependent on each other and clearly
illustrative of the great events around them, i.e. a unified
and integrated plot. But Clarke is apparently unable to
imagine a plot adequate to the scope of his framework; his
"predictive" novels are equally plotless and even his tale
of the far future is made up of a series of accidental
occurrences, set into motion almost haphazardly by the
adolescent hero's desire for change and adventure. So the
counterpoint structure was attempted for Childhood's End and
the result is a hodgepodge of pretentious chronicle, apologetic melodrama, and superficial sketches of static

unrelated, individual scenes.[19]

As it is practically plotless, so the novel is also
almost characterless. This too is due in part to the book's
ambitious theme and tremendous scope, against which individuals and their merely personal problems are bound to look
somewhat insignificant. Against the backdrop of eternal
time and infinite space, the unknown bulks extremely large,
and even the usual reaction of characters in science fiction
toward the unknown, a kind of calculated respect for size
and power, which allows for action, tends to give way in
this story to the awe and reverence that we term "religious." Man the Creator, acting, progressing, continually
making changes in his environment, the ideal protagonist of
science fiction, tends to become man the Creature, full of
fear and wonder and more than willing to follow orders, when
an encounter with an incalculable unknown power forces him
to admit how small he is and how little he really knows.

Clarke definitely does not minimize the unknown; the
Overmind is not only unknown but unknowable, and the death
of the human race is the novel's end result. However, the
fear of racial annihilation is counterbalanced by a degree
of pride in man's being chosen, and by an acceptance, on the

---

[19]Even if we regard the book as an elegy for mankind, for the end of personal and racial "childhood," the
elegiac tone is inconsistent, and insufficient to maintain
unity over 75,000 words without a more carefully wrought
"poetic structure," and the lame, pedestrian style of the
novel seems particularly incongruous for a poem.

part of the characters we meet, of the inevitable as somehow "good." Puny though man may be on an absolute scale, on the scale by which we live in the present, his future achievements are respectable; certainly his potential, symbolized by the Overlords, is by no means slighted. Although the fragmentation of the narrative prevents us from becoming acquainted with individual men, it allows Clarke to show us representative moments of what he considers their better, rational selves, and thus to preserve both the wonders of man and his science, and of the awesome realities beyond.

The four major characters, Stormgren, Karellen, George, and Jan, are not lost in a multitude of minor figures, as the chronicle form might suggest. They are practically the only characters, and one of them is involved in every episode which is acted out and not merely talked about. They are all males, representing the active principle, and all appear to be confident, as we have seen, that everything has a rational explanation. This appearance of rationality is generally reinforced by their lack of irrational behavior (unless belief in rationality in the face of the incomprehensible unknown is itself irrational), and by the glimpses Clarke gives us of their mental processes (proper grammatical sentences, with no irrational stream-of-consciousness). However, they are not really given much to say, to do, or to think, so that we hardly know them as more than marionettes in a cosmic puppet-show.

Only Karellen, who exists throughout the book, who has seen
the whole pattern of events previously, and who can observe
it with relatively detached and "scientific" curiosity, has
any real stature. Behind his posturing and lecturing, his
deceit for the benefit of his human "wards," lies a sense of
tragedy which makes him more "human" than any of them. It
is more the rational than the emotional side of humanity
which he represents, the intellectual stubbornness which
doomed his prototype, Satan, to a similarly "tragic" and
isolated immortality.

A resigned acceptance of what must be is common to
all four major characters, and is largely responsible for
the elegiac tone which pervades the book, becoming most
intense toward the end. Uncontrolled emotional outbursts
are apparently nonexistent in "the Golden Age," and
Stormgren sets the tone for Part One when he firmly rejects
the irrational rebellion led by the religious leader,
Wainwright, against the invisible Overlords. Even the
matter-of-fact "story-telling" narrator seems conscious of
impending doom, in contrast to which humanity's inconsequen-
tial behavior earns an ironic smile. Although Clarke
sometimes stumbles over awkward circumlocutions, trite
sententiae, pedantic speech-making, and labored humor, his
pedestrian style, his simple, lucid sentences, and his
uncomplicated vocabulary seldom draw the reader's attention
away from the narrative and the tone provided by events.

In scenes involving the Overlords, to be sure, they are
accompanied by a sense of melancholy, but it reaches the
reader more by means of what they stand for than by means
of Clarke's descriptive powers. Only towards the end, an
essentially flat style rises to heights of mellifluousness
and complexity, as the author succeeds in imparting a sense
of majesty to the passages dealing with the alien life-
forms and the great unknown. Clarke's attempts at generat-
ing a "sense of wonder," which range from juvenile "gee-
whiz" impressions of the Overlords and their technology to a
quasi-religious awe in the contemplation of the destiny of
man, are most successful at the closing, as the children's
testing of their powers grows more confident and culminates
in the cataclysmic shock witnessed by Jan up close, then by
Karellen far in the distance. The note of regret, although
cloying and sentimental at times (Jeff Greggson's dog mourn-
ing for his master lost in dreams, Jeff's parents saying a
final farewell just before the community of New Athens blows
itself up), also gains more depth with this ending, echoing
crescendo.

The major source of unity, besides the figure of
Karellen and the basic consistency of style and tone, seems
to lie in certain image-patterns and the repetition of
significant motifs. The dozen or so allusions to figures
from folklore and history, while they may be intended to
add depth to the narrative, are so haphazardly chosen and

introduced as to seem unrelated to the whole. On the other
hand, the apocalyptic and demonic imagery of the Overlords
and the Overmind is so persistent as to lay down at the
symbolic level a morality play contradicting the rational
message on the surface. The majority of patterns function
somewhere in between these two extremes, mainly as unifying
factors. The power and superiority of Stormgren over the
human masses is echoed by the Overlords' relationship to
him, and the Overmind's relationship to them. Karellen
refers to humans as beloved pets at one point; the image is
reminiscent of his attitude earlier toward Stormgren, and
it is reinforced again by the loneliness of the Greggsons'
dog. A continual widening of perspective is seen also in
the Overlords' intellectual striptease, in the importance
given e.s.p., in the frequent panoramic views, of Earth as
well as of time, space, and society. The frustrated takeoff
of man's first moon-rockets is echoed by Karellen's edict
that "the Stars are not for Man," and by Jan's discovery of
the proclamation's essential truth; Jan's successful flight
as a stowaway is foreshadowed by his sight of a starship
taking off, and in turn is echoed by the final departure of
the children (and of the Overlords). The final metamorphosis of the children into a fully symbiotic, super-organic
life form is foreshadowed by several other kinds of
"togetherness": a mob demonstration against the Overlords
and the gangsters' "conference" with the kidnaped Stormgren

in Part One; Karellen's entrance with the children and
Rupert Boyce's party in Part Two; the utopian community of
New Athens and the closeness of George and Jean Greggson in
Part Three.

If Childhood's End is by no means a fully satisfying
work of literature, it does illustrate certain common
characteristics of science fiction at its best, and it does
exhibit some literary virtues. Respect for rational
thought, construction of a "cosmic" perspective, relentless
pursuit of extrapolative hypotheses, faith in human dignity,
an interesting interweaving of themes and motifs, and a
genuine evocation of the "sense of wonder" are positive
achievements, however they may be undercut by deficiencies
in style, narrative structure, and characterization.

In a sense, Clarke may be considered a transitional
figure. A member of the second generation of pulp science
fiction writers, he is in many ways closer to the first
generation and to the British tradition of H. G. Wells, Olaf
Stapledon, and C. S. Lewis, all of whom are outside the pulp
field.[20] Although his subject-matter is usually the short-
range extrapolation associated with "social science
fiction," his orientation is more toward the "sense of
wonder" of the earlier writers, and his emphasis on sensational content at the expense of form, style, and psychology

---

[20]See also Moskowitz (above, note 10), pp. 374-391.

is one that the second generation was to some extent trying
to overcome.[21] Childhood's End has a high seriousness about
it that sets it apart from the ordinary pulp science fiction
novel of any generation, but still, in the growth of science
fiction as a literary genre, its combination of aspects from
science fiction's infancy and maturity make it represent a
median stage of adolescence.

---

[21]See Algis Budrys' criticisms of Clarke in this
regard, "Galaxy Bookshelf," Galaxy, October, 1967, pp. 189-
190.

CHAPTER IV

ISAAC ASIMOV: THE CAVES OF STEEL

As prolific as Arthur C. Clarke in both science
fiction and popular science, Isaac Asimov is also an influ-
ential apologist for the kind of science fiction developed
by the "second generation" writers under John Campbell in
the late Thirties.[1] First published by Campbell, in 1939,
Asimov had already published seven novels and numerous
stories before his first significant theoretical essay
appeared in Reginald Bretnor's 1953 anthology of criticism.[2]
In this essay, Asimov defined his kind of writing as social
science fiction which added concern "with the impact of
scientific advance upon human beings" to the basic setting
of science fiction in general, "a fictitious society,
differing from our own chiefly in the nature or extent of
its technological development."[3] Within the subgenre of

[1]Sam Moskowitz, Seekers of Tomorrow: Masters of
Modern Science Fiction (Cleveland and New York, 1966),
pp. 249-265. See also Contemporary Authors, II (1963), and
Current Biography (1953).

[2]Isaac Asimov, "Social Science Fiction," in Modern
Science Fiction: Its Meaning and Its Future, ed. Reginald
Bretnor (New York, 1953), pp. 157-196.

[3]Bretnor, pp. 171, 169.

social science fiction, he suggested that his own works generally tended toward what he called the "chess game" kind of story, which involves a general extrapolation of trends from "a fixed starting position . . . which assumes the socioeconomic environment we now possess," as against the "chess puzzle" variety, which tends to satirize the present by means of "some radical development or overgrowth of some aspect of our way of life."[4]

In 1957, several books and many articles and stories later, he redefined the whole field of science fiction for the readers of The Humanist as "that branch of literature which deals with the response of human beings to advances in science and technology."[5] Implying thus that all science fiction should be social science fiction, and concerned now with "human response" more than with "the impact of scientific advance," he nevertheless insisted that setting was the most important ingredient of all. Comparing science fiction with other commercial publishing categories, Asimov classified it with fantasy and social satire on the basis of setting, because in all three "the background has as little relation to reality as do the characters themselves."[6]

---

[4]Bretnor, pp. 179, 181.

[5]Isaac Asimov, "Escape into Reality," Is Anyone There? (Garden City, 1967), p. 286.

[6]Anyone, p. 284.

Stressing this unreality of the background, he contended that in these genres, background should be of major importance for itself. The disconcerting effect on the reader, he went on to say, was modified by the presence of other traditional features in fantasy (complete arbitrariness) and social satire (moral instruction), but the unfamiliarity of background was intensified by science fiction's plausible but amoral extrapolation. Far from finding fault with science fiction on this account, Asimov maintained that its innovation in the conception of setting was a positive distinction.

From the naturalistic viewpoint of most science fiction, the primacy of setting is quite understandable: the arbitrary or extrapolated setting influences physical needs, which tend to reinforce certain customs and mores, which in turn have a definite effect on individual character. Such a view of influences may well make of "human response" something rather mechanical, involving "types" or groups of characters reacting as their author would have them do to prove his point, regardless of whether they illustrate real human behavior. But if all this background activity takes place in the pre-writing of the book, in the area we have called "pure science fiction," then human character and behavior, displayed in action, dialogue, and thought, may be what change a speculative essay into a fictional experience. And the realization that "human response" is not merely a mechanical reaction to "the impact of scientific advance" may explain in part the success of Asimov's two best novels, whose publication dates fall between these two theoretical essays.

Concern for human character and for making his science fiction a felt experience was not fully developed in his early writings, Asimov admitted indirectly in the 1953 essay, by acknowledging the presence as a determining factor in Pebble in the Sky (1950) of an allegorical plot situation based on the Roman Empire's suppression of Judea.[7] With so rigid a structure and such an emphasis on the social level, it is not surprising that individual character and personal human values are relatively undeveloped in that book. Human beings are even less developed in his other books that are set against the background of a Galactic Empire: The Stars, Like Dust (1951), The Currents of Space (1952), and the "Foundation series" of stories and novelettes reconstructed into a trilogy of novels, Foundation (1951), Foundation and Empire (1952), and Second Foundation (1953).

In all of these books, the background is carefully conceived and developed in the "chess game" manner, with an emphasis on humanity, but humanity in the mass. The universe is strictly human-colonized, the Galactic Empire a relatively loose confederation modelled on the Roman Empire.

---

[7]Bretnor, pp. 179-180.

Since Asimov has written elsewhere in favor of the possibility of intelligent aliens, their absence here appears to be, as Sam Moskowitz maintains, due to a lack of interest in a world without human conflict.[8]

Human conflict in terms of human character, however, Asimov did not manage to illustrate successfully until he suppressed his fascination with the Galactic Empire. In The Caves of Steel (1953; 1954) and The Naked Sun (1956; 1957), the Empire, in its earliest stage, is reduced to some fifty-odd planets, and the vast canvas which it provided is shrunken to a limited setting on a single world. The "chess game" kind of extrapolation is still present, but the two kinds of society developed have something of the "chess puzzle" particularization about them. Against this setting, the incongruously large intrigues played out in the earlier books by people who are little more than chess pawns give way to another conventional kind of puzzle, the solving of a murder mystery, by a recognizably human detective and an almost perfectly human robot.

Of Asimov's other fiction, including six collections of stories and nine novels (six of them for children), three books are particularly relevant to this discussion. The Death Dealers (1958) is a contemporary mystery novel, whose

---

[8]Seekers (above, note 1), pp. 259-260. See also the essays on "other life" in Is Anyone There? pp. 183-213.

amateur detective is a professor of chemistry (Asimov taught biochemistry at Boston University for a number of years).

I, Robot (1950) includes nine stories of the previous decade concerning robots which had some connection with Susan Calvin, chief robopsychologist for the manufacturing firm of U. S. Robots, whose reminiscences tie the volume together. The Rest of the Robots (1964) completes the series of robot tales with eight more stories, four involving Susan Calvin, and the two science fiction murder mysteries, of which The Caves of Steel is usually considered somewhat fresher and more original, if only because it set a new pattern which its sequel followed.[9]

When it was first published, The Caves of Steel received only specialty reviews, and they were somewhat reserved. Villiers Gerson in the New York Times complimented Asimov for being aware of many other problems besides murder.[10] Fletcher Pratt in Saturday Review praised him for "a first-class detective story . . . [in which] even his

---

[9]Seekers, p. 263. On the basis of the stories in I, Robot alone, Asimov has been credited, along with Fredric Brown, with merging science fiction and detective themes in A. E. Murch, The Development of the Detective Novel (New York, 1958), p. 233. As early as 1951, a trend "toward a mariage de convenance between fantasy, scientific or not, and the detective story" (p. 16) was noted in Fletcher Pratt, "Time, Space and Literature," Saturday Review, July 28, 1951, pp. 16-17, 27-28.

[10]Review by Villers Gerson, New York Times, March 7, 1954, p. 16.

robots are completely believable."[11]   H. H. Holmes in the

New York Herald-Tribune Book Review called the book "a

splendid picture of the future technological war between

men and robots who can replace them on so many jobs . . .

[in a mystery which] states its own terms so clearly and

adheres to them so precisely that it is absolutely fair to

the reader."[12]   P. Schuyler Miller in Astounding agreed

that the novel was "honest" but he grumbled that it was

"not the virtuoso job that 'The Demolished Man' [sic] was,"

citing a recent science fictional crime novel by Alfred

Bester.[13]   Groff Conklin, writing in the magazine, Galaxy,

that had serialized The Caves of Steel, saw it as "partic-

ularly fascinating to Asimov experts, because of the way it

combines his interest in robotics with his consuming

preoccupation with the sociology of a technologically-mad

bureaucratically-tethered world of tomorrow."[14]   Damon

Knight was uncommonly generous, with special praise for

Asimov's science fictional speculation, thoroughness of

---

[11]Review by Fletcher Pratt, Saturday Review,
August 7, 1954, p. 15.

[12]Review by H. H. Holmes, New York Herald-Tribune
Book Review, February 7, 1954, p. 10. Review similarly
worded by Anthony Boucher (also a pseudonym of William
Anthony White), F&SF, May, 1954, p. 88.

[13]Review by P. Schuyler Miller, Astounding,
November, 1954, p. 150.

[14]Review by Groff Conklin, Galaxy, July, 1954, pp.
97-98. Isaac Asimov, "The Caves of Steel," Galaxy, October,
1953, pp. 4-66; November, 1953, pp. 98-159; December, 1953,
pp. 108-159.

sensory detail, and technical skill in integrating his
science fictional and mystery plots.[15] But even Knight
indicated only some of the book's strengths in ideas and
technique and none of its weaknesses in style and depth.

A novel of about 80,000 words, The Caves of Steel,
is set in New York City, around the year 5000 A.D.[16] Not
merely a murder-mystery, it is also a study in self-
discovery, a dissertation on the need for institutionalized
change to avoid intellectual stagnation, and a portrait in
some depth of life in an overpopulated and restrictive
megalopolis. Not mere accretions to the main narrative in
the form of obtrusive essays, these larger issues emerge
from the technology, politics, mores, prejudices, and everyday activities of a strange but familiar world. That world,
in surprising detail, is revealed by means of a carefully
arranged series of events which enable the detective, using
only the same information which is available to the reader,
to reconstruct the crime and identify the criminal.

Asimov establishes the background firmly in the
first seven chapters (the first installment, in the book's
serial form). Starting with a bare sketch of the locale,
the crime, and the detective, Plainclothesman Lije Baley,

---

[15]Damon Knight, In Search of Wonder: Essays on
Modern Science Fiction, rev. ed. (Chicago, 1967), pp. 90-93.

[16]Isaac Asimov, The Caves of Steel, in The Rest of
the Robots (Garden City, 1964), pp. 167-362. All page
references in the text are to this edition.

Asimov soon introduces us to the transportation system of
the City, the etiquette of the communal lavatory, the home
life of a middle-class civil servant, and the political
background of the murder. An important part of these
politics, the hostility of Earthmen toward robots and
Spacers (who are humans from the Outer Planets, Earth's
former colonies), is so much a part of Lije's psychology
that it leads him to make a serious mistake. His second
day on the case, at the scene of the crime, the Spacers'
"ghetto" outside the domed City, he erroneously asserts that
his Spacer partner, R. Daneel Olivaw, is not a perfectly
humanoid robot but a human being, the supposedly murdered
creator of the robot.

The action quickens in the next six chapters (the
second installment) as Lije, his accusation refuted, for-
given, and explained in part by Dr. Han Fastolfe's analysis
of the cultural differences between his people and Lije's,
returns to the City with Daneel. After a conference with
Police Commissioner Enderby, Lije and Daneel visit a community kitchen, escape some hostile pursuers, and retire to an
apartment distant from Lije's own. On the morning of the
third day, Lije and Daneel indulge in mutual recriminations.
Lije's second accusation of Daneel is refuted by an expert
in robotics, but Daneel's suggestion that Lije's wife,
Jessie, is involved in a conspiracy, appears to be confirmed
when she bursts into the office.

Jessie confesses in secret that she has been a member of a group of "Medievalists" opening the concluding and most rapidly-paced installment. Although she seems to corroborate Lije's belief that Medievalists are merely dreamers, wishing to restore "the old ways" (of the Twentieth Century), Lije and Daneel nevertheless proceed to "Yeast-town," where most of the City's food is grown, to question another supposed conspirator. Returning to Police Headquarters with the suspect under arrest, they find Lije suspected of destroying R. Sammy, a primitive office-robot which knew of Jessie's visit, by means of a radioactive tool taken from the power plant through which Lije and Daneel escaped the previous night. In a suspenseful confrontation (with a suddenly-imposed time limit), Lije counters Commissioner Enderby's accusation with a logical but unprovable theory, supported at the last minute by a shred of evidence visible in a three-dimensional film of the murder area obtained by Daneel from his masters. Identified as the accidental killer--he had meant to destroy Daneel--Enderby confesses; he is pardoned, at Lije's request, in return for a promise of political cooperation in the Spacers' plan to get Earthmen once again to emigrate to other worlds.

On the first page of The Caves of Steel, the reader is thrust into an unfamiliar world treated as a simple matter of fact, a world in which his major points of reference are established science fiction conventions. The background is obviously extrapolated from social organization and technological hardware of the twentieth century; the technology, sociology, politics, psychology, and sheer physical presence of this background are painstakingly built up within the novel. The major plot, although it is constructed according to the traditional pattern of the detective novel, is also science fictional, in that it involves a crime, a solution, and a team of detectives possible only within a science fictional framework. And the missionary message of science, progress, expansion, and the future, a message which the Spacers bring to Earth as part of the minor plot, is the traditional gospel of science fiction, modified in this book by the protagonist's attempt to integrate it with those aspects of culture worth preserving from the past.

The physical setting is a gigantic, domed City (the word is always capitalized) of some twenty million people, on an Earth of eight billion City dwellers, the most populous and backward of the fifty planets inhabited by human beings. A standard setting for utopian and dystopian fiction since Wells, the large, isolated, enclosed, self-sufficient community is usually little more than a dream or nightmare setting. Seen from the standpoint of a normal, imperfectly satisfied citizen, not of a utopian planner of dystopian critic, Asimov's New York is mainly a place to live, its virtues and faults being simply there, its most

important feature being that it is home, that it has a
lived-in feeling.

Seen in passing by a man at home in it, a man preoccupied with the job he is doing, the City presents a
kaleidoscope of impressions, familiar to Lije but not to the
reader. As we follow Lije across the "moving strips" which
compose the City's internal transit system, on his way to
meet Daneel for the first time, we see how that system
works, physically, geographically, and economically, and we
also overhear the thoughts with which the commuter combats
his boredom. Since Lije likes to muse about history, and to
explain things to himself (this is a part of his character),
the shapes in the kaleidoscope begin to take on consistent
outlines. His thoughts, ranging from memories of his
youthful opposition to the Spacers, to internal commentary
on immediate sensory experience, to consideration of the
City's age, size, food supply, and complexity, return to
the conflict between Earthmen and Spacers, stopping abruptly
as he remembers in time to maneuver his way to the exit for
Spacetown.

Gradually, through such indirect methods of exposition, the reader comes to know the City both from outside
(statistics, blueprints, history) and from inside (its look,
sounds, feel, and smell). He experiences it not only
physically (its moving strips, apartments, community
kitchens and toilets, underground highways used only for

emergencies, film and tape libraries, shoe stores, power plants, hydroponics laboratories, and yeast farms) but also sociologically (the observances of privacy, hatred of robots, popular entertainments, games, and songs, predilection for a romanticized past, envy and hatred of Spacers, fear of heights and open spaces, to which the New Yorker is conditioned). The reader is given no reason to wonder at the marvels of science fictional technology, as familiar to Lije Baley as they are to the average science fiction fan (and increasingly to the public at large). The real wonder is that the City is no further advanced than this after three thousand years, and even that anomaly is explained in part by the City's withdrawn and backward social psychology.

The City's technology has grown about as fast as its problems, enabling it to cope with, if not alleviate the pressure of population, the growth of which is inexorable, although the rate of growth has lowered appreciably, relative to current standards. "Moving strips," "expressways," and "lightworms" (moving directional signs) transport a huge, independently mobile population more effectively than the automobiles which used to crowd what are still called "motorways" (only police "squad cars" and other emergency vehicles still travel them, using "drive rods" supplied with "beamed power" from a central transmitter). "Trimension" (three-dimensional television), "micro-projectors" (for three-dimensional microfilm), "book-films," "video-piping," and "communos" (public telephones with vision), by improving communication, have made some travel unnecessary. The need for social control has resulted in improved spying devices, such as the "spybeam" and the "duo-beam," against which only silence can preserve secrecy with any surety; it has also resulted in destructive and non-destructive hand-weapons, primarily for police, such as the "blaster," "subetheric hand disruptor," "neuronic whip" and "tickler." The need for food has resulted in vast hydroponic gardens and yeast farms, the latter producing "zymoveal" and "proto-veg" (synthetic veal and vegetables), and requiring the expertise of "zymologists" and other technicians. Little or no creative energy has been directed toward finding a way out of the City's problems, except by those outside the City culture.

The Spacers, descendants of those who escaped Earth to explore and colonize some fifty distant planets, avoided overpopulation from the first, and continue to restrict both birth and immigration. They devote their energies to increasing their living standards, not merely trying to halt their decline. By contrast with the burrow-like Cities, their homes (although domed) are single dwellings, separated by open space, even in their settlement on Earth, Spacetown. Efficiency for them lies in the use of individu-alized robots, not mass communal services, and their basic reason for even having an "embassy" on Earth (we are told)

is to propagandize for the increased use of robot workers in
the Cities. But robots are anathema to the already under-
employed, semi-capitalistic workers of the Cities, and the
Spacers' mission is not aided by their cultural differences
from the people of Earth whom they are trying to help.

The Spacers' technology is plainly superior to that
of the City. Between their community and the City stands an
impenetrable barrier to keep out anything undesirable, from
rioters to bacteria. To keep their health perfect they have
developed quite thorough hygiene, so thorough that it
offends Earthmen, not only those few who have been subjected
to the sterilizing shower required to enter Spacetown, but
those who are even aware of its existence, or of the Spacer
precautions of distance and breathing filters in the presence of Earthmen. They have space travel, of course, and
the wealth necessary to import fresh fruits from other
worlds. The superiority of their technology, which is
sketched in more detail in the sequel The Naked Sun, is most
fully represented here in terms of their mastery of the
science of "robotics."

When Karel Čapek coined the word "robot" to describe
the "soulless monsters" of R. U. R., intent on destroying
their creators, he had in mind the traditional image of man-
made life patterned on the medieval golem and the monster in

Mary Shelley's Frankenstein.[17] Asimov's answer to this
"Frankenstein complex," explored in many of his stories, is
that robots, i.e. humanoid machines, will have safeguards
built into them to insure that they, like any other tool,
will be servants or partners for man. The technology which
will accomplish his goal of the "positronic" robot he has
explained in a rather sketchy manner at best: "My robots
[have] brains of platinum-iridium sponge and the 'brain
paths' [are] marked out by the production and destruction of
positrons. (No, I don't know how this is done.)"[18] The
safeguards, which many other writers have assumed since John
Campbell derived them from Asimov's story "Reason" (1941),
are called the Three Laws of Robotics.[19] Only partially
explicit in The Caves of Steel, they are codified elsewhere:

1--A robot may not injure a human being, or, through
inaction, allow a human being to come to harm.

2--A robot must obey the orders given it by human
beings except where such orders would conflict
with the First Law.

---

[17]Sam Moskowitz, Explorers of the Infinite:
Shapers of Science Fiction (Cleveland and New York, 1963),
pp. 208-224. For the derivation of the word "robot," see
Zdenek Nemecek, "Karel Capek," in Joseph Remenyi et al.,
World Literatures (Pittsburgh, 1956), p. 62. See also
Robert Plank, "The Golem and the Robot," Literature and
Psychology, XV (Winter, 1965), 12-28.

[18]Rest of the Robots (above, note 16), p. 42.

[19]Seekers (above, note 1), pp. 256-257.

3--A robot must protect its own existence as long as such protection does not conflict with the First or Second Law.[20]

Subject to these laws, Asimov's robots are completely logical, never complicated by emotions; designed to be obedient and constructive, they can be destructive only by accident, and even then, only if something is wrong with the circuits controlling the Three Laws. On the Earth of Lije Baley's time, robots are kept in their place as slaves by means of deliberate under-engineering; only the simplest, most ungainly, most obviously mechanical robots are employed, and even these clearly harmless machines arouse the "Frankenstein complex" in men who fear for their jobs. By contrast, the Spacer robot, R. Daneel Olivaw, represents the ultimate extension of the robot concept; completely human in appearance, sophisticated and completely logical in his thinking processes, Daneel is by far the most important piece of technological hardware in the book.

Intended to be an "information-gathering device," Daneel has been designed to enter the Cities of Earth, where the Spacers, unable to withstand the noise, crowding, and disease germs, cannot go. In New York, he is to pose as a human being, communicating directly to Spacetown such findings as may enable his masters to better understand the way the people of Earth live, thereby to understand the people

---

[20]*Rest of the Robots*, p. 43.

from their conditioning. Besides "experiencing" and measuring the environment and the overt behavior of humans, Daneel
can measure and analyze a person's "mind aura," i.e. the
biochemical-electrical reactions engendered by emotional
stress. Although he cannot "experience" an emotion, he can
come reasonably close to "understanding" emotions, presumably as close as objective knowledge can ever come to
subjective experience. Although it appears to Lije as if
Daneel does have one emotion, a "desire" for justice, from
which Lije deduces that Daneel is not a robot, this "desire"
is actually a circuit added to the robot's brain to make him
a good detective, i.e. to make him work toward what he
defines as justice, namely "that which exists when all laws
are enforced" (p. 241).

If Daneel represents the ultimate in logical, objective, scientific thinking, the men who created him are not
far from that ultimate. An emotional human being, Lije
Baley assumes at first that the Spacers, being men, have a
culture as emotionally conditioned as his own. Although he
gradually comes to understand the logical reasons behind
their behavior, he does not necessarily come to view that
behavior as attractive. Their fastidious cleanliness may
be necessary to protect them from bacteria, but the forms
it takes (avoiding physical contact with Earthmen, using
nose filters to clean Earth's air, requiring sterilizing
showers for anyone coming from the City into Spacetown)

still rankle. Their eugenics program is extremely logical,
improving the breed, keeping population down, but it runs
contrary to the traditions of free choice prevalent, if
limited, on Earth. The Spacers' liking for robots, fresh
air, and open spaces seems frightening to Lije, their
introduction of robots into the City's economy seems threatening, and their ultimate intent, to make Earthmen so
dissatisfied they will emigrate and challenge the Spacers'
complacency, seems callous and unfeeling. The summit of
Spacer egotism and inhumanity Lije sees in the act of Dr.
Sarton (the murdered man) in creating the robot Daneel "in
his own image" (p. 234). Musing over the Spacers' blas-
phemy, Lije sees them as the essence of undiluted scientism:
"He had read somewhere once that Spacers had no religion,
but substituted, instead, a cold and phlegmatic intellectu-
alism raised to the heights of a philosophy" (p. 235).

Nowhere is the Spacers' scientific outlook better
illustrated than in their experiment with Lije, himself.
Having administered to him without his knowledge a drug
which lowered his resistance to suggestion, Dr. Han
Fastolfe, the spokesman for the Spacers, lectures Lije on
the possible advantages of emigration from Earth. A practical man, Lije is persuaded only so far as to give theoretical consideration to the idea; his musing turns
gradually to daydreaming aloud, then to giving a lecture
on the subject to the Medievalist suspect he and Daneel

arrest. The experiment succeeds, since the alleged conspirator, Clousarr, appears to take the lecture seriously,
according to Daneel's cerebroanalysis. Thereupon Fastolfe,
satisfied that Earthmen will once again attempt to colonize
other planets, accedes to the request of the isolationists
in Spacetown, which is to recall Daneel and prepare to
leave Earth immediately. The fact that Lije Baley, their
"guinea pig," is in trouble on their account, disturbs them
not at all, since their mission has been accomplished.

Their lack of feeling for a single human being,
especially the one with whom the reader most identifies,
merely underlines the lack of humaneness in the Spacers'
scientific approach. Lije and Clousarr are treated not as
individual human beings but as representatives of general
psychological conditions ("practical sensibility," "romantic
longing"), factors to be controlled in an attempt to upset
the social psychology of the Cities. With part of Lije's
behavior controlled, the effect objectively observed by
Daneel confirms the Spacers' prediction; inferring the
reactions of Lije and Clousarr to be representative of
Earthmen in general, the Spacers assume an inexorable chain
of events will lead to their desired goal.

That goal, also consistent with the tenets of
scientism, is the survival of man. Man's survival, they
feel, is predicated upon full utilization of science and
technology (a goal of their cultures) in combination with

full utilization and expression of the human being (a goal of Earth's culture). Without such a combination, termed a "C/Fe" society (C for carbon, or man, Fe for iron, or machines), man will stagnate, withdraw, cease to grow (in a cultural sense) and eventually cease to exist (in a biological sense). The one-sidedness of Earth's culture is obvious from a science fictional viewpoint; cramped, regressive, passive, the people of the City recall other imaginary societies of Earth's future, usually overtly dystopian. From the standpoint of Lije Baley, conscious of emotion and humanity, the Spacers are equally incomplete; they lack a sense of history and tradition, a feeling for life and community, a sense of purpose and progress. Fastolfe even admits that they, too, have stopped growing.

Whether their ideal, the perfect C/Fe society, could ever come into being is questionable; that it would emerge in the manner and form they desire is extremely doubtful. Asimov's intention to portray it in a third volume, after illustrating the negative extremes of Spacer culture on the planet Solaria in the sequel, The Naked Sun, has never been fulfilled.[21] He claimed in 1964 that his inspiration to write fiction had failed him, and indeed relatively few stories by Asimov have seen first publication since 1957,

---

[21] Rest of the Robots, p. 555.

when <u>The Naked Sun</u> was revised for book publication.[22] But

the failure of inspiration in regard to the trilogy may have

been related more specifically to the difficulty in conceiv-

ing a properly utopian conclusion. Within the context of

the fiction, a contemporary planet of the Outer Worlds can

hardly show already in existence a <u>future</u> C/Fe society,

integrating Earth's humane culture and the Spacers' more

scientific way of life. Outside the world of fiction, the

problems of integrating machines into the life of twentieth-

century man cannot be solved by bringing two symbols

together. And if a man-machine partnership, like that of

Lije and Daneel, could be imaginatively extended to a

universal social reality on the capital planet Aurora, the

need on that world for that particular combination of man

and robot to solve a crime might be difficult to rational-

ize.

In <u>The Caves of Steel</u> (as in the sequel) their

partnership is a meaningful, unifying device, since the

cultures which produced them are presented as polar oppo-

sites. Through their partnership, Lije and Daneel manage

---

[22]<u>Rest of the Robots</u>, pp. 555-556. In 1958, nine
stories credited to Asimov received first publication (some
of which presumably were written before 1958); 1959 through
1966, fifteen "new" stories were published. In 1958, the
fifth of his novels for juveniles was published under the
pseudonym of "Paul French," in addition to his murder-
mystery, <u>The Death Dealers</u> (composition dates unknown). In
1966, his novelization of a science fiction movie, <u>Fantastic
Voyage</u>, was published and this book presumably was written
during the non-fiction period. See I[saac] A[simov], "Isaac
Asimov: A Bibliography," <u>F&SF</u>, October, 1966, pp. 36-45.

to surmount some of the negative aspects of their differences, and to emphasize some of the positive aspects, thus
proving not only the efficacy of men and machines working
together but also the efficacy of communication in breaking
down prejudices.

The negative side of each culture is generally that
side which is seen dimly by the unenlightened outsider. To
the Spacers, New York City is dark, dirty, noisy, crowded,
and foul-smelling; claustrophobic, they can only enter the
City symbolically, via Daneel. To an Earthman, Spacetown
is blindingly bright, unnaturally clean, unprotected from
sun and air, devoid of familiar sounds and smells and physical contact; agoraphobic, he could only enter the open
country symbolically, as Commissioner Enderby does, using a
robot to carry his murder-weapon. Earthmen are primitive
and regressive: they cultivate religion (as part of their
education), they study history (Lije intellectually, but the
Medievalists emotionally), and they have a tendency toward
violence (civil disturbances are endemic). Spacers are
machine-like and inhuman: they "worship" science, they
study sociology and social psychology (manipulating people
and machines in the present in order to manage the future,
but ignoring the past), and they are infuriatingly non-
violent. The fecundity of the Cities, which continually
threatens to ruin them despite population controls, is
symbolized by the vast underground farms where they grow

yeast, a blindly growing, tasteless, undifferentiated,
living organism which supplies them with food. The sterility of the Outer Planets is suggested by the figure of the
robot, capable of thought and intellectual growth, but
unable to reproduce or to feel, a perceptive, controlled,
individuated, non-living machine which supplies them with
services.

To a reader sharing science fiction's predilection
for scientific research, engineering marvels, technological
progress, and logical behavior, it would seem that the
positive aspects of Spacer culture are predominant. Since
the negative aspects were to be stressed in The Naked Sun,
Asimov could handle them mainly by implication in the first
book; indeed, most of the features of Spacer culture which
Lije finds objectionable are given favorable treatment by
the author. The reader is expected to approve of fresh air,
sunlight, private homes, robot servants, an enlightened
philosophy in lieu of religion, the scientific study of man,
eugenics, and the technological avoidance of violence. He
is expected to notice the treatment accorded to scientists
in the two cultures: robotocists (Dr. Fastolfe and the late
Dr. Sarton) act as spokesmen for the Spacers, whereas the
Earth roboticist (Dr. Gerrigel) and zymologist (Clousarr)
have no significantly favorable status among their peers.
Although Sarton is dead, Fastolfe is not autonomous, and the
task of "spokesman" to Earthmen is probably not coveted

among Spacers, the impression remains that Spacers respect
their scientists, whereas Earth does not reward those
concerned with either its present (food supply) or its
future (machines). Asimov underscores this impression by
his characterization: Fastolfe is fatherly, unemotional,
and professorial; Gerrigel is somewhat simpering, if knowledgeable and well-meaning; Clousarr is a stereotyped
belligerent conspirator, whose "professional" status is
chiefly a matter of vanity.

Via his exposure to this culture, Lije Baley comes
to understand some of his prejudices against it and in favor
of his own. On the most conscious level, he comes to appreciate the logic and the necessarily calm behavior of his
robot partner, and to allow for if not to approve of some
of the Spacers' different ways of doing things. Less
consciously he comes to feel less at ease in his old habits
and environment. Before he even meets Daneel, he thinks
favorably of New York buildings as "human hives" (p. 171)
and of the City as "a tremendous, self-contained cave of
steel and concrete" (p. 181). More negatively, on his way
to the appointment with Fastolfe, he regards the motorway
as "a blind and hollow worm" (p. 229). In Spacetown he
receives several shocks concerning differing interpretations
of what is "unclean"; his revulsions against speaking in
"Personal" (a community men's room) and eating "natural"
fruit, "straight from the dirt of a planet's soil" (p. 235)

are contrasted with the Spacers' need to avoid bacteria (in
the air, on his skin, from his breath). On his return to
the City, he discovers for the first time that "the City
smells" (p. 257) and by the end of the book he is daydreaming about sun, fresh air, and open space (despite his normal
city-dweller's phobia against all three). By the end of The
Naked Sun, he finally realizes that the Cities are "wombs"
from which man must escape, an insight which was inaccessi-
ble to him until he had himself left Earth for his visit to
Solaria.

The breaking down of Spacer prejudices concerning
Earth culture presumably takes place rather tentatively, on
a completely conscious level, and behind the scenes. Our
only evidence of it emerges from those observations by
Daneel of human behavior to which Asimov draws our attention
and from the Spacers' withdrawal from Earth at the novel's
end, supposedly motivated by the assumption that the City
culture is not now hopelessly stagnant. Daneel transmits
countless pieces of data to the Spacers, from which they,
as we, can presumably construct cultural configurations with
positive significance. Three such configurations, whose
positive values might well have been unknown to the Spacers
before they dispatched their information-gathering device,
are the rights of the individual, the tradition of the
humanities, and the role of idle fun and games.

To Spacers, the right to privacy seems to mean the
right to isolate oneself, which their level of technology
and population makes possible. On Earth, privacy must be
defended by each person, individually and as part of the
group's mores. Thus one does not speak in Men's Personal,
or look at others there or in the community dining rooms,
or, unless one's job demands it, pry into others' business
in any way. Lije's perturbation, at Daneel's violation of
these taboos, and at the thought of "cerebroanalysis" as
the ultimate invasion of privacy, is duly recorded by Daneel
as unexpected behavior. But the rights of the individual go
beyond privacy, the free choice of mates, and personal
idiosyncracies such as eyeglasses, tobacco, and real windows
to the basic concept, alien to Spacer logic, of the right to
be irrational and even to be wrong. In acknowledging Lije's
mistaken accusations of Daneel, Fastolfe and later Daneel
patiently correct him as if the error were totally a
rational one. By the book's end, Daneel has learned enough
about irrationality to be able not only to understand but
also to "forgive," even to forgive a murderer his unwitting
and misguided act.

History, enduring art, and religion are three
aspects of the tradition of the humanities to which Earthmen, at least some of them, are irrationally committed, as
Daneel discovers. All three seem to be preserved mainly via
literature, that which is available on book-films. Lije is

well-versed in history, his hobby, some of which he has
gained from historical novels; other people show a primi-
tivistic interest in historical artifacts, or copies and
reconstructions of historical artifacts, such as eyeglasses
and windows (Julius Enderby's particular fetishes). Art is
represented perhaps through architecture but most specifically through "romances" like the familiar story of "The
Wandering Londoner," who was supposedly lost in the subter-
ranean motorways. The quality of the art may not be high,
but the preservation of it is important (in contrast to the
glimpse of Spacer art we get in The Naked Sun: abstract
"sculpture" with lights, to be obliterated and replaced at
the wave of a hand). Like religion, these remnants of
tradition are representative of an observation Lije makes
at one point: "Most Earthmen were Medievalists in one way
or another" (p. 180), yearning for a time less mechanized
and efficient, more oriented toward the simpler "human"
values.

The presence of religion, of the Judeo-Christian
variety, is recurrently invoked, although not in the form
of formal worship. Lije and Jessie first met at a
"Christmas party." Jessie's Medievalist meetings, with
their speeches and songs, their "sandwiches" and "juice,"
seem to be the City's nearest equivalent to a church
service. The preservation of the names Elijah and Jezebel
for 3,000 years beyond our present era would be unlikely

without some faint hint of Biblical tradition, and Jessie
even tends to identify superficially with what little she
knows of her Biblical namesake. For Lije, the Bible seems
to be primarily a work of literature, valued for its poetry,
historical insight, and moral guidance. He shows its
relevance as a moral guide to Daneel in an attempt to
explain Jessie's irrational behavior, his own sense of
mercy, and the concept (self-contradictory, to Daneel) of
something "higher than law." That the story he recites, of
Jesus pardoning the adulterous widow, impresses Daneel is
made clear by the robot's quoting the words "Go, and sin no
more" to Julius Enderby at the end of the book (p. 362).

The third configuration, idle activity, or actions
not deliberately planned and oriented toward a specific
goal, presumably seems just as irrational to Daneel and the
Spacers as the other two patterns, but also quite functional
in context. In his youth, Lije played games such as "tag"
or "follow the leader" on the moving strips, and such as
"hide-and-seek" with "guide rods" in the City's labyrinths,
never considering the usefulness of his play. Now his
experience "running the strips" helps him and Daneel to
escape pursuit, while his familiarity with "guide rods" not
only helps him locate Clousarr in Yeast-town without warning
him, but also arouses his suspicions of the "malfunctioning"
rod which leads Dr. Gerrigel to the robot Lije is accused
of having destroyed. His adult hobby of history, as

"useless" as childhood games, gives Lije an understanding
(helpful to the reader) of Medievalism, religion, and
Earthman-Spacer relations; his historical bent, in fact,
motivated Dr. Fastolfe to have him assigned to the case in
the first place. Lije's "idle" curiosity is essential in
his professional capacity, since a detective never knows
what random piece of information may prove meaningful in
combination with others. Yet his normal curiosity is
clouded at first by his prejudices toward and suspicions of
Daneel and the Spacers. He first becomes conscious of its
importance to him when he realizes that Daneel has no
curiosity, infers that the Spacers are similarly unimaginative, and guesses that they failed to see the clue he needs
to clear himself and to identify the murderer. Besides the
practical advantage his curiosity gives him, he recognizes
in it a basic human quality distinguishing man from machine,
a quality which should eventually enable Earthmen, and
Spacers, to break out of their social rigidity and sterility.

All of these aspects of Earth culture, insofar as
they are represented by observable behavior, are recorded
by Daneel and transmitted to Spacetown. The indirect effect
is to make the Spacers confident of the likelihood of
Earth's return to space exploration. The direct effect is
upon Daneel's understanding, as he, like Lije, comes to
respect their partnership more with each lesson in

tolerating their differences.

Unlike Lije, Daneel is not actively suspicious of
his partner at the beginning; his mechanically passive
innocence, however, lacks the warmth expected of a human
partner. Despite increasing knowledge of the ability of
Daneel to remember, to reason, to act, Lije's emotional
revulsion forces him to continue to entertain irrational
suspicions; as his distrust appears to approach hysteria,
the illogic of it all compels Daneel to question his
partner's abilities. Having twice falsely accused Daneel,
Lije is taken aback by Daneel's tentative accusation of
Jessie; on the defensive, Lije begins to clear away his
prejudices against robots. Aware now of his need to feel
superior to the robot, he suppresses his resentment in order
to deal adequately with his job. Thus he eventually demonstrates his human superiority (use and control of the
irrational) as he comes to accept Daneel's mechanical
superiority. Reciprocally, Daneel comes to recognize that
logic and law alone are not sufficient for every problem.

Since man and machine can communicate and interact
in this way to solve a relatively simple problem like reconstructing a crime and finding a murderer, the implication
is that men and machines, utilizing each other's complementary abilities, can eventually solve more complex problems
involving whole societies. But man and machine or man and
man cannot solve significant problems without communication,

especially between opposing viewpoints, which are essentially different frameworks for looking at things. And communication is a key concept in this book, as in much science fiction. Within the fiction, obviously, communication is responsible for breaking down prejudices between characters and between opposing factions. But on the level of technique also, the book is designed for direct communication from the author to his readers, communication of the gospel of science to the non-scientist, communication to the scientist of the need to consider humanity. The plots, the mode of presentation, the structure, the level of diction, and the character of the hero are all directed toward this goal.

The mystery-detective plot in the foreground is smoothly handled in terms of the conventions of the detective story. All clues, leads, and possible pieces of evidence are shared with the reader before the dénouement, and no deus ex machina, in the form of a futuristic device not previously introduced, is invoked to solve the mystery. In other words, Asimov is "fair to the reader" as the rules of the detective-story demand.[23] But the plot exists not only for itself, but also to enable Asimov to use his detective as utopian novelists have often used the figure

---

[23]Holmes (above, note 12). See also Howard Haycraft, Murder for Pleasure: The Life and Times of the Detective Story (New York and London, 1941), pp. 223-258.

of a stranger from another time or place, and as science fiction writers have often used the doctor or dedicated scientific researcher who must find the deterrent to the menace from outer space. Lije Baley must learn, in order to solve the case, information which he does not already possess, and in the process, the reader can also be introduced, unobtrusively, to this unfamiliar world.

Baley is therefore a certain kind of detective, a thinking man (perhaps too conscious of his thoughts to be real), an educated man (as he must be to understand his past, and to help us understand it), but in many ways an essentially timid and conventional man, anxiety-ridden, concerned for his family, and fully imbued with his culture's insecurities. He is capable and determined in his own line or work, once he can overcome his own prejudices, but quite practical-minded in his own estimate of himself and of his position in the world. These qualities make him quite acceptable as a real person and at the same time as a kind of "everyman" figure with whom the reader can comfortably identify. These qualities also make it quite believable that he becomes involved in the background plot of Spacer-Earthman intrigue, both because he is a good detective who delves into the background of his case, and because he is the practical kind of man the Spacers need, on whom to test their arguments in favor of emigration. His growth as a person is also implicit in his character at the beginning, not merely the result of the Spacers' manipulations. They only suggested the existence of alternatives; Lije had to realize for himself the existence in himself of untapped potential. His adaptation to unfamiliar customs and ideas is subtly and gradually sketched, not as that of an experimental animal going through his predetermined paces, but as that of a human being rediscovering curiosity and wonder, and triumphing over himself and his society's rigid conventions and attitudes. Yet the contradictoriness of his character even carries over into his exultant solution at the end. He defeats, and then forgives, his friend and superior, who has proven to be his enemy. He defeats representatives of the Medievalists, with whom he has been in sympathy, yet offers them a new, futuristic solution to their frustrations. He defeats the Spacers, who had callously wanted to close the case with him still in trouble, invoking the aid of their own robot, with whom he has not been on consistently good terms, but at the same time he capitulates to their way of thinking about the need for progress and the further development of the man-machine relationship. Even in his victory over his conditioned attitudes, he is still afraid to leave Earth and the protection of the City's domes (he ultimately defeats his agoraphobia, but only in part, in The Naked Sun).

The background plot, as we have already seen, involves a good deal of communication between Lije and the

Spacers. Although we can only infer their enlightenment, and his is largely begun under the influence of a drug increasing his suggestibility, the overall impression is of stereotypes and prejudices being broken down, the most important of which are Lije's fears of space and robots. In his "everyman" capacity, then, Lije may well be considered as the average American being won over by the arguments of science fiction. Thus the secondary plot, too, is a definite tool of communication.

The use of the detective, and the detective-plot, is admirably suited to the mode of presentation generally preferred by science fiction writers of the "second generation," whom Asimov sees as writers of "social science fiction." Following the lead of Robert A. Heinlein, who is regarded by many as the master of this technique, Asimov does not detail every aspect of life in his characters' world before getting on with his story, nor does he interrupt the narrative with lengthy explanations which break the tenuous illusion of future reality.[24] Since he is telling a story, not blueprinting a utopia, he introduces through the action itself, or through short qualifying statements, as much background information as the reader needs at the moment. In some cases, where an unexplained

[24] On Heinlein, see Seekers (above, note 1), pp. 187-212; Knight (above, note 15), pp. 76-89; Alexei Panshin, Heinlein in Dimension: A Critical Analysis (Chicago, 1968).

point is an established science fiction convention, he lets
the reader familiarize himself with futuristic devices or
terms through context alone. Thus the communication is
somewhat below the surface, and the all-important background
or setting seems almost to emerge of its own accord.

Because we are mainly limited to the consciousness
of Lije, presented by a slightly more knowledgeable third-
person narrator, we have a definite focus on the action, not
a diffuse panorama of an unfamiliar world. The limitation
to one viewpoint limits us also to his knowledge; thus the
reader is kept guessing along with Lije as to the Spacers'
real motives and the identity of the killer. If we are
closed off from his mind at the moment of recognition, this
is a legitimate trick of staging for the dénouement, since
everything needed to deduce the killer's identity has been
presented to us. The third-person narrator telling us about
Lije fills in many details presumably known to Lije which
may not be in his conscious thoughts at the moment, thus
adding to our knowledge of Lije's psychological, social,
and physical environment. This results in a tremendously
compressed narrative style, introducing us to many unfamiliar things in a small space. Thus in the first chapter
alone we become acquainted with the following bits of
observation, information, and opinion: the tobacco short-
age, the problems of robot-caused unemployment, the fatuity
of Earth's primitive robots, the type of computer used in

the Police Department, the City-dweller's struggle for
status, the rarity of such old-fashioned devices as windows
and spectacles, the invasion of privacy which a window represents to Lije, the average Earthman's unfamiliarity with
rain or other natural phenomena, the primitivism of the cult
of Medievalists, the differences in the way of living in
Spacetown, the exaggerated cleanliness of the Spacers, the
recent acts of violence in the City, the existence of other
Cities besides New York, Police Commissioner Enderby's
sentimentality, the Spacers' lack of emotion, the difficult
political situation between Earthmen and Spacers, and Lije's
"special relationship" with the Commissioner. In addition,
we are presented with the opening gambit of the plot, i.e.
that Lije, in taking on the murder case, must also accept a
Spacer robot as partner and live with him, and all of this
is accomplished in ten pages, or about 3,500 words.

The chapter structure seems intended to demonstrate
to the reader that Asimov has nothing to hide, i.e. he is
neither withholding necessary evidence about the crime and
information about the background, nor is he indulging in any
subtle literary maneuvers which might please a literary
critic but deceive the average reader of science fiction.
Each chapter is not only full of information, but also
arranged in terms of action so that it has its own development and climax, its own identity as a discrete unit
complete with jejune, pulp-style subtitle (from

"Conversation with a Commissioner," Chapter 1, to "End of
an Investigation," Chapter 18). Each chapter is generally
a chronological unit, contrasted with the next in terms of
setting, mood, and action, as well. The book is unabashedly
a serial, too, with each installment ending on a melodramatic and suspenseful accusation (the first two of which are
false), thus appealing quite openly to the reader for whom
only the "action plot" is of interest.[25] Finally, the novel
is also a part of a trilogy and, while the allusions made by
Lije and others to other worlds and their customs are very
much a part of this particular book, they also point beyond
it to the sequel or sequels.

Asimov's prose style is superior to that of many
writers of pulp fiction, but here too he seems to be aiming
at a mass audience. Aside from the few dozen terms describing future technology, most of which are quickly explained,
his vocabulary is simple and familiar, even trite. His
sentences are relatively uncomplicated and generally cast
in the active voice, resulting in a breathless, but not
staccato, narrative pace. His language is relatively full
of imagery and analogies, making the most unfamiliar science
fictional conventions immediately accessible. The apparent
impersonality of his style, a common feature of much science
fiction, is modified by a serious, earnest, and optimistic

---

[25]Norman Friedman, "Forms of the Plot," in The
Theory of the Novel, ed. Philip Stevick (New York, 1967),
p. 158.

tone which is characteristic of Asimov's fiction.[26]

Dialogue predominates over exposition and narrative in The Caves of Steel, as is more typical of detective stories than science fiction, thus giving us more of the feeling of what it is like to live in that world, and less of the awe and wonder an innocent stranger or a highly impressed and omniscient third-person narrator might well create by stressing description. Thus, too, Asimov can show us more and tell us less of his characters' behavior, letting the characters tell us, by act and speech, what he advocates in the way of progress and decency. The dialogue is usually introduced by the word "said," frequently modified by adverbial stage directions establishing the mood of the speaker which may not be clear from his speech. Such a reliance on adverbs, as a kind of verbal shorthand substituting for precise and effective dialogue, is often overdone in pulp fiction, but Asimov's use of this device is seldom obtrusive.

The dialogue itself is generally suited to the character and whatever emotion there is in the situation. Even the one-dimensional characters are appropriately characterized by their speech patterns, including the fatherly Fastolfe, the blustering Clousarr, the simpering

---

[26]William Atheling, Jr. [James Blish], The Issue at Hand: Studies in Contemporary Magazine Science Fiction, ed. James Blish (Chicago, 1964), pp. 29-30.

Gerrigel, the timid Jessie, and less successfully the
stereotyped adolescent, Bentley Baley, and the caricatured
bureaucrat, Julius Enderby. The most important characters,
whose conversation is most often before us, Lije and Daneel,
are also the most recognizable by their speech patterns.
Daneel speaks a slightly stilted, awkward, grammatically
perfect English which just misses being idiomatically
correct, as when he offers refreshment to Lije in Spacetown:
"These are the fruits of natural plant life grown on Aurora.
I suggest you try this kind. It is called an apple and is
reputed to be pleasant" (p. 234). Everything he says must
be letter-perfect, including the way he addresses humans:
Lije is "Elijah" to Daneel, and he hesitates to use the
diminutive "Jessie." Lije, by contrast, is perfectly comfortable with the idiomatic language, frequently on a level
of colloquialism which is confusing to the literal-minded
Daneel. Baley frequently uses the approach of the traditional "tough cop"; somewhat effective with Clousarr, it is
a bit inappropriate with Jessie, and completely useless with
Daneel, for whom the pose's artificial emotionlessness
carries no meaning to supplement the actual words involved.

The conventional tendency of dialogue in detective
fiction to communicate far more information than speech
carries in real life is particularly appropriate to Asimov's
purpose. Content in general is more important than style in
The Caves of Steel, and every aspect of Asimov's technique

seems dedicated to communicating content in as direct a manner as possible. The possibility of clear, direct communication is itself a part of the content, not merely in an implicit way, inferred from the erasure of prejudices, but also explicitly, as in Asimov's assumptions within the fiction concerning future linguistic change. At one point, Lije's thoughts include the following sentence: "English might not be the 'English' of Shakespeare or Churchill, but it was the final potpourri that was current over all the continents and, with some modification, on the Outer Worlds as well" (p. 266). Even allowing for the tendency of communications technology to standardize language and retard change, such a situation after 3,000 years in a civilization of fifty-odd planets not in constant contact with one another is at least improbable, from a linguistic point of view. The bias for English as the standard tongue is an established convention, even in the science fiction of other countries, and the necessity for a common language between characters in a work of literature is not peculiar to science fiction at all. But the wishful thinking which lies behind the science fictional assertion of one common tongue in the future is, I suspect, related to the scientist's desire to communicate across international or interlingual borders as freely with words as with mathematical and technical symbols.

As a writer of science fiction as well as a scientist, Asimov is also concerned with communicating the missionary gospel of progress to a non-scientific and non-science-fictional audience beyond the science fiction community. To this end, I believe, not merely because such a _tour de force_ was a challenge to the craftsman in him, Asimov has attempted to amalgamate the detective story with the science fiction novel. In addition, the combination of reservations about over-reliance on scientism with the optimistic anticipation of perfect communication and man-machine progress, while it may well represent the author's personal sense of balance between the sciences and the humanities, also seems calculated as a message of caution to the zealous prophets of science, and as an attempt to show both the masses and the literati that science fiction isn't quite as wild and radical as they may believe.

As a _tour de force_, The Caves of Steel is a remarkable feat of craftsmanship. As a work of science fiction, it is an unqualified success. As a piece of literature, fairly narrow in scope and limited in aim, it is an adequate entertainment. It communicates its message clearly, but without preaching--not that space is the answer to the population explosion, nor that the future is necessarily utopian or dystopian, but that what we call progress, expansion, or growth is essential to the survival, for good or for bad, of civilization and of the individual man. In

addition, the book makes its hypothetical future, its physical and social setting, a felt and remembered experience,
long after the details of the murder investigation are
forgotten.

CHAPTER V

THEODORE STURGEON: MORE THAN HUMAN (1953)

In his first book review column, which appeared in
the July, 1957 issue of F&SF's short-lived companion magazine, Venture Science Fiction, Theodore Sturgeon declared
that he personally did not read science fiction for its
science, its fiction, or its entertainment value, since all
three could be obtained elsewhere and better. Referring to
himself in third person, he wrote: "he reads s f [sic]
because of its expansion of the known--its thrusting back
of horizons. S f has no inhibitions when it penetrates or
extrapolates or makes extensions. S f is bold and unabashed
and not embarrassed by its speculations. This is the
quality which, when added to good fiction, makes good s f;
but this wonderful reach of the field is its heart."[1] This
statement would not seem exceptionable coming from any
writer developed by John Campbell around 1940, but Sturgeon
is far from a typical Campbell product.[2] Although he was

[1]Venture, July, 1957, p. 78.

[2]Sam Moskowitz, Seekers of Tomorrow: Masters of
Modern Science Fiction (Cleveland and New York, 1966),
pp. 229-248. See also Judith Merril, "Theodore Sturgeon,"
F&SF, September, 1962, pp. 46-55, and James Blish, "Theodore
Sturgeon's Macrocosm," F&SF, September, 1962, pp. 42-45.

discovered by Campbell, who bought most of his stories of fantasy and science fiction in the Forties, Sturgeon seldom wrote the "pure" science fiction which he saw in Campbell's own space operas: "narrative which could not occur without its science."[3] And since the rise in literary quality of Astounding's competition since 1949-50, only one story of Sturgeon's has appeared in Campbell's magazine.[4]

Sturgeon's understanding of such key terms in the above passage as "extrapolation" and "good fiction" is quite different from that of Campbell, for whom the kinds of content and of story-telling manner are rather limited.[5] In another short essay, dealing largely with the mechanics of extrapolation and the study of science in science fiction, Sturgeon asserted (giving credit to Murray Leinster) that extrapolation could also be applied to people; understanding a character in terms of his responses to real life situations, one should be able to "extrapolate" what his behavior would be in a less likely situation.[6] On other occasions,

---

[3]Theodore Sturgeon, "On Hand . . . Off Hand: Books," Venture, November, 1957, p. 82.

[4]Sources of bibliographical information include indexes (above, Chapter I, note 35), personal collections, and Sam Moskowitz, "Fantasy and Science Fiction by Theodore Sturgeon," F&SF, September, 1962, pp. 56-61.

[5]See John W. Campbell, Jr., "Science Fact and Science Fiction," Writer, August, 1964, pp. 26-27. See also Chapter I, above, pp. 25-28.

[6]Theodore Sturgeon, "The Other IF," IF, May, 1962, pp. 107-112.

he has stated opinions far from Campbell's concerning the subject matter and function of science fiction. "With the admission of psychology and political criticism to legitimate s f, all things acting upon human beings, and acted upon by them, fall within s f's province."[7] "S f is what any f is--an expression, by the creative mind, of human values and human experience."[8] And in a personal note to readers, after he had been chosen Guest of Honor for the Twentieth World Science Fiction Convention in Chicago in 1962, Sturgeon acknowledged his debt to the science fiction community for enabling him to write in a way which was not particularly bound to science fictional techniques at all:

> I know why world science fiction . . . called me up. It's because I have a great facility with words, an odd kind of detachment, and an unabashed way of putting them together. These things all put into one word make a thing called Talent. A better word for it is Gift. . . .
>
> The reason that it's so hard, in these specializing times, to say what sf [sic] is about is that it isn't about anything--it's about everything. It begins at the most remote horizons of any other form of expression except, possibly, poetry. As such, it is big enough for a talent--a gift--like mine. Sf has been the only place for it, and what I'm most grateful for is that sf coexisted with its birth and growth.

---

[7]Theodore Sturgeon, "On Hand . . . Off Hand: Books," Venture, January, 1958, p. 78.

[8]Theodore Sturgeon, "On Hand . . . Off Hand: Books," Venture, March, 1958, p. 68.

The Gift knows where it wants to be. It is at home there.[9]

Despite his professed liking for pure science fiction, for extrapolation based on scientific studies, Sturgeon's own science fiction is frequently based on impossible or incredible assumptions which have little or no "scientific" stature. His real starting points often seem to be things about which he, and many people, have strong emotional commitments, things that we very much want or fear to be true. And his extrapolations, from present or future situations, from bases in technology or fantasy, involve at times extremely arbitrary plots, designed more for an aesthetic than a realistic pattern. Unrealistic in origin though they may be, many of Sturgeon's stories and characters do have, within the fictional world, a vivid reality rarely equalled in science fiction.

Besides an uncounted number of non-fantasy stories (usually published in detective, adventure, and other pulp magazines), Sturgeon has published over one hundred stories of fantasy and science fiction.[10] More stories by Sturgeon have been anthologized than stories by any other science fiction writer but Isaac Asimov, and nine collections of

---

[9]Theodore Sturgeon, "Most Personal," IF, November, 1962, p. 6.

[10]See above, note 4.

his tales have been issued.[11] In addition to these books, seven novels by Sturgeon have been published.

Two of his novels were potboilers, written for quick sale, the pseudo-historical I, Libertine (1956, by "Frederick R. Ewing"), and a "novelization" of the motion picture, Voyage to the Bottom of the Sea (1961). The other five were original works, extending the borderlines of science fiction, imaginative projections dealing with love and sex, emotions and perversions, symbiosis (biological interdependence, like that between the shark and the pilot fish) and syzygy (union between related things, which with Sturgeon comes to mean a kind of emotional and mental interpretation, like the intercourse of Milton's angels). The Dreaming Jewels (1950) concerns, among other things, syzygy and crystalline life forms. The Cosmic Rape (1958) envisions the attempt by an alien "group-mind" to take over Earth; all Earthmen become one and take over the alien, instead. In both cases, the story is told mainly from the standpoint of an outcast, an "isolato," such as figures in many of Sturgeon's tales. Venus Plus X (1960) contrasts

---

[11]W. R. Cole, A Checklist of Science Fiction Anthologies ([New York], 1964), p. v. Concerning collections of Sturgeon's stories, personal holdings confirm the bibliography in Three to the Highest Power: Bradbury, Oliver, Sturgeon, ed. William F. Nolan (New York, 1968), pp. 105-108. The collections are as follows: Without Sorcery (1948), E Pluribus Unicorn (1953), A Way Home (1955), Caviar (1955), A Touch of Strange (1958), Aliens 4 (1959), Beyond (1960), Sturgeon in Orbit (1964), Starshine (1966).

America's changing sexual mores with those appropriate to a
"utopia" of physiological hermaphrodites. In Some of Your
Blood (1961), Sturgeon manages to make of a traditional
fantasy theme, vampirism, a novel of borderline science
fiction, by making it into a scientific (psychoanalytic)
case-history. Not well received, it was one of his last
efforts in science fiction to date; except for a very few
stories, his connection with the field has been primarily
through science articles (as Feature Editor for IF, 1961-64)
and book review columns (in the National Review, since
1961).[12]

The novel usually considered his best, More than
Human (1953), won the International Fantasy Award for 1954,
against unusually strong competition.[13] Ostensibly an
examination of various kinds of e.s.p., it is also very
much about love and community; as James Blish has noted,
Sturgeon's telepathy might better be called "telempathy."[14]

---

[12]Sturgeon's brief articles on science and speculation appeared in every bimonthly issue of IF from July, 1961
through March, 1964, according to the MIT Index (see above,
note 4); I have so far been able to confirm only ten of
these seventeen issues. In National Review, Sturgeon's book
review column appears irregularly; the first appearance was
September 23, 1961, the nineteenth May 30, 1967.

[13]Seekers (above, note 2), p. 244. Other winners,
1951-1955 and 1957, were: Earth Abides by George R.
Stewart, Fancies and Goodnights by John Collier, City by
Clifford Simak, A Mirror for Observers by Edgar Pangborn,
and Lord of the Rings by J. R. R. Tolkien, according to
Moskowitz, Seekers, pp. 244, 422, and personal letter.

[14]Blish (above, note 2), p. 44.

Reviewed in some general periodicals, it got a fair reception. Maurice Richardson in the New Statesman and Nation said Sturgeon's psychological fantasies interested him as a sociological phenomenon, but he found the author's style "maddeningly turgid" and his science "nonexistent."[15] Kingsley Amis in the Spectator regretted that Sturgeon had not fully imagined a "composite individual" in his homo gestalt, giving us rather "a lot of people milling about [and not] doing anything."[16] Fletcher Pratt praised the book in Saturday Review: "As far as I know, Mr. Sturgeon is the first writer to produce a plausible theory of how [psi powers] could work instead of merely saying they do."[17] Villiers Gerson wrote in the New York Times: "Their adventures, their growing realization of their power and its responsibilities, aided by a poetic, moving prose and a deeply examined raison d'être, make this . . . one of the best science fiction novels of the year."[18]

In the science fiction community, Sturgeon and More than Human were highly acclaimed. P. Schuyler Miller in Astounding compared Sturgeon favorably to Ray Bradbury,

[15]Review by Maurice Richardson, New Statesman and Nation, October 30, 1954, pp. 554-556.

[16]Review by Kingsley Amis, Spectator, September 17, 1954, p. 350.

[17]Review by Fletcher Pratt, Saturday Review, August 7, 1954, pp. 14-15.

[18]Review by Villiers Gerson, New York Times, November 22, 1953, p. 34.

saying "His [Sturgeon's] stories are always about real
people, whose basic trouble is that they are only people,
with the limitations as well as the powers of people."[19]
Groff Conklin in Galaxy reacted similarly: "It is something
of a relief to find a piece of science fiction that is
concerned with odd but astonishingly real people and with
parapsychology maturely used [rather] than with hopeless
mobs and violent disaster."[20] The editor of F&SF, as "H. H.
Holmes," hesitantly used the words "profundity" and "great-
ness" in the New York Herald-Tribune Book Review, and as
"Anthony Boucher," praised the book on several levels: "In
its crystal-clear prose, its intense human warmth and its
depth of psychological probing, it is a first-rate
"straight" novel; its ingenious use of telepathy, psycho-
kinesis, and other 'psi' powers make it admirable science-
fantasy; and the adroit plotting and ceaseless surge of
action qualify it as a distinguished suspense story."[21]
Damon Knight, although he called Sturgeon "the most accomplished technician this field has produced, bar nobody, not
even Bradbury," apparently felt unequal to the task of
describing the book; after two brief quotations and a

---

[19]Review by P. Schuyler Miller, Astounding, June,
1954, pp. 144-145.

[20]Review by Groff Conklin, Galaxy, January, 1954,
pp. 128-129.

[21]Review by H. H. Holmes, New York Herald-Tribune
Book Review, November 22, 1953, p. 19. Review by Anthony
Boucher, F&SF, February, 1954, p. 93.

reference to its genesis as a novelette, he concluded:
"It's a single story that goes from here to there like a
catenary arc, and hits one chord like the Last Trump when it
gets there, and stops. There's nothing more to be said
about it, except that it's the best and only book of its
kind."[22] Obviously, there _is_ more to be said about it, not
all of which is wildly complimentary; it may well be "the
best and only book of its kind," but that begs the question
of just what kind of book it is.

A novel of about 75,000 words, More than Human is
divided into three subtitled sections, roughly equal in
length, each separated from the others by a number of years,
and each subdivided into numerous episodes separated only by
spacing.[23] It tells the story of the combining, and the
growing to maturity of a superhuman "gestalt"-being, whose
unique and disparate members are "children" with parapsychological talents.[24]

---

[22]Damon Knight, In Search of Wonder: Essays on
Modern Science Fiction, rev. ed. (Chicago, 1967), p. 115.

[23]Theodore Sturgeon, More than Human (New York,
1953). All page references in the text are to this edition.
This is the Ballantine paperback edition, which has recently
been brought back into print. I have not been able to
locate a copy of the hard-cover edition by Farrar, Strauss,
and Young.

[24]Moskowitz claims Sturgeon's indebtedness to
"gestalt philosophy," Seekers (above, note 2), p. 244.
Sturgeon himself suggests something similar in the text,
when Gerry lifts the term "gestalt" from the mind of the
psychiatrist, Stern (pp. 142-143). My readings in gestalt
psychology, however, have turned up little that is explicitly related to the novel. Some relevant quotes

Part One, "The Fabulous Idiot," introduces us, by means of impressionistic sketches of loosely related events, to the original members of the gestalt, before and after they have been gathered together by Lone, an "idiot" with hypnotic and telepathic talents. Lone's coming to awareness, via a bizarre, unfulfilled, telepathic love affair with Evelyn Kew, repressed fifteen-year-old daughter of a sexually obsessed maniac, is related in the beginning. After Lone, who was almost killed by Kew, has been nursed back to health and "miraculously" educated by a farmer couple named Prodd, we are introduced to Gerry Thompson and Hip Barrows, who will dominate Parts Two and Three, and we are given a glimpse of Evelyn's sister, Alicia, who will play a major role in Part Two. The nucleus of the gestalt is soon formed, as the telekinetic Janie makes friends with the teleporting Negro twins, Bonnie and Beanie, and the three escape to the woods. Lone joins them, then adds the mongoloid idiot son of the Prodds, Baby, who has a brain like a computer, and the group begins to "blesh" (minimal

---

follow. "The whole is more than the sum of its parts," Raymond Holder Wheeler, The Science of Psychology: An Introductory Study (New York, 1929), p. 16. "[Gestalt psychology offers a] general thesis concerning the primacy of wholeness in mental life," John Elmgren, Gestalt Psychology: A Survey and Some Contributions, in Göteborgs Högskoles Årsskrift, 44 (Göteborg, 1938), p. 4. "A configuration cannot be considered as built up out of the 'parts' of which it consists, if these parts are regarded as independent and self-contained elements," Aron Gurwitsch, The Field of Consciousness, in Duquesne Studies, Psychological Series, 2 (Pittsburgh, 1964), p. 114.

definition: blend and mesh), but with Lone at its head the gestalt is no more than a "fabulous idiot."

Part Two, "Baby is Three," was originally published in Galaxy as a compact and tightly unified novelette, with slight but significant differences from the present version.[25] With the aid of the psychotherapist Stern, the fifteen-year-old Gerry relives in one afternoon the momentous experiences of the seven years since Lone picked him up out of the gutter and added him to the group. Seeking the reason why he killed Miss Kew (Alicia), their "governess," Gerry probes his memory, encountering a great deal of resistance at the phrase "Baby is three." Three years earlier, with Lone dead, Gerry had brought the orphaned group to Miss Kew, who Lone had said would care for them, and that phrase, we discover, had loosed a flood of her memories, concerning her relations with Lone and her attempts to help him understand the creature of which he was a part, into Gerry's mind. Overcoming the mental block which has made him repress his identity and that of the gestalt, Gerry now realizes that he has killed Miss Kew because she was smothering the gestalt with love and kindness. Defying Stern's warning that he is not "cured," that without a sense of morality to guide him, his feelings of guilt and loneliness may make him psychopathic, Gerry

---

[25]Theodore Sturgeon, "Baby is Three," Galaxy, October, 1952, pp. 4-62.

"calls" Bonnie to erase Stern's tape recorder (with advice
from Baby), and proceeds to erase hypnotically from Stern's
mind all memory of the afternoon's discussion.

In Part Three, "Morality," the plot device of
restoring a memory is repeated, but this time from outside
the person's mind. Janie helps Hip Barrows recover from
the hypnotic commands implanted by Gerry, to whom Hip's
chance discovery of and search for the group constituted a
threat some years before. After reconstructing his past,
Hip learns of Janie's connection with that same group, and
with Gerry (whom he knew as Major Thompson), and goes with
her to the old Kew residence, the home and prison of the
gestalt, which is now pathologically withdrawn under Gerry's
leadership. After some melodramatic scuffling, Hip succeeds
in making Gerry "ashamed," and the gestalt, having come to
recognize through Hip its kinship with homo sapiens, is
welcomed by the mental voices of the community or race of
homo gestalt.

The fiction in More than Human far outweighs the
science, as might be expected from Sturgeon's definition of
a good science fiction story: "a story built around human
beings, with a human problem, and a human solution, which
would not have happened at all without its scientific
content."[26] The science fictions, or science fictional

---

[26]Sturgeon's definition is quoted in William
Atheling, Jr. [James Blish], The Issue at Hand: Studies in
Contemporary Magazine Science Fiction (Chicago, 1964),

themes, are presented in terms of individual, personal

problems. The extrapolation is taken to a point of almost

utopian perfection, where wish-fulfillment seems more

determining than practical possibilities. Setting and tone,

structure and style all contribute to a kind of fairy-tale

form, in which science and logic are almost out of place.

And the whole work, although it communicates on the popular,

superficial level of most pulp science fiction, also pulses

with a kind of literary "feel" associated before the mid-

Fifties only with Ray Bradbury, Alfred Bester, and Sturgeon.

The scientific basis of More than Human is rather

fuzzy at best. The "science" of parapsychology is still a

rather controversial research area, as are spiritualism and

psychical research in general. Over sixty years since the

Rhines began their studies at Duke University, conclusive

proof has not yet been offered even of the existence of

extra-sensory perception (e.s.p.).[27] The psi phenomena

described in the novel, moreover, have been extrapolated to

---

p. 14. This definition is also referred to, in a shortened
version, in Robert A. Heinlein, "Science Fiction: Its
Nature, Faults and Virtues," in Basil Davenport et al., The
Science Fiction Novel: Imagination and Social Criticism,
rev. ed. (Chicago, 1964), p. 19. It is implicit in some of
Sturgeon's writings (above, notes 1, 6-8), as well, but I
have not been able to locate it explicitly in his writing.

[27]See especially C. E. M. Hansel, ESP: A Scientific
Evaluation (New York, 1966), which, besides demolishing most
of the "evidence" presented by others, also contains a good,
brief, selective bibliography on the subject, including
writings by proponents as well as opponents.

a point far beyond the meager findings laboriously arrived
at in the parapsychology laboratory. At least as far beyond
today's alleged laboratory evidence of e.s.p. as another
science fiction staple, travel to the stars, is beyond the
Wright Brothers' first flight, the talents of Sturgeon's
characters are perfected to a degree which may never be
achievable except in literature. Gerry explains this to
Stern, toward the end of Part Two, borrowing Stern's
terminology to do so:

> I'm the central ganglion of a complex organism which
> is composed of Baby, a computer; Bonnie and Beanie,
> teleports; Janie, telekineticist; and myself, tele-
> path and central control. There isn't a single
> thing about any of us that hasn't been documented:
> the teleportation of the Yogi, the telekinetics of
> some gamblers, the idio-savant mathematicians, and
> most of all, the so-called poltergeist, the moving
> about of household goods through the instrumentation
> of a young girl. Only in this case every one of my
> parts delivers at peak performance. (pp. 142-143)

Although each of these talents has been documented,
the documentation--which is often full of exaggeration and
fraud--does not indicate an ease and facility comparable to
what is exhibited here. Lone, and later Gerry, can reach
into someone else's mind at will and select whatever information and vocabulary he wants, or implant an all but
irresistible hypnotic command, with no visible effort except
that, to the victim, it appears as if the telepath's irises
are about to spin. Janie's telekinesis (parapsychologists
usually call it psycho-kinesis or PK), although it has to
be trained and disciplined, enables her not only to throw

things (as any good poltergeist should be able to do) but also to create rather subtle and delicate effects, with no apparent effort other than a momentary look of concentration. The ability Bonnie and Beanie have, of being able to travel long distances instantaneously, is so casual a possession they are not even aware at first of having willed it. And Baby's computer-speed thinking reveals no expenditure of energy at all, outwardly, although his mode of communication does involve physical movements.

Materialistic theory, unable to cope at all with precognition or communication with the dead, is also extremely uncomfortable with the concepts of clairvoyance and teleportation, barely allowing the possibility of mental energy (involving electro-chemical reactions) sufficient to allow wordless communication or the movement of small objects. As a result, many scientists--like the biologist, Herman J. Müller, contributing to a symposium on science fiction in The Humanist magazine--would banish most if not all e.s.p. from probability-conscious science fiction to the purely literary realm of fantasy.[28]

Not sharing the preference of many writers and fans for "pure" science fiction, Sturgeon is conscious nevertheless of the need to overcome the reader's disbelief of the improbable. He does so, however, primarily by literary,

---

[28]Hermann J. Müller, "Science Fiction as an Escape," The Humanist, XVII, 6 (1957), 333-346.

rather than by "scientific" (science fictional) means. Sturgeon by no means assumes a lawless universe--psi powers in More than Human are subject to rules and limitations--but he does not feel it incumbent upon him to give a detailed explanation of the laws of nature which apply to his fictional world. Little or no explicit rationalization is offered for his characters' ability to defy natural laws apparently operable in the real world; he merely demonstrates their abilities in action, as they appear both from outside and from within the characters' minds.

Sturgeon does not attempt to anchor his fantasy in the basic assumptions of science; empiricism, determinism, and relativism are all somewhat subverted in this novel. Psi powers may be an objectively observable reality in the fictional world, but they are not subjected to or described in terms of quantitative measurement, and their objective reality is subordinated to their subjective reality, with which empiricism is not qualified to deal. Naturalistic determinism is invoked, in a way: the children's loneliness and rejection, resulting from some kind of maltreatment, is implied as a causal factor--necessary but not sufficient-- in their parapsychological development. But loneliness and rejection are at least partly subjective, Sturgeon indicates, relieved by positive social interaction (love, affection, belonging). And the real determinism of the book is teleological: the goal of maturity, explicit in the characters and implicit in the structure of events, requires the success of the gestalt. Scientific relativism is operable in that each individual gestalt is regarded as an experiment of nature; the race (homo gestalt) welcomes each success, but it destroys each failure which does not dissolve or destroy itself. Moral relativism is more heavily stressed, especially in the character of Gerry, for whom the gestalt is largely a means to his playing the role of superman. Having no respect for merely human beings, laws, or institutions, he feels no obligation to use his power for good, nor does he even recognize a distinction between "good" and "evil" until his final confrontation with Hip.

The basic goals of science, prediction and control, are clearly present in More than Human, but they are also basic desires of every man, which fantasy can achieve in literature where science cannot in the real world. The lesson of science, that we can achieve what we want only if we accept and take advantage of how the world is really constructed (i.e. not in accordance with our wishes alone) seems not to matter here. The ease with which certain "elect" persons achieve goals unreachable in the world outside the fiction is reminiscent of the ease with which seduction is managed in works of pornography. Sturgeon avoids intellectual pornography to some extent, however, by making his characters suffer and struggle in other ways,

and by leading them toward a sense of ethical values. By
treating psi powers as other writers treat mechanical technology, Sturgeon even avoids drifting completely beyond the
borders of science fiction. By showing psi powers at work,
as a matter of "fact," not of mystery, and by showing the
skepticism of other characters overcome in the novel, he
undermines our disbelief somewhat, even though we know he
is using the literary equivalent of a conjuror's tricks.
Since he does not refute the basic assumptions of science,
and since the world he displays is still an orderly one, we
are not so much led to a belief in "disguised spiritism,"
as Müller charges, as we are reminded that there may be
charges, as we are reminded that there may be wonders in
the world which are still unexplained.[29]

The concept of a gestalt being, by which Sturgeon
extends these marvels still further, seems to belong exclusively to science fiction, and even there his predecessors
were generally content to refer vaguely to an alien "group
mind" or "hive mentality," as in Clarke's Childhood's End.[30]
By contrast, Sturgeon has imagined a composite entity of

---

[29]Müller, p. 338.

[30]Henry Kuttner, however, wrote a series of stories
in the late Forties about a strange hillbilly family, whose
members all had bizarre talents, and who occasionally worked
together. Two of these stories were reprinted recently:
"Cold War," in Henry Kuttner, Bypass to Otherness (New
York, 1961); "See You Later," in Henry Kuttner, Return to
Otherness (New York, 1962).

individual human beings, each of whom has his own distinct
problems and abilities, which he preserves at the same time
that he consciously cooperates with others, not as a matter
of instinct, but as a matter of social and emotional interaction. Thus the author makes possible a very human kind of
conflict between individuals, complementing each person's
inner conflict between superior powers and normal human
emotions.

By choosing children as the bearers of abnormal
powers, Sturgeon is following another established convention; superchildren have frequently appeared in science
fiction, their powers evoking fear as their psychological
state arouses pity.[31] Since it is primarily their sensa-
tions in which Sturgeon is interested, rather than the
sensational values for which their powers can be exploited,
we can expect some variation on the convention for the sake
of believable character. The old stereotype of childhood
innocence and purity is incomplete, although it is alluded
to in Baby's eternal youth, in Lone's mental childishness,
in the enforced innocence of fifteen-year-old Evelyn Kew,
whose telepathic love call brings Lone to some degree of
consciousness, and in the dwindling of the twins' ability
to communicate with Baby as they grow older. But the
destructiveness of childhood is also apparent, in the

---

[31]See, for further illustration of science fiction's
use of children, Children of Wonder, ed. William Tenn
(New York, 1953).

careless mischief of the twins, in the hatred of Janie for
her playgirl mother, in the mindless malevolence of an
urchin whom Hip and Janie happen upon at a carnival, and in
the behavior and character of the whole gestalt under the
leadership of Gerry.

As children, of course, they are not fully in
control of themselves, or of their powers. Their emotional
needs, which are frustrated by a hostile or indifferent
world, have in their cases enabled them to encourage rather
than inhibit their parapsychological powers, but have also
built up in the children a high degree of suspicion and
hostility toward strangers. In order for the whole gestalt
to approach the sum of its parts, the parts must come to
accept each other, and if the gestalt is to be more than a
simple addition of talents, the individuals possessing
those talents must also come to accept themselves, and the
outside world which frustrated them in the first place.
This integration, which takes place gradually, provides the
novel with its basic pattern; a kind of Bildungsroman, it
shows the education and the coming to maturity of a single
member, not of homo sapiens, but of homo gestalt.

As they grow, relatively secure in each other's
company, the children gradually perfect their technique as
individuals, and the total powers of the gestalt are also
increased. Bonnie and Beanie learn to control their
travelling with precision, though they never overcome the

impossibility of taking anything (including clothes) with them. Janie learns to handle extremely difficult and subtle engineering problems, including the pressure of bodily fluids in others (Gerry's need to urinate in Part Two, Hip's premature sexual desire in Part Three). Gerry, like Lone before him, first becomes fully conscious of his telepathic ability, then learns to direct it within another person's mind.

The experiences of each are added to Baby's store-house of information, available to all (through Janie), but otherwise the powers of the gestalt are mainly to be taken on faith. In its childhood and adolescence, the gestalt does not perform as well and as consistently as its potential presumably would indicate. As children, its members cooperate for survival, but Gerry's partial amnesia and his later paranoia cause them to withdraw, mentally and phys-ically. An actual demonstration of their mature capabili-ties would be beyond the limits of a book whose central concern is bringing them to maturity, not following their superman-like exploits, alien to our experience and sympathies, after maturity.

They are given one concrete achievement within the book, "Earth's first anti-gravity generation" (p. 73), but that machine is important primarily as a symbol and a pivotal plot device. Invented near the end of Part One, it illustrates the potential of the group, but also its idiocy under Lone's direction; the purpose of the invention was to make a farm truck maneuverable on muddy ground, as a favor to the Prodds who no longer occupied the farm. Recurring in Part Three, it is seen as a device Hip has sought to find and to understand, pitting his curiosity against Gerry's determination to obliterate all trace of the gestalt; Janie uses a fragment of the device to reawaken Hip's curiosity, assisting him in his recovery from the effects of Gerry's persecution. As the only example of advanced mechanical technology in an otherwise contemporary world, it calls attention to itself, but not as an example of the powers of science, rather as an example of a group mind's unlimited possibilities.

The real technology in More than Human is parapsychological, not mechanical; like all technology it offers power and the problems of control. The fear of runaway technology, which often gives rise in science fiction to what Asimov calls the "Frankenstein complex," is rechannelled here. Within the mind, parapsychology should logically be controllable by psychology, making the question of controls over technology largely a matter of maturation or character development. Each of the six major characters is involved with this problem, four within the gestalt (involved both as an individual and as a member of something greater) and two outside (of whom one is closely associated with the group, while the other is professionally distant).

Gerry is a variation on the stereotype of the "mad scientist," the selfish inventor who wants only to take personal advantage of his discovery, regardless of its effects on others. With all the power he has available, he has no sense of direction, no sense of responsibility except to himself and his appetites. He seems to regard the group more as an extension of himself than as something of which he is only a (replaceable) part. A runaway orphan living by stealth at the time he is taken in by Lone, he retains a surly, vengeful attitude toward the world at all times, fitting in well with the group's survival program of petty thievery. For the sake of his own ego he kills Miss Kew instead of merely deserting her when he discovers she is smothering the group with love (the absence of which drives them together). For sheer perversity he tortures Hip with hypnotic commands, but he gets no enjoyment even from sadism. Having learned he can do whatever he wants, and not desiring anything, he withdraws self-protectively, to a kind of mental womb position. The demonstration of Hip's existence as a person, not merely as a thing to be manipulated, draws Gerry out of himself. He discovers in himself a sense of shame, not only because of Hip's message of ethics but also because of Hip's demonstration of ethics, sparing Gerry's life and offering his own. Hip's act may be quixotic, but it is also more mature than anything Gerry has ever done, and it works: the "mad scientist" is cured.

Hip, too, had to achieve that level of insight which he transmits to Gerry, and he also started far away from it. His childhood affluence is juxtaposed to Gerry's poverty in Part One, but both are seen as emotionally starved and full of hate. As he grows, from one easy achievement to another, Hip develops an allegiance solely to science or truth, and places himself on the open market for others to exploit. His abstract belief that whatever he finds to be true must be made available to the world disregards both the potential of any discovery for power and the tendency of the strong to manipulate the weak. Specifically, he seeks the anti-gravity generator, then an understanding of why it has been denied him. Tenaciously resisting Gerry's attempts to destroy him, Hip learns self-control not through that punishment, but through the rewards offered him by Janie, the simple joys of living, loving, and being needed. The son of a doctor, Hip (short for Hippocrates) Barrows heals himself, then brings to the gestalt the sense of ethics he has learned. Of his own free will he goes to meet Gerry and help him, only half aware that he is thus completing both himself and the gestalt. He recognizes that he has been foolhardy in thinking before that he should "go headlong into the presence of this--this monster--without his sanity, without his memory, without arms or information" (p. 203). But besides being whole he recognizes that he is now less than something else, that all his adolescent wants are overshadowed by something new, although he admits he doesn't know what that something is.

Of all the major figures, Janie reaches a degree of maturity the youngest. Apparently hard-shelled and mischievous when we meet her in Part One, she has already learned in dealing with her mother that "power without control has its demerits" (p. 32). After making friends with, then running away with the twins, she has to "mother" them, then to overcome Lone's suspicions of and hostility toward mere childish minds in order to adopt him as a father. No longer alone, she learns to control her power for mischief; in Part Two, her telekinetic talents are said to have subdued Gerry when he arrived at the cave, and to have convinced Miss Kew that she must not break up the group by sending Baby to a home for special children. Somewhat fulfilled by her responsible role, and by the chance to express herself in painting, she makes a faithful but not unquestioning helper for Lone, then Gerry, not only by her ability to use force, but also by her ability to read Baby's "semaphore system" of communication. By Part Three, she has seen tremendous unchecked power in Gerry and feels the need to exert some control over it; her interest in Hip stems largely from this need, since she feels that he may be able to introduce that control which will integrate the gestalt. Her patience, tenderness, and joy with Hip have a more romantic cause, but she is hesitant to give in to it until she knows he will fit in, not only with her, but with the entire group.

The pivotal figure in the novel is Lone, the idiot who emerges from his mental twilight world to become spiritual father to a child which far surpasses its parents. A real challenge in character-drawing, he is largely typified in terms of a single human emotion, loneliness. Loneliness drives him to seek something beyond himself and figures predominantly in his labored thinking, even to the extent that, when Prodd asks his name and he manages his first word, trying to say "alone," he accepts "Lone" as an adequate description of himself. Largely driven by instinct, he can only communicate with telepathic babies, until he is touched by the mind, then by the hand of Evelyn. Trying to recapture the feeling of that contact, he accepts the limited human contact of the Prodds, then joins with Janie and the twins, learning along the way a bare minimum of speech and social amenities but never really growing in intelligence. Perfectly happy to get by, he regards the gestalt as a remedy for his loneliness and as a means for solving problems. Lacking judgment, he sees nothing strange or wonderful in the gestalt's ability to create an anti-gravity generator to improve the performance of a farm truck, as a thank-you gift for the Prodd's care of him, after the Prodds are no longer around to notice. "We can do practically anything," says Janie, interpreting for Baby, "but we most likely won't. He says we're a thing, all right, but the thing is an idiot" (p. 73). Only with the death of Lone (the father) and the emergence of Gerry (the son) can the gestalt grow in Part Two, and even then not until Gerry overcomes certain memories of Lone. The shadow of Lone is also present in Part Three, directly, as the gestalt re-establishes at a higher level the equilibrium it had with Lone and missed with Gerry.

Outside the gestalt, but closely associated with it, is Miss Kew (Alicia), who is defined largely by her relationships with others. A forbidding sister to Evelyn, she has developed a taste for her father's whip, with which he would "purge" them of behavior which seemed to him at all sexually motivated. "Cured" by a psychiatrist, she is still beset with memories of her "demon" father, against which she perhaps overreacts, periodically dancing nude in the fields to fulfill Evelyn's dying request that she "take a bath in [the sunlight]." During one of these ritual expiations, Lone enters her life, seeking information rather than sex, and she feels almost compelled to throw herself at him. At her request, he reads her mind, finding a "damned mishmash inside," which perhaps suggests the inevitable result of life and emotions bottled up, rather than shared, in contrast to the apparent clarity and health of Evelyn in her innocence, and Janie, later, in her emotional security made possible by the gestalt. Within the mess two demands stand out: to know who or what Lone is, and to lose (at age thirty-three) her virginity. Made a woman at last, she is hardly freed from her prejudices, sexual or otherwise, but she is thus able to take on the role of foster mother to the children. In this role, she shows real love and motherly care in conflict at times with a set of rigid social conventions (a shield against her father's rules), and ironically, it is her better qualities, overwhelming the gestalt, which result in her death.

Completely outside the group is the psychiatrist, Stern, who functions to some extent as a "control" figure by contrast to the other characters, by virtue of his maturity, individual humanity, professional distance, and scientific status. He is by no means representative of the physical scientist, who deals ideally with quantitative measurements, isolated phenomena, and detached observation. Since his province is the mind, Stern must take the subjective seriously but not gullibly, and if he is to help his patients adjust, he must keep them in touch with the outside world. Not just a disinterested engineer of the psyche, who knows which emotional buttons to push, he becomes involved and even afraid. Once he realizes that Gerry's "fantasies" are real (after Gerry demonstrates his mind-reading ability), he realizes, as Gerry does not, that Gerry is incomplete and alone, covering over feelings of guilt with hostility and amorality, and therefore extremely dangerous.

Although he is presumably meant to be a mature

human being, an example in homo sapiens of the ideal of
completeness desired by homo gestalt, Stern is extremely
limited by his role as a technical device of the author's.
His existence is circumscribed by his office and by a single
afternoon (quite a display of instant analysis); his role is
defined by its success in illustrating and getting beyond
Gerry's mental blocks so that Gerry's story can be told.
Even Stern's completeness is in a sense created by Gerry,
who identifies him with Lone, transferring to Stern his love
for his foster father, and however complete Stern may be as
a human being, he is no match for Gerry's incomplete,
immature gestalt.

 A striving for maturity, for experience, for understanding is central to the development of all the major
characters, except for Stern, and in each case it is related
to a central event in the person's life. Lone's contact
with Evelyn awakens his consciousness and he strives to
complete himself with the cooperation of others. Alicia
becomes a woman when Lone takes her virginity, thus enabling
her to mother his children, who come to her after his death.
Janie and Hip find themselves in each other, making it
possible for the gestalt to awaken to sexual love. Gerry
and Hip first seek subsidiary goals--for Gerry, the reason
for his killing Miss Kew, for Hip, the reason for certain
puzzling phenomena--but they finally force each other into
maturity.

Sharing, in each case, is the necessary act which overcomes initial hostility and makes possible the tolerance required for cooperation and understanding. Lone and Evelyn share a pure love which ends both her innocence and his idiocy. Lone tries to share something with the Prodds, the farmer couple who take him in after his fight with Evelyn's father (Lone was physically, Kew mentally ravaged). Mrs. Prodd's pregnancy drives him away, but he returns and finds Baby, who seems as much his brother as their child. Janie and the twins share fun, then running away, then fear with no one to take care of them. Lone shares food with the girls, the group shares food with Gerry, and Janie shares food with Hip, along with love and care. Hip shares thought with Gerry, a sense of shame, a sense of ethics. The whole group at times shares a greater consciousness, a "bleshing" which begins under Lone, is almost extinguished by Miss Kew, then torn apart by Gerry, only to be restored by Hip and expanded to include the society of homo gestalt.

At each stage, hostility of some kind must be overcome. Kew is hostile to Lone as a man, threatening his daughter's perversely preserved innocence. After his experience with Evelyn, Lone is hostile to children, whom he has at last outgrown, and this dislike extends at first to Janie and the twins. Janie and the twins go through a period of hostility to each other before they run away, and Janie opposes the additions to the group both of Baby (whom she

accuses Lone of kidnaping) and of Gerry (whose behavior is
rather obnoxious). Gerry's hostility to the whole world is
overcome in part when he comes to see the group as an extension of himself, but it is adequately dealt with only when
he comes to feel shame for what he has done to Hip (and
other normal humans represented by Hip).

Where this hostility is not overcome, where assimilation does not take place, the result can be dangerous,
even fatal. One-sided mind-sharing (by Gerry and Lone) and
one-sided or unconsummated love (Alicia and Evelyn Kew,
respectively) do not amount to assimilation. Stern's memory
is tampered with, Hip is nearly driven insane, the Kew
sisters die, after contact with the gestalt. Passive
acceptance is also one-sided; in order for Hip to become a
member of the gestalt, he must learn what he has to offer
it, then actively share it with them, practically forcing
tolerance from Gerry. Of all the members of the gestalt,
Hip must overcome the most resistance, as the group after
years of adolescence faces a new stage of maturity; accepting him means admitting incompleteness, recognizing sexual
love, and assimilating an outsider without psi powers.

For Gerry, confronting Hip is a reminder of his own
humanity. Treated as an object when he was a child, Gerry
has come to show the same lack of regard for others, for
human beings who are in terms of power as inferior to the
gestalt as children are to adults. In Hip, he sees that he

and the gestalt must seem a kind of monster when looked at from outside, with the eyes of someone who does not share the power and the psychological security of the gestalt. Assimilating Hip's message of ethical responsibility, Gerry comes to realize that some learning can only come from personal experience, not from reading others' minds and writings. And recognizing the humanity he can and does share with Hip and with others, Gerry finally achieves the respect and tolerance for others necessary for his own maturity (or sanity). At the same time, the gestalt, by admitting Hip as its "conscience," becomes complete and can thus be welcomed, albeit as a child again, to the world-wide community of homo gestalt.

Viewed figuratively, this concluding union with homo gestalt can be seen as a metaphor, representing an integration of personality, and an achievement of community, at least equal to the utopian ideals of the psychiatrist and the social reformer. The talented individual, or the individual who feels himself marked in some way, may well find himself alone, and a kind of monster, even if he has not been maltreated in his childhood. Until he grows to learn love, and matures enough to learn enough respect for others, to whom personal love does not extend, he cannot become a fully functioning part of the community. Without the community, however imperfect it may be, he cannot know how he appears to others, and cannot complete himself. He must become socialized, and fully human, if he aspires to be more than human.

In the fictional world of <u>More than Human</u>, love becomes syzygy, symbiosis, or "bleshing," the community is first the family (the gestalt) and then the race (<u>homo gestalt</u>), and the special talent becomes e.s.p. or psi powers in general, such as folklore suggests that man has always wanted, in order to make his social adjustment easier or even unnecessary. This externalization of the psychological is not uncommon in science fiction, and its fictional reality may disguise even a personal level of meaning. The talented individual could be interpreted as the writer himself, who turns his fantasies into stories, entertainments, and artworks, who has the equivalent of psi powers in his ability to manipulate and understand his characters, and who must learn to respect the tastes, backgrounds, and prejudices of his audience, as well as the powers and limits of literary technique, in order to share his writing, and himself, with a community of readers. I do not mean to suggest that this novel must be read as a personal allegory, but Sturgeon is unusual among science fiction writers in his personal involvement with his stories, and he has given similar treatment elsewhere to the concepts of need, belonging, and love, and even the idea of a "maturity" which is never complete (since full maturity is over-ripeness or readiness for death).[32]

However we may view More than Human as a psychological novel, a novel of character, or a Bildungsroman, the
book remains primarily a science fiction novel. Interpreted
literally, didactically, or personally, it can be seen to
involve technology (as a means to attaining a sense of
community) and its prediction and control (as matters of
maturity and understanding). The general movement of the
narrative is outward, toward larger and more inclusive definitions of community, toward external manifestations of subjective desires, toward conscious and relatively superficial
explorations of internal psychological states. Although
there is no emphasis on the widening vistas of time (the
future) or space (beyond the Earth), discovery of something
new, something as yet unknown but not unknowable, creates an
expanded and expanding perspective, consistent with more
conventional methods of extrapolation. The psi phenomena
are not just allegorical counters, whatever they may be
taken to mean on various planes of interpretation; they are
not just story-tellers' fantasies or daydreams of the dis-
advantaged. E.s.p. is treated rather as an objective reality within the fictional world of the novel, as a technique
which can be developed and perfected by the right people
with the right attitude, even as a means for the salvation

---

[32]Seekers (above, note 2), p. 243.

of the world and the advancement of the human race. The
concreteness and importance of the concept are, in fact, so
emphasized that they make individual human beings and problems pale somewhat by comparison.

That Sturgeon should be able to keep this external
reality of action and situation alive and in the foreground,
and at the same time involve the reader in personal human
problems, is one indication that a considerable amount of
craftsmanship is involved in the construction and writing
of More than Human. Although the book functions as a
science fiction exercise, it goes beyond that; although it
communicates on the surface, and even with some of the tools
of pulp fiction, it also suggests multiple levels and meanings. Indeed, an examination of the technical virtuosity
displayed in the book might make it seem that the action and
the philosophical-psychological content had been chosen as
pretexts for the purpose of challenging the author's versa-
tility with literary form, style, and technique.

Calling attention to himself and to his writing in
a manner unusual for a pulp writer, Sturgeon is always up
to something new, surprising the reader with startling sense
impressions, fresh turns of phrase and figures of speech,
unexpected psychological insights and shocks of recognition,
numerous twists in plot and variations of established
conventions of literature in general and science fiction in
particular. He dwells on nothing long enough to give us

more than a vivid, fleeting impression, be it of an event,
a character, a manifestation of psi phenomena, a setting,
an image, or a symbolic identification. Everything is
vividly sketched on the surface, but also points beyond
itself, suggesting more, as ripples in water spread outward
from a disturbance toward the boundaries of the water's
container. This suggestiveness allows for a rapid juxtaposition of ideas, events, and episodes, which makes the novel
appear extremely fast-paced and filled with action when in
fact very little of a dramatic nature ever happens, and the
movement is largely of abstract concepts, sensuous images,
and especially language. Every element of language, of
style, and of literary form is fair game for manipulation,
for repetition with variation, for parallel and antithesis.
The general effect approaches that of a large bright canvas,
filled with somewhat abstracted and vaguely symbolic
figures, each caught straining to continue its movement
toward another figure, as in a never-to-be-completed pattern
of dance.

Even the conclusion, with its crescendoing recapitulation of themes and suggestion of a resolution, is only a
coming together of partners about to separate again into
another dance-figure; the long-awaited maturity turns out to
be another beginning, and the book ends on a diminuendo:
"And humbly, he joined their company" (p. 233). Beginning
with short bursts of telepathic dialogue, and an evocation

of the presence of music, the conclusion utilizes short and long sentences, italics, parenthesis, and ellipsis marks, paragraphs of description and paragraphs of explanation, to create an effect of complexity and immense potential, with a surface clarity which is childishly simple.

His technique is illustrated in one paragraph of the conclusion, sandwiched between description and explanation, which in turn lie between snatches of telepathic conversation. Gerry (representing his group) has just become aware of the community of homo gestalt welcoming him, and now "meets" telepathically several "beings" who have supposedly engineered certain human cultural developments: "Here was one who had whistled a phrase to Papa Haydn, and here was one who had introduced William Morris to the Rossettis. Almost as if it were his own memory, Gerry saw Fermi being shown the streak of fission on a sensitive plate, a child Landowska listening to a harpsichord, a drowsy Ford with his mind suddenly lit by the picture of men facing a line of machines" (p. 232). Quickly thereafter, the reader discovers that homo gestalt is not above, but rather a part of humanity, which explains that the gestalt actors are not to be regarded as gods handing down the above series of discoveries, even though Gerry, and Sturgeon's prose, both turn worshipful. In the background is the idea that homo gestalt has been with us a long time, seeing that things are no worse than they are, staying out

of our awareness deliberately, but there is also the suggestion that gestalts do not arise frequently ("There hasn't
been a new one for so long . . . [sic]") for some unknown
(sinister?) reason. All this, and more, physical and mental
sense impressions, suggestions of religious and philosophical thinking, is compressed into a little more than seven
hundred words.

That single paragraph, almost lost in the whole of
the conclusion, illustrates Sturgeon's technique in both
form and content. It offers five events of discovery or
revelation, two from music (one of composition, one of
performance), two from science and technology (one of more
or less basic research, which resulted eventually in the
unleashing of atomic energy, the destructiveness of which
generally outweighs its constructive potential in the public
mind, the other of industrial technology, whose economic
constructiveness is more visible than its contribution to
worker fatigue and air pollution), and one from literature
and the pictorial arts (and more, since Morris was a utopian
planner and something of a "Renaissance man" and the Pre-
Raphaelite Brotherhood suggests community, mysticism, and
decadence, among other things). The paragraph offers these
events as a discovery to Gerry of what it is he is a part
of (symbolically, humanity, and human culture, artistic and
scientific, as well as homo gestalt in the fictional sense,
which is actually more figurative, while humanity is the

more literal meaning). The syntax is varied to impress on us the differences within the similarity: "here was one" introduces the first two slightly passively, but each is shown acting ("whistled," "introduced"); Gerry is the actor in the other three cases, since he "saw" them, <u>almost</u> as part of his own remembrances, and each of the figures he sees is shown in a relatively passive reaction ("being shown," "his mind suddenly lit," "listening"). At the same time, the language is extremely simple and clearly rhythmic, and sends the reader's eyes and mind flying along several different images, of varying sensory impressions, which combine with the complex suggestiveness of the allusions, so that each sentence, almost each phrase, is a minor discovery in itself, yet they all coalesce into one general impression, of revelation in history, which itself is only a small part of the whole effect of the conclusion.

The concept of discovery is the key to Sturgeon's technique, in this book at least (his style varies with his subject matter and purpose, in other works).[33] Varying his tone to some extent with character and situation, Sturgeon consistently produces an air of wonder, as if he has just discovered that words can rhyme or alliterate, that images

---

[33]"Sturgeon was a literary phenomenon. In every one of his stories he strove not only for originality of idea or approach, but for a style to fit the story line as well. No two stories were even remotely alike. He was forever experimenting." Sam Moskowitz, <u>Explorers of the Infinite:</u> <u>Shapers of Science Fiction</u> (Cleveland and New York, 1963), p. 341.

can shift and even pun, surrealistically, as in Gerry's free

association in Part Two:

> Eight. Eight, plate, state, hate. I ate from the
> plate of the state and I hate. . . . Eight, Eight
> years old. Eight, hate. Years, fears. Old, cold.
> Damn it! I twisted and twitched on the couch,
> trying to find a way to keep the cold out. I ate
> from the plate of the--
>
> I grunted and with my mind I took all the eights
> and all the rhymes and everything they stood for,
> and made it all black. But it wouldn't stay black.
> I had to put something there, so I made a great big
> luminous figure eight and just let it hang there.
> But it turned on its side and inside the loops it
> began to shimmer. It was like one of those movie
> shots through binoculars. I was going to have to
> look through whether I liked it or not. (p. 84)

The narrator seems to have just happened upon unusual simi-

larities, as in the last sentence of the following descrip-

tion of breakfast prepared by Janie for Hip, after she gets

him out of jail, and as she begins to try to bring him back

to sanity:

> The girl was spooning fragrant bacon grease over and
> over three perfect eggs in a pan. When he sat down
> on the edge of the bed she slid the eggs deftly onto
> a plate, leaving all the grease behind in the pan.
> They were perfect, the whites completely firm, the
> yolks unbroken, liquid, faintly filmed over. There
> was bacon, four brief seconds less than crisp, paper
> dried and aromatic. There was toast, golden outside,
> soft and white inside, with butter melting quickly,
> running to find and fill the welcoming caves and
> crevices; two slices with butter, one with marmalade.
> And these lay in some sunlight, giving off a color
> possible only to marmalade and to stained glass.
> (p. 156)

Even where he is clearly striving for the striking effect,

it seems to take the form of a revelation, as in the novel's

opening paragraph:

> THE idiot lived in a black and gray world, punctu-
> ated by the white lightning of hunger and the
> flickering of fear. His clothes were old and many-
> windowed. Here peeped a shinbone, sharp as a cold
> chisel, and there in the torn coat were ribs like
> the fingers of a fist. He was tall and flat. His
> eyes were calm and his face was dead. (p. 3)

This air of discovery is shared by the characters

themselves, not merely in terms of events and other charac-

ters, but in relation to themselves, their powers and

potentialities, and their sharply aware sense impressions

of the wonders of everyday life and nature. Fifteen and

innocent, not knowing she wants an end of innocence, Evelyn

sits outdoors and observes:

> It was spring, the part of spring where the bursting
> is done, the held-in pressures of desiccated sap-
> veins and gum-sealed buds are gone, and all the
> world's in a rush to be beautiful. The air was
> heavy and sweet; it lay upon lips until they parted,
> pressed them until they smiled, entered boldly to
> beat in the throat like a second heart. It was air
> with a puzzle in it, for it was still and full of
> the colors of dreams, all motionless; yet it had a
> hurry to it. The stillness and the hurry were
> alive and laced together, and how could that be?
> That was the puzzle. (pp. 8-9)

Two days later, she is shown looking again, this time from

behind a window:

> It rained for a day and a night and for half the
> next day, and when the sun came out it rained again,
> upward; it rained light from the heavy jewels which
> lay on the rich new green. Some jewels shrank and
> some fell and then the earth in a voice of softness,
> and leaves in a voice of texture, and flowers speak-
> ing in color, were grateful. (pp. 10-11)

When the starving Gerry enters Lone's cave he notes that

"the air had a haze of smoke and such a wonderful, heart-

breaking, candy-and-crackling smell of food that a little

hose squirted inside my mouth" (p. 88). And a little later

Gerry reflects on the pleasantness of living with Miss Kew:

> And the morning goes by like that, school with a
> recess, there in the big long living room. The
> twins with the ends of their tongues stuck out,
> drawing the alphabet instead of writing it, and
> then Janie, when it's time, painting a picture, a
> real picture of a cow with trees and a yellow
> fence that goes off into the distance. Here I am
> lost between the two parts of a quadratic equation,
> and Miss Kew bending close to help me, and I smell
> the sachet she has on her clothes. I hold up my
> head to smell it better, and far away I hear the
> shuffle and klunk of filled pots going on the stove
> back in the kitchen. (p. 122)

In passages like these, where nothing dramatic or

melodramatic "happens," the language is alive, and a great

deal happens in terms of poetry. In the last quotation,

for instance, the senses of sight, hearing, smell and touch

are all evoked, the latter via physical gestures or move-

ments. The spatial relationship of kitchen and living room

is established, and complemented by the expansion of the

scene which the painting introduces, comparing the outdoors

(fenced) with the confinement of school in a "big long"

room. Parallels are developed between the drawing of

pictures and the drawing of words, and between the language

of words and the language of mathematics. The naivete and

earnestness of childhood envelops the other children and

also Gerry, describing them, and getting lost in the mental

haze Miss Kew's sachet recalls to him. The habitual

passage of mornings invoked at the beginning is reinforced

by the sense of class periods suggested by "recess," a

special time for painting, and the approach of lunch time.
The pace is continually rapid, but varied by alliteration,
punctuation, and the use of small words and what in verse
we call spondees. And the extremely limited vocabulary
conveys a sense of artless simplicity with its predominance
of everyday, one-syllable words, in which the technicality
of "quadratic equation," the formality of "sachet," the
onomatoepoeia of "shuffle and klunk," and the subdued
cleverness of such conceits as "drawing the alphabet" and
being "lost between the two parts of a quadratic equation"
create an unobtrusive charm.

The paragraph is also full of clichés, the "real
picture," the helpful, loving schoolteacher, the incompetent
Negro children, the sentimentality of childhood remembrance
all being extremely overworked in popular fiction, yet
Sturgeon manages to reinvigorate them by the lightness of
his style, the barest suggestion of description, and the
rapidity of juxtaposition. Throughout the book, his reliance on pulp stereotypes of character, situation, emotion,
and description is not always as successfully disguised as
it is here; yet the pace and the psychological and parapsychological foreground generally keep it under control.
That the use of such "subliterary" tools is deliberate is,
I think, clear from the contrast in style between passages
in which they are more and less overt; Miss Kew's memories
inside Gerry's head are related in a pastiche of "true

romances" style, which clearly separates it from the two
styles of Gerry, dealing with his dreamy remembrances and
his belligerent present; Mr. Kew is even more of a caricature, and cleverly mocked by the passage where, after his
death, the young Janie considers the books available, in what
we know to be his library, for reading aloud to the twins.

In each of the passages quoted, we can also see the
way in which motifs recur or are set up for later recurrence. Other worlds, both inside and outside the book, are
symbolized and alluded to, even as the worlds themselves
beautifully evoke the experience or sensation. The light-
ning and flickering of the opening suggests Lone's hypnotic
talent, the cold chisel of his shinbone is echoed in the
coldness of Gerry's introduction to us and his capitulation
to Hip, the fingers of a fist suggest the gestalt and anger,
and the bleakness and angularity of the whole passage
conjure up the aloneness, ineptness, and desolation which
is the alternate fate, not only of Lone, but also of most
of the book's characters. The sense of tension and pressure
in nature describes Evelyn's internal revolt against her
father's restrictions; the synesthesia which follows pre-
pares us for her telepathic contact with Lone. The perfect-
ness of breakfast, and the symbol of potentiality in eggs,
foreshadows Hip's recovery, his making himself and the
gestalt whole. And the final passage quoted, with its
fence, and the slightest suggestion of smothering and

intoxication evoked by Miss Kew's sachet, symbolizes the gestalt's captivity within her home, even as it emphasizes the sweetness of that captivity.

Frequently striking in themselves, and aptly expressive of a particular emotion or situation, images in Sturgeon's work also contribute to a strongly sensuous impression, even as they work in fairly intellectual patterns. Their concreteness, color, and appeal to several senses in succession give the narrative an almost physical presence, and make it seem extraordinarily full and vivid, even though its many actions are mainly small and of an ordinary, everyday variety. In addition to functioning as leitmotifs, as shown above, they produce a background of contrasts--hot and cold, dark and light, indoors and outdoors, etc.--and contribute to underlying patterns, such as the pattern of sexual symbolism which supports the basic movement of the book (toward enlightenment, understanding, maturity). The entire novel is an extended metaphor of birth, which the myriad individual discoveries (intellectual and emotional "births") recapitulate in miniature. And a good deal of the imagery suggests penetration, gestation, and a bursting out of confinement to achieve something new.

Telepathic penetration seems to involve the eyes (sight connoting understanding) and the incipient realization of potential (Lone's and Gerry's irises seem about to spin just before penetration), but its sexual connections

are also made clear. Gerry describes Stern's violated mind
as a "tunnel," Lone and Evelyn "awaken" each other through
telepathic love, and Lone discovers in Alicia's mind her
desire that he end her virginity. In a bravura exhibition
of technique, Sturgeon shows us Gerry breaking through his
mental block in Part Two, and releasing a flood of Alicia's
memories with which he had been inundated when he first
spoke to her. The transition into her remembrances is
identical with her closing memory, of sex with Lone: "There
was a pressure, a stretching apart, and a . . . [sic] a
breakage. And with a tearing agony and a burst of triumph
that drowned the pain, it was done" (pp. 129, 139). Since
Lone and Alicia are the gestalt's parents (symbolically, at
least), the memory of their love-making would probably have
to be suppressed by their twelve-year-old son, especially
since it was obtained by a virtual fulfillment of the
oedipal desire, and Gerry has even gone so far as to sup-
press any knowledge of his own talent which enabled him to
possess his mother and her memories.

The recurrent images of confinement and escape seem
clearly allied to the concepts of pregnancy and childbirth.
Images of bursting are not uncommon (as in Evelyn's intoxication with spring, quoted above), the unusual phrase
"encysted need" occurs three times, and there is a general
sense of things (people) trying to come to fruition.
Evelyn, Alicia, Janie, and the twins all manage somehow to

burst out of confinement, and the gestalt manages three
times to escape limiting physical and emotional environments: Lone's cave and idiocy, Miss Kew's home and
emotional asphyxiation, and (presumably, since the book ends
on a hopeful note) Kew's mansion and withdrawal. Outdoor
imagery contrasts favorably with the indoors; trees and
grass, sun and sky are associated with openness, freedom,
and light, whereas the cave, the Kew estate, Hip's jail cell
and his apartment (and cells and wards in his memory) are
dark, close, even too warm and moist (like a womb), and must
be escaped. Toward the end, as Hip approaches his confrontation with Gerry, he observes the labyrinthine paths and
corridors of the Kew house, and its "mossy" wall which has
one gate, he experiences a feeling that he is "walking . . .
in a great sick mouth" (p. 218), and he notes that his
apparently final destination is an inner room with a door
that fits perfectly flush, the door through which Gerry
(and the others) will enter. In this context, Hip
(Hippocrates) seems to have the role of the doctor presiding
over a difficult delivery, but a successful one, since the
gestalt is welcomed into the world of homo gestalt, as a
child.

The figure of the gestalt is central to the complex
pattern of relationships between the characters. Among the
many explicit similes, mechanical, biological, and social,
that Sturgeon employs to describe it, the most picturesque

are those comparing it to the fingers of a hand, or the
organs of a person, but those comparing it to a gang of
workmen or a marching band may be more accurate. Implicitly, it is presented to us as a family, whose members are
distinct, interacting, and somewhat interchangeable. It
has a spiritual father in Lone, a foster-mother in Alicia,
a capable older sister in Janie, a sullen adolescent son in
Gerry, and three younger children, one a perpetual baby.
The relationships are complicated by Gerry's telepathic
knowledge of his "mother," through which he has sexual
knowledge of his "father," and by Lone's and Janie's outside
contacts. Lone's first love was of Evelyn, which makes his
possession of Alicia symbolically incestuous. Lone was
"raised" by the Prodds as an adopted son, and then adopted
as his "child" the baby whose coming demanded that he and
the Prodds part. The last addition, Hip, who "marries in"
to the family, has to overcome Gerry's hostility toward a
love of his "sister" (or "mother," since Janie also performed that role for the group, and we know Gerry has
oedipal conflicts). Within this extended family, additional
parallels and antitheses can be seen: wealthy Hip and
destitute Gerry feel unwanted in childhood, and pass through
stages of delayed adolescence, in which they are emotional
"monsters"; Lone and Baby are rather different varieties of
idiots; Janie's fire and flexibility contrast both with the
softness and innocence of Evelyn and with the prudishness

and masochism of Alicia; Gerry, brilliant and hostile, has little in common with the feeble-minded, passive Lone, except that each is a capable telepath and an inept head for the gestalt.

Patterns of imagery, individuated and external, provide a large amount of Sturgeon's characterization, especially of the minor characters. Least effective of all are the Negroes, for whom stereotyped blackness seems to be their single character trait; Miss Kew's maid, Miriam, and the janitor who is ostensibly the twins' father, are indistinct and scarcely distinguishable, while Bonnie and Beanie, themselves, identical in appearance and practically unable to speak, appear to exist merely to indicate that gestalt membership is not restricted by race. Also close to nonentities are the male friends of Janie's mother, the sheriff from whom Janie obtains Hip's release, and the Army psychiatrist who "treated" Hip for his idée fixe (the anti-gravity generator) each of whom is simply defined by his occupation. Others are slightly advanced beyond them: Kew, characterized by his whip, his library, and his obsession of repressing sexuality in his daughters; Evelyn, who finds nature so full to bursting and insists on exposing herself to it, physically; the Prodds, who struggle vainly with their farm and its machinery, and not so vainly with Lone, whom they nurse to health and manage to educate, but who abandon Baby, their hope for the future, Mrs. Prodd by dying, Prodd by deserting; and Wima, the lonely tramp who is Janie's mother, for whom life is nothing more than a mindless search for fun. Not always avoiding cliché and perhaps not trying to, Sturgeon does not belabor the stereotype, but sketches the character in terms of a few marked impressions, suggesting hidden aspects that might round the character off if we only knew more about them: Prodd's delusion that his dead wife will return, Wima's conviction that her missing soldier husband could have handled the unruly Janie.

There is no apparent pattern involved in the naming of characters, although considerable local symbolism is apparent. The Prodds are blunt farmers, laboring people who don't talk too much, and who "prod" Lone into working for a living and learning to speak. Lone is lonesome and alone, and Hip Barrows is aware ("hip"), a doctor's son who is himself a healer (Hippocrates), and a man returned almost from the dead ("barrows"). Kew may be a question mark ("Q.") or a source ("Quelle"), and his older daughter, in her stepmother role, is perhaps a mistake for the gestalt ("miscue"). Stern, not sternly characterized, could be a punning abbreviation of Sturgeon, thus a stand-in for the author, amazed and overcome by the creations of his imagination. As the first woman (for Lone), Evelyn might be an allegorical Eve, while her sister's name may allude to Lewis Carroll's Alice, although Alicia refuses to accept the evidence of her senses, that her house is a wonderland

of psi phenomena. As they stand, the names Evelyn and
Alicia carry a connotation of gentility, and emotional
connotations carry the only significance I can see in Gerard
(a bit snotty) or Janie (a bit cuter and more little-girlish
than Jane). Least ambiguous of all is the name Baby, and
the names of Bonnie and Beanie signify little except that
they are twins.

Names, like external imagery, are useful, even
necessary devices for suggesting certain qualities of a
character without subjecting him to a detailed analysis,
and for connecting him with events, issues, and other
characters. But more information, particularly of a more
subjective nature, is needed for a major character,
especially since subjective states are so important to the
novel's theme and development. The subjective aspects of
Sturgeon's characters, examined only to a limited extent,
are introduced in several ways. Least directly, there are
the external images already mentioned, including names and
their allusions or connotations, and there are the character's functions, both overt and symbolic, in the plot and
in various patterns. More obviously, there is the assumption of a specific character's point-of-view, from which to
present his actions, speeches, and even thoughts, the last
of which are given to us at times by third-person narration,
at times by internal monologue, fitted, as is the novel's
dialogue, to the specific character.

Point-of-view is handled in a different way in each of the three parts of <u>More than Human</u>. The narrator of Part One is presumably omniscient, but he chooses to alternate glimpses inside and outside various characters. In the first fourteen segments separated by spacing, Lone, Evelyn, Alicia, Kew, Prodd, Mrs. Prodd, Gerry, and Hip are each given some subjective treatment in this manner. The same viewpoint is used for two consecutive segments only once, and single viewpoints are varied with multiple or alternating viewpoints and an objective viewpoint outside all the characters. Janie dominates the next ten segments, although three are given over to Lone, and the last eight, although they involve Janie, Baby, and the twins, are dominated by Lone. The minds most effectively entered are Lone's and Evelyn's, both of which are fairly simple, and can be sketched in rather broad strokes, but Janie, Gerry, Hip, and Alicia are also internalized with some success.

Parts Two and Three are alike in their almost total restriction to a single consciousness, but there are significant differences between the two handlings of point-of-view, differences which are not limited to the nature of the character whose consciousness is penetrated. Gerry is the first-person narrator of Part Two, the frame of which takes place in Stern's office, but the action of which takes place mainly in Gerry's memory, including the ten-page excerpt, in her own thoughts, of Miss Kew's remembrance of Lone.

Hip is the separate character to whom the third-person
narrator of Part Three mainly limits himself, although he
also describes things about Hip and actions in his presence
which Hip does not observe, and the conclusion reverts to
Gerry, as head and representative of the completed gestalt.

This manipulation and variation of the point-of-
view accomplishes several things. It takes us inside the
characters to some extent, yet it prevents us from being
dominated by the thinking of any single character. A somewhat internalized treatment complements the psi motifs, and
lets us see the longings within the characters which will
draw them together. The diffuseness and rapid alternation
of viewpoint in Part One ties together these longings, but
it also contrasts the characters with each other. It sets
up a tolerance for varying attitudes, supporting the theme
of learning regard for others. Thus a sense of aesthetic
distance is established which prevents us from identifying
too strongly with the wrong-headed Gerry in Part Two, before
the corrective of Part Three can be applied.

In terms of the structure of the novel as a whole,
the rapid alternation of viewpoints in Part One establishes
the formal identity of the spaced segments as significant
narrative units. The gradual centralization of viewpoint
as the gestalt begins to take shape results in a kind of
funnel effect, whereby the restriction of viewpoint in Part
Two, if not inevitable, is certainly a natural sequel. The

third-person omniscient narrator of Part Three, also not an
inevitable structural feature, complements Gerry's first-
person narration of Part Two, supporting the two parts'
complementary relationships of character (Hip vs. Gerry),
plot (both centering on a search for lost memories), and
theme (power vs. mercy, difference vs. likeness, two kinds
of accomplishment and completion).

If there is a problem of unity in the book, it is
largely due to its genesis as a novelette. A masterful
display of control of form and technique, "Baby is Three"
ended on a sentimental note, as Gerry, having discovered he
only imagined killing Miss Kew, decides to buy her flowers.
In the revised form, with Miss Kew actually dead, Gerry's
erasure of Stern's mind and Bonnie's erasure of the tape
recorder seem more sinister, demanding correction or retri-
bution, but Part Two is still complete in itself. Because
it is so self-contained, the parts surrounding it could not
be done in the same form or style, but must fit together
more like movements in music. Part One is quite successful
on its own terms, full of color, action, and confusing
variety, and it establishes the themes for its successors,
even introducing Gerry and Hip at an early stage to complete
the cast of major characters (except for Stern). Part Three
is more conventional and pale alongside its predecessors:
the development of love between Janie and Hip is handled
with charm as well as sentiment, but it lacks the shock of

Lone's contact with Evelyn, or Gerry's mental penetration of Alicia; Hip's and Janie's retelling of his past is not nearly as vivid as Gerry's re-living of his; the melodramatic scuffling among members of the gestalt is no match for the venomous violence Kew wreaks on Lone; and the explanation of the book's "moral" is a bit too pat, somewhat too overtly speech-making.

Even the conventionality and relative obviousness of Part Three, although they may be failures in execution, may also be understandable, in terms of the demands of the science fiction audience, the analogy of musical form, and the role of surprise and discovery in More than Human. The reader's demand that major points be clearly communicated and explained was stronger in 1953 than it is today, now that literary indirection has penetrated science fiction somewhat more. In the third and last movement of a musical composition, it might not be wholly out of place to repeat themes or motifs in a minor key. And such a recapitulation might be intended, not only to allow further development and completion of the book's major ideas, but also to contrast, by its subdued quality, with the attempt at transcendence and grandeur which marks the conclusion.

Surprises are hardly out of place in More than Human. Although Sturgeon has accounted to some extent for scientific disbelief, he has also constructed his book so as to make questions of logic and scientific probability inapplicable. Days and years passing are very much and quite specifically a part of the story, yet the only reference point in the historically real world is the fact that, in Janie's childhood, her father was involved in World War II. Even the approximate city or state is impossible to discern from the descriptive data given, yet the settings are given in some visual detail, and are geographically located close together, in a narrowly circumscribed area at the center of which lies the ominous Kew estate. The recurrence of this "home," the allusions to the characters' "family" relationship, and the importance given to subjective longings as early as Part One, all combine to make the gestalt's success seem almost inevitable. Within the scope of this poetic, rather than scientific logic, minor plot surprises, "discoveries" by the narrator and his characters, and literary "experiments" by the author are part of the "expected" pattern.

Thus we may understand the logic behind some of the author's choices in Part Three, even though we do not fully appreciate the result. Lone's shocks of love and violence can hardly be repeated, or even matched, using normal characters. Hip's past is related, rather than shown, in the middle of Part Three for reasons of balance. Complicated though it is, Hip's past is not as important to the total gestalt as is Gerry's past, involving the others, in Part Two, or Hip's present with Janie, both of which are

shown directly. The length of time it takes Hip, a normal
human being, to recover, must be contrasted with the single
afternoon of Gerry's (incomplete) self-examination, but
dramatizing what is in Hip's memory would make that section
too long. The scuffle with Gerry at the end is needed, too,
to illustrate Hip's selflessness, Gerry's resistance, and
the dissension within the gestalt which has turned everyone
against Gerry. Finally, even the talkiness of Hip's
thoughts, as he prepares to give Gerry his moral lesson, has
some justification, although it might have been handled less
repetitiously: a normal human being can only communicate
with words, and Sturgeon has even managed to make words
pictorial, as he described Hip's preparation of the message
in his mind for Gerry to scan telepathically.

In a good year for science fiction novels, More than
Human perhaps came closest to being great science fiction,
or really good fiction in general. It succeeded, however,
almost by not being science fiction; Sturgeon won the International Fantasy Award for his book, not the "Hugo" for best
science fiction novel.[34] Yet the book is built on science
fiction conventions, it does involve an exercise in

---

[34]The Demolished Man by Alfred Bester won the "Hugo"
for best novel of 1953. Other competitors included:
Mission of Gravity by Hal Clement, The Caves of Steel by
Isaac Asimov, Childhood's End by Arthur C. Clarke, Bring the
Jubilee by Ward and Out of the Deeps by John Wyndham (all of
which are on the MLA list noted above, Chapter II, note 52).

extrapolation, and it does subject a kind of technology as well as some scientific assumptions to examination. The success of More than Human was also achieved almost by its not being literature, i.e. by exploiting, not avoiding conventions of pulp fiction. Sturgeon's fairy tale would be insupportable in a long novel, or one with a heavy style, full of psychologizing. Sturgeon's conception demands characters who are to some extent grotesques, variations on stereotypes, and in general, the variation is capably performed. Sturgeon's prose, too, is derived from the simplicity and directness of pulp style, although it has a suppleness and suggestiveness rarely found in pulp fiction, and it generally avoids the staleness and mawkishness frequently found in pulp fiction. In summary, then, I would say that Sturgeon, in handling a concept which can hardly be done justice to outside the genre, has extended the boundaries of the genre considerably, and has done about as well as can be done within those boundaries.

CHAPTER VI

WALTER M. MILLER, JR.: A CANTICLE FOR LEIBOWITZ (1959)

In Science and the Shabby Curate of Poetry (New
York, 1965), Martin Green recounts his experiences and discoveries as an English man of letters who subjected himself
to a year's study in "science," objectively demonstrating to
himself the validity of C. P. Snow's diagnosis of a split
between the literary and scientific cultures. One result of
that separation, Green notes, is the popular manifestation
of science and scientific thinking in science fiction, which
he respects for what he feels it is trying to do, even
though he believes it is doomed as literature and will, at
best, be absorbed into the mainstream the way that nineteenth century American folk humor was. In a perceptive
essay, Green writes: "The split between the cultures, the
purification [sic] of the literary mind, which has so
specialized the subject-matter of serious fiction, has
provoked a kind of rebellion, or separatist movement. . . .
Quite major themes of the imagination are developed there
in a way that the non-scientific reader recognizes as both

221

authentic and at the same time deeply alien to him."[1]

One of the books which Green chooses to exemplify his thesis is A Canticle for Leibowitz (1959), by Walter M. Miller, Jr., a novel in which history and religion are given science-fictional treatment and science fiction is given a relatively literary voice. Contrasting Miller's novel with Buddenbrooks and War and Peace, he points out that whereas Mann and Tolstoi illustrate their ideas through an in-depth treatment of character and proto-typical if not actual event, in science fiction "the historical imagination is encouraged to a much freer play; the writer invents a new version of the Renaissance, re-creates with variations the life of a medieval monastery."[2] Although he grants that "there are some beautiful moments in the book, some imaginative feats that succeed by the most conventional standards," Green insists that "the thing to emphasize here is the oddity, for the literary man, and yet the authenticity, of its treatment of a familiar theme."[3] Reasoning from the artistic success of this book, and of one or two others in which church machinery, rather than church dogma, is varied and extrapolated, Green derives a general conclusion about religion in science fiction, a conclusion which a wider

---

[1]Martin Green, Science and the Shabby Curate of Poetry (New York, 1965), pp. 12-121.

[2]Green, p. 124.

[3]Green, p. 124.

examination, despite uncovering exceptions, would also bear out: "Instead of probing into rationalistic experience to expose its limitedness, its incoherence, its inadequacy, under strain; or introducing unnatural or supernatural phenomena in close combination with the most ruthless naturalism; instead of this the science-fiction writer moves outward, constructs new religious systems, applies them to new worlds."[4]

Green's interest, if not his perceptivity, was shared by many in the literary community at the time of the book's publication. Miller's novel won high praise from Edmund Fuller in the Chicago Sunday Tribune, Robert Phelps in the New York Herald-Tribune Book Review, and Orville Prescott in the San Francisco Chronicle.[5] General approval with some reservations came from Stanley J. Rowland in Christian Century, Roy Perrott in the Manchester Guardian Weekly, Maurice Richardson in the New Statesman, and John Coleman in the Spectator.[6] Martin Levin in the New York

---

[4]Green, p. 125.

[5]Review by Edmund Fuller, Chicago Sunday Tribune, March 6, 1960, p. 1. Review by Robert Phelps, New York Herald-Tribune Book Review, March 13, 1960, p. 4. Review by Orville Prescott, San Francisco Chronicle, March 8, 1960, p. 27.

[6]Review by Stanley J. Rowland, Christian Century, May 25, 1960, pp. 640-641. Review by Roy Perrott, Manchester Guardian Weekly, April 7, 1960, p. 13. Review by Maurice Richardson, New Statesman, April 9, 1960, p. 533. Review by John Coleman, Spectator, March 25, 1960, pp. 444-445.

<u>Times Book Review</u> expressed definitely mixed feelings, as
did Edwin Kennebeck in <u>Commonweal</u>, and the reviewer for
<u>Time</u>.[7] Marcus Klein in <u>Nation</u> treated the novel purely as
a symbol of national complacency in the face of world
conflagration, while Whitney Balliett in the <u>New Yorker</u> and
James Yaffe in <u>Saturday Review</u> saw almost nothing good in
it at all.[8]

The number of general periodicals which thought
<u>A Canticle for Leibowitz</u> worth reviewing was unusually large
for a science-fiction novel. None of them reviewed it in a
special science-fiction section and some of the reviewers
even seemed totally unaware of the science-fiction background of Miller, and even of the book, whose three parts
had originally appeared in <u>F&SF</u> between 1955 and 1957.[9]
Those who were aware of this background attempted to dismiss
it, or found fault with the book on that account. Coleman
felt there was "mercifully little 'imaginative' S F jargonry
[sic]," Rowland complained of "flaws that are apparently

---

[7]Review by Martin Levin, <u>New York Times Book Review</u>,
March 27, 1960, pp. 42-43. Review by Edwin Kennebeck,
Commonweal, March 4, 1960, pp. 632-634. Anonymous review,
<u>Time</u>, February 22, 1960, p. 110.

[8]Review by Marcus Klein, <u>Nation</u>, November 19, 1960,
pp. 398-402. Review by Whitney Balliett, <u>New Yorker</u>,
April 2, 1960, p. 159. Review by James Yaffe, <u>Saturday
Review</u>, June 4, 1960, p. 21.

[9]Walter M. Miller, Jr., "A Canticle for Leibowitz,"
<u>F&SF</u>, April, 1955, pp. 93-111; "And the Light is Risen,"
<u>F&SF</u>, August, 1956, pp. 3-80; "The Last Canticle," <u>F&SF</u>,
February, 1957, pp. 3-50.

indigenous to its genre," Phelps wrote that it was not
typical of science fiction, and Perrott claimed to be
astonished that "space fiction" [sic] had produced a genuine
"novel."[10] Miller's craftsmanship was generally applauded,
even by those who felt it was wasted, but that was a secondary consideration or perhaps a basic qualification for
reviewing the book at all. Most of the reviewers used the
novel as a pretext for a brief article justifying religion,
faith, hope, or humanism at the expense of everyday
politics, public complacency, science, and science fiction.

Inside the science-fiction community, Miller's book
was recognized as science fiction, with a not uncommon
religious theme and framework, written by an established
science-fiction writer. Floyd C. Gale in Galaxy gave it his
highest rating and the following praise: "Practically all
SF stories dealing with religious themes have been top-
drawer, written with a careful eye toward perfection because
of their controversial nature. Miller's belongs at the very
top of the top. It has many passages of remarkable power
and deserves the widest possible audience."[11] P. Schuyler
Miller in Analog commended the author on his characters and
the depth and handling of his theme, calling the book "an

---

[10] Coleman, Rowland, Perrott (above, note 6); Phelps
(above, note 5).

[11] Review by Floyd C. Gale, Galaxy, February, 1961,
p. 139.

impressive piece of writing."[12] Having praised the novel's

parts, when they were originally published, F&SF, for whom

Damon Knight was then reviewer, merely noted the publication

of the whole.[13] Knight inexplicably omitted reference to

the book in his collected reviews, and James Blish, in an

article dealing with religion in science fiction, called

Miller's book a "deservedly admirable" contribution.[14] The

highest praise came in September, 1961, when the Nineteenth

World Science Fiction Convention, meeting in Seattle,

awarded Walter M. Miller, Jr. his second "Hugo," naming

A Canticle for Leibowitz the best science fiction novel of

1960.[15]

Up until then, Miller had been regarded, in Sam

Moskowitz's words, as "the perennially promising author."[16]

An engineer-turned-writer, he had published some forty-odd

stories in the major science fiction magazines in the

---

[12]Review by P. Schuyler Miller, Analog, November,
1960, pp. 165-166.

[13]F&SF, June, 1960, p. 87.

[14]William Atheling, Jr. [James Blish], The Issue at
Hand: Studies in Contemporary Magazine Science Fiction,
ed. James Blish (Chicago, 1964), p. 55. Damon Knight, In
Search of Wonder: Essays on Modern Science Fiction, rev.
ed. (Chicago, 1967).

[15]See The Hugo Winners, ed. Isaac Asimov (New York,
1962), for a listing of the award winners through the 1961
World Science Fiction Convention.

[16]Sam Moskowitz, Seekers of Tomorrow: Masters of
Modern Science Fiction (Cleveland and New York, 1966),
p. 413.

Fifties; several were chosen for anthologies, sometimes of the best stories in the field, but many of his tales are rather conventional and far from distinguished.[17] "The Darfsteller," a story about a human actor struggling quixotically to compete in an age of automated stage plays, won for him a "Hugo" in 1955 for the previous year's best novelette, but he was not able to publish a collection of stories until after the success of his novel.[18] The first collection, Conditionally Human (1962), combines "The Darfsteller" with two other novelettes, demonstrates his proficiency with fiction of medium length dealing with serious intellectual and emotional themes, and shows a generally prosaic and sometimes plodding style. The second collection, The View from the Stars (1964), consisting of nine stories from the period 1951-1954, exhibits a considerable range of subject matter, various degrees of control over style, and a talent for compression, and makes it clear that the ability to construct effective scenes and dramatic contrasts was present early in Miller's abbreviated career. Ironically, by the time these books were published, their

---

[17]See MIT Index and supplements (above, Chapter I, note 35) for bibliographical data. See also W. R. Cole, A Checklist of Science Fiction Anthologies ([New York], 1964). With reference to Miller's biography, mention of his engineering background is made in Richardson (above, note 6), on the dust jacket of A Canticle for Leibowitz, and in Donald R. Tuck, A Handbook of Science Fiction and Fantasy, rev. ed., 2 vols. (Hobart, Tasmania, 1959).

[18]See Hugo (above, note 15).

author was no longer writing science fiction; aside from the
considerable revisions of earlier material embodied in his
novel, no new science fiction has appeared under his name
since 1957.[19] Nevertheless "the perennially promising
author" had fulfilled his promise; his last work was one of
the best novels ever to emerge from the pulp science fiction
field.

A novel of about 100,000 words, A Canticle for
Leibowitz is composed of three parts, roughly equal in
length, sharing the same basic setting in space but separated in time by gaps of approximately 600 years.[20] Each
part is a coherent novelette, an original variation on a
conventional science fiction theme, carefully plotted and
constructed for its own particular effects. Each individual
story, dealing with individuals' personal struggles, brings
to life the issues and ideas of the whole which, because of
the interplay between the novelettes, is thus something
greater than its parts. Making good use of science
fictional conventions, methods, and philosophy, Miller has
gone beyond them to produce a dissertation on the ambiguity
of advance and the relativity of knowledge, against a

---

[19]The only item I have been able to locate which was
published since 1960 under Miller's name is a political
article on the Kennedy-Hoffa feud: Walter M. Miller, Jr.,
"Bobby and Jimmy," Nation, April 7, 1962, pp. 300-303.

[20]Walter M. Miller, Jr., A Canticle for Leibowitz
(Philadelphia, 1960). All page references in text refer to
this edition.

background of history as an aesthetic pattern, a seamless fabric into which individuals and institutions, actual events and folklore are inextricably interwoven. Yet for all the complexity, solemnity, and high seriousness that such a description (aptly) suggests, the book is first of all an entertainment, full of fun and occasional thrills, presenting sympathetic characters in a narrative of curious and interesting situations and events.

Part One, "Fiat Homo," originally published as "A Canticle for Leibowitz," consists of eleven chapters covering 109 pages. It tells the story of Brother Francis Girard, covering twenty-two years of his life at Leibowitz Abbey in the twenty-sixth century, in what was the Southwestern United States before the Atomic Deluge. Fasting in preparation for taking his vows at age seventeen, Francis comes upon a fallout shelter in which it appears there are relics of the engineer who founded his monastic order to preserve what scientific knowledge was left in the Dark Ages of the twentieth century. Like his colleagues, Francis has no idea of the true meaning of the relics (a grocery list, a blueprint, some scribbled notes); unlike them, he refuses to speculate and contribute to the folklore growing around his discovery (including the conjecture that the old Jewish pilgrim who directed Francis' attention to the shelter might have been the blessed Leibowitz himself). A simple soul, Francis is delayed seven years in professing his vows

because the apparent miraculousness of his discovery
threatens to discredit the claims of the order for its
founder's canonization; admitted at last, he becomes an
apprentice copyist, and spends fifteen years making an
illuminated copy of the blueprint in his spare time, while
investigators from New Rome examine and eventually accept
his findings as evidence supporting the canonization.
Entrusted to take both copies to the Pope for the canonization ceremonies, Francis is set upon by robbers, radiation-
deformed monsters, whose preference for the gilded copy
allows him to get through with the relic intact. After
seeing the shabby capital, he is killed and eaten by the
same robbers on his way home, and buried by the same old
wandering Jew who appeared at the story's beginning.

The science fictional framework set up in this
story, a framework which embraces the whole novel, should be
obvious; the problems of survival and rebuilding after a
global catastrophe have long been staples in pulp science
fiction, and warnings in science fiction of the dangers of
atomic war (including the likelihood of radiation-produced
mutations) predated the Manhattan project. Within that
framework, however, Miller has also made use of other
conventions frequently seen in science fiction.

The science-fictionist's concern with social
mechanics frequently demands that he briefly characterize
the government operating within his tale; not infrequently,

that government is a theocracy, empty of belief, employing
ritual and dogma for purely political purposes. In Miller's
vision of the Church, political power is of practically no
consequence, ritual and dogma maintain a small oasis of
order in a wholly chaotic world, and belief is uppermost,
belief in the justice and mercy of God, and in the potential
intelligence and constructiveness of man. Parallels with
the European Dark Ages are explicit, including the primary
worldly function of the Albertian Order of Leibowitz, which
is to preserve what scraps of written knowledge it can,
regardless of how little sense they make, until someone can
again make use of them.

Another science fictional theme, the lack of communication between societies on different scientific and
technological levels, is fundamental to Part One. The
Church is the only civilization there is, and no one in it
understands the original meaning of the artifacts it discovers and preserves. This point is brought out by Brother
Francis' fear of the fallout shelter, and of the "fallout"
itself, believed to be a monster, by his recollection of the
priestly expedition which "disappeared" after reporting the
finding of an "intercontinental launching pad," and by
various other bits of scholarly, often folkloric information. Most of all, however, the fundamental misunderstand-
ing between eras is brought out by the central symbol of the
novelette, the blueprint. Because electricity and

electronics are merely meaningless terms at this time, the
blueprint's only comprehensible value stems from the fact
that it was designed by one I. E. Liebowitz, whom everyone
comes to believe must be identical with the "Isaac" or
"Edward" Liebowitz who founded the Order. As a relic of
past civilization, it must be kept intact, therefore it must
be copied exactly before it fades. As a relic of the
Beatus, soon to be Saint, it deserves to be revered and in
some way glorified. As a design, supposedly conveying
information, it appears to Brother Francis "to be no more
than a network of lines connecting a patchwork of doohickii,
squiggles, quids, laminulae, and thingumbob" (p. 78). And
when he discovers that the color scheme is accidental, the
idea of "illuminating" the blueprint follows almost inevitably:

> With the color scheme reversed, no one would recognize
> the drawing at first. Certain other features could
> obviously be modified. He dared change nothing that
> he did not understand, but surely the parts tables and
> the block-lettered information could be spread sym-
> metrically around the diagram on scrolls and shields.
> Because the meaning of the diagram itself was obscure,
> he dared not alter its shape or plan by a hair; but
> since its color scheme was unimportant, it might as
> well be beautiful. He considered gold inlay for the
> squiggles and doohickii, but the thingumbob was too
> intricate for goldwork, and a gold quid would seem
> ostentatious. The quiggles just had to be done jet
> black, but that meant that the lines should be off-
> black, to assert the quiggles. While the unsymmet-
> rical design would have to stay as it was, he could
> think of no reason why its meaning would be altered
> by using it as a trellis for a climbing vine, whose
> branches (carefully dodging the quiggles) might be
> made to furnish an impression of symmetry or render
> asymmetry natural. When Brother Horner illuminated
> a capital M, transmuting it into a wonderful jungle

of leaves, berries, branches, and perhaps a wily
serpent, it nevertheless remained legible as M.
Brother Francis saw no reason for supposing that the
same would not apply to the diagram.

The general shape, over-all, with a scrolled
border, might well become a shield, rather than the
stark rectangle which enclosed the drawing in the
print. He made dozens of preliminary sketches. At
the very top of the parchment would be a representa-
tion of the Triune God, and at the very bottom--the
coat of arms of the Albertian Order, with, just
above it the image of the Beatus. (pp. 82-83)

This passage, quoted at length, which is fairly

typical of Miller's style, is one of the highlights of Part

One. A breakdown in communication, usually a good basis

for comedy, here gives rise to a train of thought completely

dissociated from the original purpose of the object being

contemplated, but which is perfectly functional and logical,

given the circumstances. As each new detail of design comes

to Brother Francis' mind, the joke is elaborated one more

step, until it seems to transcend itself, like madness

producing inspiration. As Francis muses lovingly over his

scheme, we become drawn in by Miller's empathy with him;

knowing Francis' conscious thoughts, following his bursts

of inspiration, which seem entirely authentic for a man of

his hypothetical world, we come to know him and his era

better.

For the most part it is the era which occupies

Miller's attention, an era in which survival, never too

certain, has the first priority, as is indicated by the

title ("Fiat Homo," "Let there be man"). The survival of

the Church and its ways, of the Order and its Memorabilia, of the fallout shelter and its contents, is balanced by the survival of the Wandering Jew, of the mutations (called "the Pope's children" because of edicts demanding that all "humans" be allowed to live), even of Francis himself. The Age of Simplification which followed the Atomic Deluge encouraged the survival only of those who denied their intelligence and education or who had none; centuries later, the effect of that period is still strong. Francis, a runaway slave from the hill tribes of Utah, has learned at the Abbey to read and to write, and has pored over much of the written materials available to him, but he is still a very simple man, at age thirty-nine as at age seventeen. Ill-trained for any kind of work outside the monastery, physically weak (his propensity for fainting is a running joke), intensely aware of his ignorance (not only regarding ancient science, but also in that large area of experience between natural and supernatural, the preternatural), he leads an existence made only slightly less precarious by faith, obedience, and allegiance to his Order. Timid and mildly superstitious, he can be brave when curiosity or duty demands it, as he demonstrates before the fallout shelter and the band of robbers. Devout and obedient, he is yet stubborn enough in his scrupulous honesty to endure seven annual Lenten fasts in the desert, because he cannot swear to his Abbot that the old man he met on the day of the discovery was <u>absolutely</u> nothing more than an old man.

Seen from his point of view, the world in which he
lives is made up of many seemingly disconnected ideas and
events, as is fitting, since communication has been lost
not only between temporal eras and the concepts which
compose them, but also between geographical areas in the
same time period. The years are the only sure connection
between things, years whose passing is measured by the
yearly celebrations, by the ageing and death of fellow
monks, by the progress Brother Francis makes on his illuminated blueprint, by the fact that decisions are made in
distant places, news of which eventually makes its way to
Leibowitz Abbey. Since every year is essentially the same
as every other year, the narrative can focus on the few
events out of the ordinary which have special significance
in Francis' life. His discovery, his becoming a monk, his
interviews with the Abbot, with the postulator for and the
devil's advocate against the canonization of Leibowitz, with
the Pope, his confrontations with the robbers, these scenes
stand out against the confessions, conversations, and other
everyday activities, taking up the bulk of his time, which
are given to us in representative snatches.

Most of the scenes in Part One, but not all, involve
Francis as a participant, a not completely reliable observer
who is observed in turn by a sympathetic and understanding
narrator of our time. The difference in perspective,

between Francis, who understands very little, and the narrator, who seems to understand everything, provides most of the humor and irony, but the mockery is gentle, and implicit only, for the narrator never comments directly in his own person.

Concentrating on Brother Francis, and his view of things, the narrator caricatures the rest of the characters: Arkos, the shaggy, blustering Abbot, whose shrewdness we see only in his scene with Prior Cheroki, Francis' confessor, out of Francis' perception; Fingo, the jovial carpenter with the spotted hide, whose major function for the story is his carving of a wooden statue of Leibowitz; Brother Jeris, the mocking sophist and practical man whose appointment over Francis stops work on the blueprint for a while; Monsignor Malfreddo Aguerra, the postulator, who countermands Jeris' order, and whose kindliness causes Francis to idolize him; Monsignor Flaught, the devil's advocate, whom Francis cannot see without horns and fangs; Pope Leo XXI, a wise ruler, despite the fact that his technical ignorance is the same as Francis', who takes time away from his political socializing to welcome Francis and reassure him as to the value of his work, and whose "wink," a delightful artistic touch in itself, amounts almost to a divine revelation to Francis of the simultaneity of poverty and dignity; and the old Jewish pilgrim, ugly, irascible, and mysterious, who is dressed like the founder, whose mocking smile appears on Fingo's

statue, and who reminds us of the central incongruity of a
monastic order founded by a Jew, and a scientist, at that,
who becomes canonized even though his very existence cannot
be demonstrated. These are caricatures in the dictionary
sense--"exaggeration by means of deliberate simplification
and often ludicrous distortion of parts or characteristics"--and they are not out of place in a story in which so
many years are compressed, in which simplicity and simplification are virtues, and in which the era itself is being
characterized in terms of such "representative men."[21]

Part Two, "Fiat Lux," originally published as "And
the Light is Risen," comprises twelve chapters and 110
pages. Taking place for the most part in the same Leibowitz
Abbey, little changed by another six centuries, it focuses
not on a single man but on a confrontation between two men,
taking place in the relatively small space of a few months,
as against the many years which pass in Part One. Invited,
at his own request, Thon Taddeo Pfardentrott, a humanist
scholar from the feudal court at Texarkana, comes to the
Abbey to examine the library collection, allegedly dating
from before the Flame Deluge, and to give the secluded monks
a glimpse of the new age of science and enlightenment.[22]

---

[21]Webster's Third New International Dictionary,
ed. Philip Babcock Gove (Springfield, Massachusetts, 1961).

[22]Thon Taddeo is a "humanist" scholar in that he is
participating in a revival of "classical" learning, and in
that he has a man-centered, rather than a god-centered,
viewpoint. In that context, science is just one of many

In some ways, Taddeo himself is enlightened, since the Memorabilia appear to be genuine, and the Thon's own theories regarding electricity are demonstrated in practice; Brother Kornhoer has developed a carbon-arc lamp, fed by a monk-powered dynamo, which provides the scholar with illumination in the library, to the eternal outrage of the conservative librarian, Brother Armbruster. In some ways, the monks are given a glimpse of a new barbarism, since the Thon's cousin Hannegan II, illiterate ruler of Texarkana, is beginning a war of conquest which knows no boundaries (the soldiers in the Thon's party are busy making thorough sketches of the Abbey's fortifications), and the fascination of the Thon himself with new theories and old heresies causes the ageing Dom Paulo to wonder if knowledge can ever be used properly. The continuing debate between science and faith, which takes place largely in Paulo's mind, is expanded by the inclusion of other viewpoints, the positions of doubt and art represented by old Benjamin Eleazar, a hermit who claims an existence of thousands of years, and the Abbey's most unwanted tenant, its anonymous Poet-in-residence. In the end, nothing is settled, but the Thon and the Abbot do achieve a measure of understanding, and the Abbey, retaining

---

human activities. To call him a "scientist" and Dom Paulo a "humanist," on the analogy of C. P. Snow's "two cultures," would be even more anachronistic, and would equate "humanism" with only one human activity, religion, which is differentiated from science, to be sure, but also from other human areas of endeavor.

control over its library, is left alone again for a while.
In an epilogue, the Poet dies a most unromantic death,
blasphemously administering "last rites" to a cavalry
officer whose men had shot the Poet, leaving him and the
officer to the buzzards.

Besides the basic framework of life in the future,
and a continuation of the theme of contact between technological unequals, Part Two demonstrates its science-
fictionality by its exploitation of the old motif of the
marvelous invention, by allusions to two fragments of
science fiction within the science fiction, and by treating
one of its major characters as an archetypal scientist.

As in Part One, the background is allegorical, the
wars of conquest, the relative power and wealth of the
Church, the slowness of transportation and communication
hampering the inevitable growth of diplomacy and intellectual ferment clearly parallelling the developments of the
European Renaissance. The major differences lie in the
American setting, and the knowledge of prior technology.

The desirability of scientific and technological
advance is accepted by three different cultural levels: Mad
Bear and his tribe of nomads (descendants of the "Pope's
children" and similar outcasts) are interested purely in
weapons; Hannegan differs from Mad Bear only in the scope
of his ambitions, although some of his own people are more
theoretically inclined; even the Abbey adds a printing press

and electric lighting, within limits and with reservations.
In the case of the Abbey, the picture is perhaps more
complicated; besides being unequal to the secular Renaissance in technology (i.e. inferior), the Church prides
itself on being unequal in the area of responsibility (i.e.
superior). Superiority, however, depends somewhat on context: Mad Bear and his people have their pride, too, and in
their own eyes, only warriors, braves, and buccaneers like
themselves have the right to be called "men."

The marvelous invention in this story is of course
Brother Kornhoer's light-machine, certainly a marvel for its
era. Like the illuminated blueprint of Part One, it seems
to involve an inordinate amount of labor relative to the
result: "it was necessary to keep at least four novices or
postulants continuously employed at cranking the dynamo and
adjusting the arc-gap" (p. 187). The result itself is
somewhat ambivalently viewed: its blue-white brilliance is
as "ghastly" to Dom Paulo as it is unexpected; its aid to
Thon Taddeo's researches is offset by a double injury to
his pride. Thinking at first that the lamp was preserved
from the past, and its existence kept secret, he is embarrassed not only by his error but also by the fact that it
was someone else (and a monk at that) who demonstrated the
practical applications of his theories of optics and
electricity.

The lamp is a symbol of enlightenment, not only to

the Thon, but also, and especially, to Brother Kornhoer and
his assistants. During the experimental period of the
invention's development, Brother Kornhoer's continuing confrontation with Brother Armbruster, the librarian, provides
a comic illustration of the war between science and faith,
parallelling and foreshadowing the Abbot's conflict with
the Thon. Every move and change in the library's normal
pattern of activity is greeted by the librarian as sacri-
lege, especially the decision, condoned by the Abbot, to
hang the lamp itself on a hook in the alcove of the Memorabilia, replacing a crucifix. Armbruster's approval is never
won, as he demonstrates toward the end of the story by
deriding the research of the Thon and his colleagues, but
his tacit obedience to the Abbot is apparently gained,
since we hear of no comments from him when Kornhoer and his
assistants stage a quasi-blasphemous welcome for the Thon,
in a marvelously effective scene.

> The monk who watched from the head of the stairs
> turned solemnly and bowed toward the fifth monk on
> the landing below.
>
> "In principio Deus," he said softly.
>
> The fifth monk turned and bowed toward the
> fourth monk at the foot of the stairs. "Caelum et
> terram creavit," he murmured in turn.
>
> The fourth monk turned toward the three who
> lounged behind the machine. "Vacuus autem erat
> mundus," he announced.
>
> "Cum tenebris in superficie profundorum,"
> chorused the group.

"Ortus est Dei Spiritus supra aquas," called Brother Kornhoer, returning his book to its shelf with a rattling of chains.

"Gratias Creatori Spiritui," responded his entire team.

"Dixitque Deus: 'FIAT LUX,'" said the inventor in a tone of command.

The vigil on the stairs descended to take their posts. Four monks manned the treadmill. The fifth monk hovered over the dynamo. The sixth monk climbed the shelf-ladder and took his seat on the top rung, his head bumping the top of the archway. He pulled a mask of smoke-blackened oily parchment over his face to protect his eyes, then felt for the lamp fixture and its thumbscrew, while Brother Kornhoer watched him nervously from below.

"Et lux ergo facta est," he said when he had found the screw.

"Lucem esse bonam Deus vidit," the inventor called to the fifth monk.

The fifth monk bent over the dynamo with a candle for one last look at the brush contacts. "Et secrevit lucem a tenebris," he said at last, continuing the lesson.

"Lucem appellavit 'diem,'" chorused the treadmill team, "et tenebras 'noctes.'" Whereupon they set their shoulders to the turnstile beams.

Axles creaked and groaned. The wagon-wheel dynamo began to spin, its low whir becoming a moan and then a whine as the monks strained and grunted at the drive-mill. The guardian of the dynamo watched anxiously as the spokes blurred with speed and became a film. "Vespere occaso," he began, then paused to lick two fingers and touch them to the contacts. A spark snapped.

"Lucifer!" he yelped, leaping back, then finished lamely: "ortus est et primo die."

"CONTACT!" said Brother Kornhoer, as Dom Paulo, Thon Taddeo and his clerk [sic] descended the stairs.

The monk on the ladder struck the arc. A sharp spfft!--and blinding light flooded the vaults with a brilliance that had not been seen in twelve centuries. (pp. 183-184)

As in the case of Brother Francis' blueprint, the incongruous combination of technological practicality and Christian ritual is a joke to the twentieth-century reader, but also a matter of profound importance to the participants. The recitation of the first verses of Genesis is as much a magical incantation, a prayer for success, as it is a spectacle (it is seen only by Brother Armbruster, whom it would not be calculated to impress favorably). And the manner in which the light is received, both by Paulo and by Taddeo, is humorous only to the reader; the embarrassment suffered on all sides is significant, and results gradually in somewhat changed attitudes on the part of all three principals, reviving Kornhoer's humility as it increases the doubt and suspicion of the Abbot and the scholar for each other.

Other science-fictional features of the novelette include a pseudo-biblical pastiche purporting to be an account of the Flame Deluge and its aftermath, apparently written "a few decades after the death of Saint Leibowitz" (p. 182), and read to Thon Taddeo as an example of what little there is in the way of accurate written records of the catastrophe. Acknowledged by the Church to be somewhat fanciful and allegorical, it is received by the Thon with a skepticism which is curiously lacking in his analysis of a contrasting, but similarly symbolic document he comes upon in the Memorabilia. This document--described by Paulo in these words: "a fragment of a play, or a dialogue, it seems. . . . It's something about some people creating some artificial people as slaves. And the slaves revolt against their makers" (p. 223)--the reader can recognize, without its being quoted, as an excerpt from Karel Čapek's play, R. U. R. The Thon, anxious to avoid thinking of human beings as responsible creatures, leaps to the hypothesis that "Man was not created until shortly before the fall of the last civilization" (p. 222). The ensuing argument, wherein the Thon preaches the need for "freedom to speculate," at the same time that Dom Paulo recites to him the story of the Fall of Man, is the climax of the novelette. The Abbot reveals Hannegan's edict, abolishing the Church (cf. England's Henry VIII), Brother Kornhoer replaces the lamp with the crucifix, and the Thon departs in an atmosphere of strained, but determined politeness.

Perhaps the central science-fiction motif of Part Two, and of the novel as a whole, is the Thon himself, the one character in the whole book who stands unequivocally in favor of science, research, and speculation. Since he is also the only character concerning whose background we are given any specific information, we may find his single-

mindedness somewhat suspect. Illegitimate, but the only
heir of Hannegan's uncle, he was raised by Benedictine
monks, and not restored to his birthright until age fifteen,
from which time he excelled in learning, the one area in
which his rival the Prince was not adept. But whatever its
emotional source, and however unjustified we may regard his
conviction of its superiority over other viewpoints, a
detached, unemotional rationality is his key characteristic.
We see it accompanied by a cynical contempt for mankind in
general when we first meet Thon Taddeo in company with
Marcus Apollo, the papal nuncio to Hannegan's court. Chaf-
ing at the need for diplomacy with a fellow-intellectual,
Taddeo demonstrates a practical command of it, along with a
talent for languages and a tolerance for cultural differences, when next we see him among the savages of Mad Bear's
clan, whose political arrangements with Hannegan he chooses
to ignore, as long as they enable him to travel safely to
the Abbey. By the time he arrives there, we fully expect
him to deal politely with the monks, but skeptically with
their Memorabilia, as with their beliefs, and we can understand Dom Paulo's anxiety over what should be an occasion
for rejoicing, the rediscovery of the Order's papers by
someone who can understand them.

    Surprisingly enough, relations are fairly smooth for
most of his visit. The embarrassment caused by the light-
machine is dismissed, if not forgotten, and the political

tensions outside the monastery are not talked about; the
Thon's enthusiasm over the authenticity of the Memorabilia
is a comfort to Paulo, diminished only slightly by the
scholar's unhappiness at the documents' relative inaccessi-
bility. Paulo is so pleased that he coaxes Taddeo to give
a lecture to the community, and even hopes to get the Thon
to act politically, to do something about Hannegan's
officers who are mapping the Abbey's fortifications.
Despite the risk of failures in communication on both
sides--Taddeo fears the distortion of mathematical ideas in
lay language, and expects the resistance of religious
prejudice--the scholar agrees, setting the stage for a
festive, and embarrassing occasion.

In a well-constructed chapter, the Thon reveals the
nature of his researches and also, despite the formality of
the setting, the nature of his own character, therefore by
implication of the scientific mind in general. During the
dinner, the Poet embarrasses everyone by showing up, by
talking about the soldiers' sketches, and by direct and
indirect slurs on Taddeo's sense of responsibility. Each
of the three parts of the lecture has implications beyond
its surface: the Thon's amazement at his rediscoveries is
coupled with resentment that the Memorabilia were not
recognized before; his report on the research in which his
colleagues are involved offends Brother Armbruster, whose
outburst embarrasses the community; the conclusion of the

lecture, a prediction of change, unwilled, inevitably bringing suffering, earns Taddeo the silent scorn of Dom Paulo,
who sees what the Poet saw, an evasion of responsibility.
This insight, twice voiced, is underscored by another inter-
ruption, practically ending the speech and the chapter:
Benjamin, the old Jew, enters the hall, examines the Thon at
arm's length, and pronounces his judgment, "It's still not
Him" (p. 208).

The Thon, of course, had never claimed to be the
Messiah, and would have scorned the idea if it were broached
to him. The sense that he might be more than a man of
superior intellect was fostered by the involvement of
others, especially the desire on the part of Dom Paulo for
objective proof that his, and the Order's worldly occupation
was not in vain. Sharing Paulo's viewpoint throughout most
of the novelette, sharing the thoughts, insights, and
philosophy of only his mind, which is preoccupied with his
own doubts in the face of a gastric illness bringing him
close to death, the reader is required to make a difficult
judgment regarding the Thon. However much in favor of
reason and enlightenment, and opposed to superstition and
ignorance we may be, we tend to sympathize with the Abbot
over the savant.

Taddeo's attempt at bribing Kornhoer to come to
Texarkana, his absurd interpretation of R. U. R., and the
actions of his cousin, abolishing the Church and barbarously

murdering Marcus Apollo, merely confirm our judgment, so that we may overlook the significance of his farewell scene with the Abbot. The fact that their shaking hands is, in the Abbot's eyes, "no token of any truce but only of mutual respect between foes" (p. 227), represents a gain for the Church. The Thon is no longer actively contemptuous toward it and, while he promises nothing on their behalf, he has already performed one political act, in confiscating the sketches of the Abbey's fortifications. If he is not an ally, he is at least a determined neutral, and he seems to have learned something intangible, in terms of people, as well as to have filled his notebooks with practical, scientific knowledge.

The Thon is but one member of a well-drawn gallery of significant character in this novelette. The spirit of the age, which dominates Part One, and which plays an important role here, seems secondary to the individual persons, although their very individuality seems to be one of the cardinal features of the Renaissance era, as Miller envisions it. Kornhoer and Armbruster are not mere comic relief; their arguments stem from differing interpretations on how best to serve their God. Marcus Apollo, urbane, witty, even flippant, provides a good introduction to the court of Hannegan; Miller's choice of him for Hannegan to make an example of is calculated to wrench our emotions. Hongan Os, or Mad Bear, the nomad tribal chieftain, for all

his stereotyped bravado and ostentatious cunning, is seen as
"just and kindly" in his own cultural context, as was the
robbers' leader in Part One, and his cruelty and brutality,
perhaps because they are less effective and of narrower
scope, pale beside the barbarity of the supposedly civilized
leader whom we never meet, Hannegan.

The most important characters, however, after the
Thon and his opponent in argument, Dom Paulo, through whose
wise but ageing mind we see so much of what takes place,
are the Poet and the Jew. As representatives of art and
doubt, they widen the scope of the intellectual world from
what might otherwise be merely a debate between science and
faith. Each is involved in a confrontation with each of
the major disputants, but merely by their existence, being
the characters that they are, they provide a commentary on
the inadequacy of single categories of thinking to provide
answers to human problems.

The Poet, like the Thon, is creative and irresponsible; unlike the Thon, he knows he is irresponsible.
Playing the fool, he pricks the conscience of others; this
function of his is made especially clear by his clowning
with his artificial eye, the "removable conscience" which
he cedes to Thon Taddeo, who will have greater need of it.
Distrusting both religion and science, both the Church and
the State, he is nevertheless dependent upon one or the
other for patronage. Indeed, the Poet is somewhat more

committed to and affected by their values than he would have us believe. For all his sour cynicism and apparent isolated self-sufficiency, it is an act of senseless gallantry that gets him shot when, having left the Abbey, he happens upon some soldiers mutilating a girl refugee they have already killed. And when he is already dying, it is a sense of duty as much as it is annoyance which causes him to parody the role of a priest, i.e. to "absolve" the sadistic officer he has already mortally wounded, and on whose behalf he himself has been shot, by cutting his throat.

The old Jewish hermit, Benjamin Eleazar, also acts as a conscience, a passive and almost eternal one. He claims to have spoken with, and to have buried Brother Francis, during his "former career" as a "wanderer," and gives his age alternately as 3,209 and 5,408 years. Since the year is A.D. 3174, the first figure would make him at least a contemporary of Ahasuerus, the legendary "Wandering Jew," commanded by Christ to await his return; the second figure would make him as old as the Jewish people.[23] Dom Paulo prefers to believe that the Jew is merely identifying himself with his community (as Paulo identifies himself with

---

[23]The Creation is supposed to have taken place in 3761 B.C., according to Webster's (above, note 21), p. 2648, but Miller's character makes no claim to be as old as that. Five thousand four hundred eight years before 3174 A.D. would bring us to 2234 B.C., which is even earlier than Abraham, according to most scholarly estimates: Bernhard Anderson, Understanding the Old Testament (Englewood Cliffs, New Jersey, 1957), pp. 16-22.

his), but Miller provides us with enough impressions of the uncanny for us to see that in this fiction, at least, the Wandering Jew is a reality. Proud of his heritage, Benjamin is shrewd enough to compromise it, in difficult times; the basic invocation of Judaism stands by his house as it should, but it faces the wall rather than the outside world. Bearing a burden for all mankind, he shames the Abbot who comes to visit him and who finds it so difficult to bear his own individual burden. The hermit's mocking smile, so similar to the smile on the wooden statue of Saint Leibowitz in the Abbot's study, measures against bitter experiences of the past the desire of the Abbot, and of his times, to proclaim a new dawn, if not a new Messiah. That he may see for himself, the old Jew asks Paulo to bring the Thon by his hermitage; since the request is refused, Benjamin's visit to the Abbey, and the shock it produces, is motivated well in advance.

The strength of these characters, their dramatic confrontations, the philosophical focus provided by the Abbot's point-of-view, his dialogues, and his internal monologues, combine with other effective devices to make this story an excellent novelette, and a powerful midsection for the novel. The third section, like the first, has its own peculiar virtues, but the weight of the action and thought of the whole turns on this middle portion, where the powers and ideas dominant in the other eras meet as equals.

Part Three, "Fiat Voluntas Tuas," originally published as "The Last Canticle," is the shortest of the three parts, consisting of seven chapters and eighty-five pages. The scene is still Leibowitz Abbey, much the same after another 600 years, but having added an annex of modern buildings, including scientific laboratories, across the road which is now a six-lane "robot highway." The time is once again the beginning of an atomic war, from which the Church hopes, once again, to salvage something. While Brother Joshua, of the Order of Leibowitz, struggles with his conscience, trying to determine whether he is worthy to command the starship full of clergy and children which the Church is sending off to Earth's colony at Alpha Centauri, Abbot Jethrath Zerchi tries to keep alive a shred of religious teaching in this world, particularly that part of it which is collapsing near the Abbey. Zerchi's problems, which occupy the foreground of the novelette, include: Dr. Cors and the secular forces which seek to restrict the definition of evil to "pain," and to eliminate pain via euthanasia camps; Mrs. Grales, a two-headed crone who seeks baptism for her new head, "Rachel," trying to get "born"; the daily business of the Abbey; and perhaps most important of all, himself. Beaten at everything, Dom Jethrath finally comes to terms with himself when, trapped in the rubble of the bombed-out Abbey, he awaits death in extreme pain, receiving "last rites" from Rachel, who has at last emerged, unbaptized, to take over the body of Mrs. Grales. The last chapter, an epilogue, recounts briefly the departure of the ship which carries what hope for culture, civilization, and humanity the Church can offer, but which carries as well its share of doubt and fear, for all that the Wandering Jew and a decimated Earth are left behind.

The era and its futuristic technology being clearly identified with our own near future, barring catastrophe, this part of the novel is the most obviously science-fictional of the three. Compressed into a time span of only a few days, wherein all actions are dwarfed by the menace of total annihilation, limited to a few characters, superficially developed, and relying to a large extent on narrative gimmicks and science-fictional gambits, this novelette seems also the least effective composition of the three. As inevitable a sequel to Part Two, given Miller's cyclical view of history, as Part Two is a sequel to Part One, it seems nevertheless more random and arbitrary in the selection of scenes and actions that it displays.

The futuristic hardware, so unreassuringly familiar, includes robot highways, spaceships that have reached other planets, world-wide television relayed by artificial satellites, atomic weapons, and refined devices for measuring and predicting the weather. One machine, an electronic translator, Miller devotes several pages to; the failure of the "Abominable Autoscribe" to serve Abbot Zerchi provides the author with an opportunity for slapstick humor, at the same time that it introduces us to the hot temper of Dom Jethrath and to the feeling that man once again has become overly reliant on machines which he cannot control. Another machine, the atomic bomb, the Church refers to as "Lucifer," bent again on causing man to decree his own destruction. Another, the starship which carries away the pilgrims, is also a science-fictional cliché, but here it is viewed with some irony; like the blueprint and the light-machine of Parts One and Two, the starship seems an inefficient use of man's resources, involving as it does long hours and awkward methods for what may well be a meager result.

As endurance and the clash of wills provide the frameworks for Parts One and Two, fragmentation is the key to Part Three. Episodes are more or less peripherally related to one another, the scene changing jerkily within each chapter. Televised press conferences enter the Abbey in chapters 24 and 25, as Joshua is made acquainted with his task, Mrs. Grales and an old Jew named Lazarus are introduced, and the Abbot starts to face his own responsibilities. Chapter 26 mainly concerns Joshua's night of decision, and his departure for New Rome. Chapters 27 and 28 set Zerchi against Dr. Cors, who wins from the Abbot a young girl and her child, burned by radiation. Chapter 29 is the scene of Dom Jethrath's death, and of Rachel's birth,

while 30 is a detached epilogue. The motivation of persons'
actions is generally presented as selfish, even where it
appears to be altruistic or "for the good of the community."
Characters seem to avoid contact with each other, Joshua
with Mrs. Grales, Zerchi with Rachel, Dr. Cors with Zerchi,
Lazarus with the world. Even the machines, which can provide such efficient means of communication, transmit only
diplomatic exercises in non-communication, or they don't
work at all, e.g. the translator breaks down, the radio
transmitter of the Abbey is closed by the authorities.

The narrative form is also discontinuous, beginning
with a free verse poem, entering into two press conferences
reported in dialogue style, involving typographical tricks
in its demonstration of the automatic translator's failures,
and including letters, telegrams, and radio newscasts, as
well as the more conventional devices of debate and internal
monologue. What continuity there is in this world apparently lies in its connections with the past. Francis and
Leibowitz, Hannegan and Thon Taddeo (whom history has
confused with a colleague, Thon Esser Shon) are alluded to,
the wooden statue of Brother Fingo and a slim book of verse
by "Saint Poet of the Miraculous Eyeball" have survived
within the Abbey, an old Jew named Lazarus exists, whose
smile seems familiar, and names from our own history are
mixed into the stew as well. The most important reference
to history, repeated and dwelled upon by both Joshua and

Dom Jethrath, is the apparent conclusion that nothing is learned from history, that man is doomed to repeat his own mistakes over and over, including acts of self-annihilation.

But with death, in some cases, can come rebirth, the only hope held out for man by this third novelette. If there is an Abbot killed, and a Mrs. Grales must die, perhaps a Rachel may spring forth, embodying the Immaculate Conception, though she seems to grow out of the corruption of radiation-induced mutation and of fornication. If there is wholesale destruction in the world, and a Dr. Cors to ease the pain with voluntary death, there may also be a Brother Joshua to lead a tiny remnant to a promised land, much in the manner of his namesakes in the Old and New Testaments. The hope is slim, but it is all there is, if Miller is right about man's predilection to use power and knowledge destructively.

In such a doom-laden atmosphere, carrying such symbolic loads, it is not too surprising that the characters of Part Three are not well developed. Dr. Cors, polite but legalistic, a pacifist and an atheist, is little more than a symbol for the moral helplessness of science. Mrs. Grales-Rachel, though she is vividly described, is never allowed to show that she has a personality, in either guise; only the symbol, the suggestion, the obscurity remains. Brother Joshua, a low comedy caricature with his red beard and his propensity for bathing naked without making sure of his

privacy, is not perfectly convincing as the dedicated monk
who agrees, after long soul-searching, to accept command of
the starship. The only character developed at any length
is the Abbot, whose flaming temper seems to be matched in
intensity only by his fear of death and the uncertainty of
his belief, all of which we share at times from the inside.
His failures, to deal with machines, to communicate with
Lazarus, to overcome the arguments of the wounded young
girl, to withstand the power of Dr. Cors and of his own
temper (Zerchi punches the doctor in the nose), to baptize
Rachel, to face his own death (until he has seen in Rachel
the promise of resurrection), are failures of twentieth-
century man, and of man in general. He has no successes,
nor does mankind in Part Three, or perhaps in the whole of
A Canticle for Leibowitz.

Part Three in the novel varies considerably from the
magazine version. The press conferences, the episode of the
translation machine, the Abbot's tale of the mercy-killing
of his cat as an argument against euthanasia, the rejection
by Rachel of his baptism and her administration of last
rites are all additions to the original version. Many
episodes, paragraphs, and lines are completely rewritten,
or at least significantly revised, to reduce the melodramatic, telegraphed, too direct style and treatment of
characters, symbols, issues. Yet the whole does not fully
hang together, nor does the effect of fragmentation fully

succeed, so that we are left with a novelette which does not seem complete in itself, and which depends to a large extent upon its relationship to the total book for meaning and for success as a story.

The relationship between the three distinct stories is multifaceted, some elements remaining constant throughout, some being repeated with variations, some forming a continuous progression. Tone and style are fairly constant, allowing for deliberate variations and special effects, conveying the character of an omniscient narrator, whose sympathy for individuals and their plights is tinged with mild irony, an observer not completely detached, who is yet able to rationalize and explain, as well as to observe and report. The physical setting of most of the action, Leibowitz Abbey, is relatively constant, although even there, as outside, the phenomena of growth are in evidence. In keeping with the setting and the role of Churchmen as protagonists, the use of Church ritual and the Latin language is continuous. Each of the three parts in fact displays a pastiche of Church writing and of a significant ritual of its times: Part One finds Francis whispering "versicles from the Litany of the Saints" (pp. 26-27) and observing canonization ceremonies in New Rome; Part Two gives us the narrative of the Flame Deluge and the chanting which accompanies the rediscovery of light, as well as the relatively secular ritual of a public lecture; Part Three

opens "Versicles by Adam, Rejoinders by the Crucified"
(pp. 235-236), and presents Brother Joshua's ritual of soul-
searching, as well as the secular rituals of press conferences and news releases.

Each section has its Abbot as a major figure, with
his point-of-view being adopted by the narrator in Parts
Two and Three. Each section has a Wandering Jew, who may
be the same man under different names, identified by the
initials L Z, the names Benjamin and Eleazar, and the name
Lazarus in that order.[24] Besides sharing letters of his
name with the Abbey's Saint Leibowitz, the old Jew shares
the Saint's ethnic background, and has the same kind of
mocking smile as the wooden statue of the Saint carved in
Part One and occupying a featured place in the Abbots'
studies of Parts Two and Three. Each section has its
radiation-induced deformities, the blue-headed goat of Part
Two playing a rather small role in comparison with the band
of robbers in Part One and Mrs. Grales (not to mention her
six-legged dog Priscilla) in Part Three. Each section has
its buzzards, who feast on Brother Francis and on the Poet,
and who await the death of Abbot Zerchi; in the epilogues
to Parts One and Two, Miller offers a buzzard's-eye view of
the world as being intended for their nourishment and even
for their philosophical consideration, whereas the lone

---

[24]See Joseph Gaer, The Legend of the Wandering Jew
(New York, 1961).

buzzard of Part Three is wet and singed and presumably dying from radiation, and a shark, far out at sea, deep under water, and "very hungry that season" closes the final epilogue. Formal similarities between the novelettes include the repetition of a 600-year gap between the stories, the consistent use of epilogues, and the employment of a varied point-of-view. Although one character is at the center of consciousness for most of each story, some episodes, even whole chapters, involve a break with that point-of-view; each part has scenes in nature, scenes at court, an epilogue involving death which that character could not witness, making perfectly clear the narrator's role in arranging and juxtaposing the material presented to us.

Progression in time is indicated both within and between the chapters. The chapters are continuously numbered, and the action within them is handled in chronological order. All three eras share the same ancient history (the reader's real world), but they distort it somewhat. Fact and folklore tend to blend events, individuals, and institutions into a homogeneous past, even if professional historians try to guard against such distortion. This process is shown in operation not only in terms of our hypothetical future's remembrance of us, but also in terms of the assessment by each of these hypothetical eras of its predecessors in the novel. The whole pattern, kept in mind

for us by the narrator's choice of historical parallels, as
well as by philosophical observations made by his characters, is a pattern of history repeating itself, in essen-
tials rather than detail, as a result of a kind of racial
hybris. Miller's Dark Ages, Renaissance, and Age of Technology succeed each other not merely in time, but also in
growth, biological, sociological, and especially technological. The world outside the Abbey becomes progressively
larger, richer, and more powerful, as we see from glimpses
of its courts, its spread of civilization, even the growth
of population in the neighborhood of the Abbey, itself; the
town of Sanly Bowitts which interacts with the Abbey in
Part Two did not exist in Part One and has grown into a city
by the time of Part Three. Man's geographical dominance
expands progressively, even reaching other stars by Part
Three, and the contact of the Abbey and of the Church grows
with it. More area is involved in each novelette than in
its predecessor and, coupled with a reduction in the time-
span allotted to the action of the narrative, this expansion
of horizons results in a sense of increasing speed, of more
frenetic activity (however directed) with the passage of
years.

In each period, the level of scientific knowledge
and the rate of technological advance, i.e. the degree of
man's command over his environment is suggested as one of
the most important measures of a culture's status, even of

its identity. The narrator's sympathy for this view is apparent in Parts Two and Three, where he shows his own knowledge to technology and of technical terminology to be superior to that of his characters. The apparent cynicism of Part Three illustrates a bitterness over man's continued inability to control himself and his technology, but not an abandonment of the position that an increase in control over the environment is a good in itself. His intellectual commitment to the preservation and increase of scientific knowledge is not single-minded, however, nor is he blind to the defects of the amoral scientistic mentality. Thus he balances science against art, and doubt, and especially faith, in the form of characters in Part Two, as general modes of inquiry and forms of knowledge throughout, and sets the pattern of interrelationships against a backdrop of the centuries, of uninvolved nature, and of a blank and opaque universe.

The Order of Leibowitz is also committed to the expansion of knowledge, including but not restricted to scientific knowledge. And since we see almost everything from the viewpoint of the Abbots and monks of Leibowitz Abbey, we are involved with them in a curious, or perhaps rather a darkly ironic, contradiction of beliefs. As the level of scientific knowledge rises with the passage of time, a growth to which they are pledged, the balance of power changes drastically between secular and religious forces. Thus science and technology are put to use in the service of political power and, as in our own world, discoveries which are neutral in themselves are both good and evil in practical application.

This progression is underscored by the central image pattern of light. "Illumination" in Part One is an artistic process, used anonymously to glorify, for religious reasons, the presumed maker of a blueprint which no one living can read or understand ("make light of"). The age is far from "enlightened" about its past, or about the knowledge possessed by the people of that past, mere remnants of which are retained. The unimportance of the blueprint as a conveyor of information is stressed by Brother Francis' discovery of the fact that its color scheme is arbitrary and accidental, making it possible for him to reverse the pattern of "light on dark," much as time has reversed man's relationship to the vast unknown. "Light" in Part Two is a technical process, a symbol for knowledge, and a symbol of desecration. Brother Kornhoer's light-machine brilliantly illuminates the dark alcove of the library which holds the Memorabilia, in order that Thon Taddeo may be able to read, understand, and take advantage of what no one has been able to comprehend for centuries. The charge of desecration, which Brother Armbruster levels at the inventor, is perhaps not meant to be taken seriously, but Dom Paulo calls the brilliance of the lamp "hellish," and the monk who checks the spark yells "Lucifer!" as he leaps back from it in the middle of the ceremony which attends the machine's introduction to the Abbot and the Thon. And Taddeo is "enlightened" only in a narrow, secular, scientific sense, not in terms of faith, morality, or personal responsibility. Taddeo's description of Kornhoer's light as "bright as a thousand torches" (p. 185), recalls descriptions of the H-Bomb in our world as "brighter than a thousand suns." Appropriately enough, the nuclear weapons of Part Three are referred to as Lucifer, thus identifying them with light (they are an end-product of centuries of "enlightened" research), with the evening star (Venus, goddess of love, but also a symbol of twilight, and of approaching death), and with a certain archetypal dark angel (who fell through pride, like that which man displays in his own power, in his own reason, and in himself). But even in Part Three, light is not totally denigrated, as we see from Brother Joshua's meditation on fire as he keeps his vigil, making up his mind to accept the role allotted him:

> Someone had opened the abbey doors. Monks were leaving quietly for their cells. Only a dim glow spilled from the doorway into the courtyard. The light was dim in the church. Joshua could see only a few candles and the dim red eye of the sanctuary lamp. The twenty-six of his brethren [who would also be on the starship] were just visible where they knelt, waiting. Someone closed the doors again, but not quite for through a crack he could still see the red dot of the sanctuary lamp. Fire kindled in worship, burning in praise, burning gently in adoration there in its red receptacle. Fire, loveliest of the four elements of the world, and yet an element too in Hell.

While it burned adoringly in the core of the Temple,
it had also scorched the life from a city, this
night, and spewed its venom over the land.   How
strange of God to speak from a burning bush, and of
Man to make a symbol of Heaven into a symbol of Hell.
(p. 273)

How strange of God to speak at all, the context sug-

gests, as Brother Joshua hears a slithering sound, which may

issue from a snake (in the garden, of course), and inter-

prets it as an omen from God at the same time that he throws

a rock at it. How foolish of man, from some perspectives,

to make a symbol of things that do not exist, and yet how

typical. For all of Miller's irony and satire, his sympa-

thies are clearly with the monks, who at least have some-

thing to believe in and, believing in it, behave like decent

human beings. The rituals of the Church, for all that they

may be perfectly useless in any objective sense, do at least

offer subjective comfort, uniting men in hope and brother-

hood, even in the face of death and annihilation. The

progression of titles of the novelettes shows what hope, and

what little hope, the Church can offer. Fiat Homo, "let

there be man," is a plea for survival, for a chance to do

something "worthwhile." Fiat Lux, "let there be light,"

echoes God's command in Genesis, and suggests the inevita-

bility of the rise in secular learning. Finally, Fiat

Voluntas Tuas, "(let) thy will be done," with its echoes of

Christ's acquiescence to death, suggests an abandonment of

any hope that man, without any reference point outside

himself, can guide his own destiny.

From this religious or quasi-religious viewpoint, secular forces, including empirical science, must be regarded as having failed man, not just once (the nuclear holocaust in our own immediate future) but twice (the total disaster of Part Three). Power, with regard to people as well as environment, seems to beget only more power; the growth of society demands ever more growth; science recognizes as goals only the acquisition of more knowledge, and the perfection of more tools and techniques to obtain it. The growth of science and technology seems to lead to a more mechanized way of living and thinking, whereby society as a whole becomes more or less scientistic. Empirically, like Dr. Cors, it recognizes only pain as being "evil"; relativistically, it recognizes no values except its own aggrandizement, like Hannegan and by implication the political blocs of the thirty-eighth century; deterministically, it follows the "inevitable" path of growth and destruction suggested by Thon Taddeo.

But for all of its dangers, the scientific world-view seems to appeal to Miller, intellectually, in this novel. His language is often technical or quasi-technical, and he assumes a superiority to his characters not only in terms of technological training, but also in terms of his grand perspective overlooking the centuries, quite similar

to that of John Campbell's "Universe-Directed" scientist.[25]
The time spanned by the whole, the irony directed at
characters whose command of history is weak, as is their
ability to distinguish between history and folklore, the
historical allusions contained in characters' names, apparently unknown to them, all these suggest the narrator's
role as a historian, a kind of social scientist. But the
view of man as a creature subject to natural laws (much as
the buzzards are), about which he can dispute (much as the
buzzards do), but which can be determined and plotted in
terms of arithmetical and geometrical progressions, involves
theory as well as the observation and selection of materials
necessary for history. The theory involved is at least
agnostic, if not atheistic, positing no knowable God or
meaning in the universe and eternity which form the backdrop
for this mere 1,800 years of narrative. From this perspective, both science and religion are inadequate in themselves
to supply man with knowledge and to guide his conduct. And
indeed it is not merely the irony of historicism with which
the Wandering Jew views the world and its happenings that
causes Miller to hold up almost everything he describes to
a kind of melancholy ridicule.

It may be that the Poet's "slim volume of verse"
which Dom Jethrath Zerchi reads in Part Three contains a

---

[25]John W. Campbell, Jr., "Science Fiction and the
Opinion of the Universe," Saturday Review, May 12, 1956,
pp. 9-10, 42-43.

clue to the meaning of the novel:

> The book was a satirical dialogue in verse between
> two agnostics who were attempting to establish by
> natural reason alone that the existence of God could
> not be established by natural reason alone. They
> managed only to demonstrate that the mathematical
> limit of an infinite sequence of "doubting the cer-
> tainty with which something doubted is known to be
> unknowable when the 'something doubted' is still a
> preceding statement of 'unknowability' of something
> doubted," that the limit of this process at infinity
> can only be equivalent to a statement of absolute
> certainty, even though phrased as an infinite series
> of negations of certainty. The text bore traces of
> St. Leslie's theological calculus, and even as a
> poetic dialogue between an agnostic identified only
> as "Poet" and another only as "Thon," it seemed to
> suggest a proof of the existence of God by an epis-
> temological method, but the versifier had been a
> satirist; neither poet nor don relinquished his
> agnostic premises after the conclusion of absolute
> certainty had been reached, but concluded instead
> that: Non cogitamus, ergo nihil sumus. (p. 289)

This passage about a satire is itself a satire of theolog-

ical disputation, of mathematical-scientific means of

reaching a decision, and of poetry and literary criticism,

and suggests that Miller, too, in A Canticle for Leibowitz,

is denying the reader any "conclusion of absolute cer-

tainty." Although he appears to be sympathetic toward all

of the characters with whom he deals, he also views them

all with a sense of irony suggesting they are all agnostics;

those religious persons whom we see going beyond mere fear

and ritual in their thinking are doubters, as all the non-

religious persons appear to be. Miller's irony does not

stop there; it comes out also in events (and their misinter-

pretation), in situations (some of which are broadly

humorous), even in phrases (where puns and comic allusions

frequently lurk). In some cases, since the various perspectives adopted (religion, science, history, art, eternal skepticism) tend to subsume each other, the irony cuts two ways (or more). As we saw was the case with the blueprint, and with the light-machine, the Poet's book of verse, seen from other perspectives, has its serious meaning as well.

Although the Poet's book, according to Miller's description, satirizes theology, science, and poetry, it may be that it treats them as mistakes, due to human limitations, but mistakes which are accepted, because of the limited viewpoint of isolated disciplines, as Truth. This interpretation would seem to bring the Poet's book into alignment with Miller's book, in which each discipline is seen as inadequate from others' perspectives. Taken at all seriously, the Poet's book asserts not only the impossibility of knowing, or of proving God in any objective manner, but also the necessity of using whatever tools we have-- observation, reason, mathematics, science--however faulty their approximation to truth may be, in order to know anything at all. In other words, man may be doomed to fail ultimately at whatever he attempts, but he is also doomed (or destined) to keep trying.

The Poet's book stops at the nihilistic positions arrived at (and also started from) by two individuals. Miller's book carries the problem of knowledge further, into its relationship with society, culture, the community.

Society may be ignorant and blind, but without its support
and transmission of culture, each individual would be
totally ignorant and uncomprehending. And whatever knowledge an individual may be able to arrive at is likely to be
passed on only by those who care, i.e. a community of like-
minded persons. Such a community, caring even for that
knowledge which they do not understand, is the Albertian
Order of Leibowitz, but some kind of community, or subculture, stands behind the characters outside the Church, as
well. The process of transmission is perhaps best seen at
work within the monastic community where, theoretically at
least, problems of sex, family, and biological inheritance
do not complicate what is essentially a matter of the
intellect. Verbal and mathematical language, and to an
extent the lines and shapes of art, in relatively permanent
form (i.e. capable of enduring generations, perhaps
centuries), communicate from mind to mind what best (and
worst) approximations of truth individuals are capable of.
And a monastic community, which cannot breed its successors,
can only survive and perpetuate itself through education,
appealing to individuals through their mental faculties.

Biological survival by mankind may come first, but
once it is assured (as in Parts One and Three), the purely
cultural phenomenon of the community (even anti-biological
in the case of religious orders) is needed to safeguard what
knowledge is needed for cultural survival. This at least

would appear to be the theory accounting for the establishment of the Order of Leibowitz, before Miller's novel begins, and for its mission to the colonies on other worlds, as the novel ends. In keeping with the satiric intent of the Poet's book, however, Miller's book also implies that the theory is flawed, that mankind as a whole does not want the kind of knowledge that the Church has to offer, and that a tiny remnant at best is all that the Church can ever salvage from the ruins of civilization.

The Poet's book also suggests another level of interpretation. Miller writes that "Abbot Zerchi soon tired of trying to decide whether the book was high intellectual comedy or more [mere?] epigrammatic buffoonery" (p. 289). But neither the Abbot nor the narrator suggests that the book is not poetry, i.e. not entertaining and aesthetically pleasing. Clearly, A Canticle for Leibowitz is entertaining and aesthetically pleasing, whatever interpretation we may give to its philosophical content.

As an entertainment, the novel is a story, or three stories, about people, about their joys and pleasures, about their thoughts, and about their personal struggles, with their faith, with their environment, with themselves. At this level, the reader is made to feel such things as survival, discovery, and frustration, which bulk so large in the intellectual content of the book, even as the comic effects amuse him and predispose him to sympathy with the characters. The comedy, however, and the irony congruent with the narrator's vast perspective make it nearly impossible to identify with the characters, leading us more toward a position of relating ourselves intellectually, to their philosophical stances, and to the oblique historical parallels with our own past and present. The characters, themselves, seem to find complete commitment to an idea difficult to achieve, however strongly they may be shown as wanting to believe in it, and their relatively cerebral involvement is reinforced by the narrator's rationality and perspective.

The typically science-fictional tendency to involve the head before the heart is evident in Miller's style, too, which is entertaining in the way that cultured, intelligent conversation is. Seldom startling, his style is witty, yet relatively formal, and distinctive enough to maintain an aesthetic distance between reader and story, encouraging critical observation and appreciation. Although the directness, obviousness, and simplification of pulp style had not been blatant in the original versions of the novelettes, Miller added dignity to his revised narrative by means of longer sentences, more sonorous rhythms, and less use of colloquial diction. Specialized words from technology and theology were already in frequent use in the earlier versions, as were words and sentences from foreign languages, from Latin of course, but also from Hebrew (in

Hebrew script, the English translation of which is given),
with an additional snatch of German to bring us into the
industrial totalitarianism of Part Three. The net effect is
a certain measure of weight and seriousness and scope,
contributing to the narrator's air of omniscience but also
to the dignity of the characters, whose speeches often seem
somewhat elevated and self-conscious. From the perspective
of the centuries, dignity may seem a bit incongruous for
such puny and even comic figures, but within each story,
some characters manage to stand out, as if to decree their
own significance on a purely human scale of values.

The mixture of comedy and weightiness which penetrates so much of the book is visible also on the symbolic
level. The allegorical identification of Miller's three
eras with eras in Western civilization suggests a certain
solidity which we associate with historic grandeur. The
allegory also impresses upon us the idea that these are
representative men and times about which we are reading.
But the disparity between Miller's relatively simple men
and the inflated figures of history, and between his relatively uneventful narratives and the supposedly grand
movements of history is essentially comic, a sympathetic
but knowing commentary on the difference between aspirations
and achievements.

Similarly, the allusiveness of their names suggests
an additional dimension to some of Miller's characters, at

the same time that it suggests a reassessment of the reference figure's image. Brother Francis is gentle, obedient,
and devout, but unlike Saint Francis of Assisi he founds no
order, receives no stigmata (unless we so regard the arrow
through the skull from which he dies), and seems an
extremely simple man, almost a simpleton. Dom Paulo is no
great theoretician or organizer, as was Saint Paul, yet he
may be said to have given new direction to the Church, or
at least the Abbey, by encouraging active relations with
secular scholars. Brother Joshua is clearly to be identified with the Old Testament Joshua, who led his people into
a promised land, as well as with Christ, whose Hebrew name
is also Joshua. His struggle with himself in the Abbey's
garden over whether to accept the role thrust on him recalls
Jesus' night in the Garden of Gethsemane, but his relationship with Dom Jethrath parallels that of Joshua to Moses,
whose father-in-law's name (Jethro) is similar to the
Abbot's. With Mrs. Grales-Rachel, the symbolism of the
names essentially serves to deepen the mystery about her,
combining the mystical significance of the Holy Grail with
that of the Immaculate Conception. The name of the second,
and more beloved wife of the Old Testament patriarch Jacob,
in order to marry whom he labored a second seven years for
the bride-price, may suggest that man (or perhaps the
Church, the "bride" of Christ) will be more beloved of God
after this second "resurrection"; a secondary allusion could

be intended to the ship that rescues Ishmael in <u>Moby-Dick</u>,
"the devious-cruising Rachel, that in her retracing search
after her missing children, only found another orphan."[26]

In the case of certain other names, the allusions
seem to be exploited more for puns or rather localized and
humorous symbolism. Marcus Apollo and Brother Claret,
whose names suggest sophistication, even voluptuousness,
are emissaries from the Church to the neo-Renaissance court
of Hannegan II. The name of the postulant for Beatus
Leibowitz, Aguerra, connoting war, is hardly less intimidat-
ing than that of the devil's advocate, Flaught, with its
connotation of flogging. Brother Fingo, who sculpts the
wooden statue of Leibowitz, bears a name which means in
Latin, "to make or form," and old Brother Horner, the master
copyist under whom Francis serves, vaguely suggests the old
nursery rhyme figure, Little Jack Horner, in that the monk
may be thought to "sit in a corner" where he does his work,
and that he "pulls out a plum" in getting Francis as an
apprentice. Cors, suggesting "body" and "corpse," is the
name of a doctor who abhors pain (that which the body finds
evil) prescribes euthanasia, and faces the "wrath" of the
Abbot Jeth<u>rath</u> Zerchi. A rather elaborate pun on the
figures of Cain and Abel seems intended by the contrast in
Part Two between Brother Armbruster, whose name means

---

[26]Herman Melville, <u>Moby-Dick</u> (Signet Classic
edition, New York, Toronto, and London, 1961), p. 536.

"crossbow" and suggests "hunter" (Abel was a hunter), and Brother Kornhoer, whose name suggests "farmer" (Cain was a farmer) and whose activities are branded as desecrations by the librarian (his spiritual "brother"). And an excellent play on words is implicit in the name of the town near the Abbey, Sanly Bowitts, a justifiable linguistic corruption of Saint or San Leibowitz.

The structural design of the book has an almost geometric simplicity. Historical movements are treated as direct progressions, such as could be plotted on a graph, if history could be resolved into a science; seeing this pseudo-history fulfill its implications creates the same essentially "aesthetic" effect as observing a successful experiment demonstrate the validity of its hypothesis. The linear progressions, the cycles, and the repetitions with variations by means of which this pseudo-history advances are too smoothly continuous to correspond to actual history, except where it is treated in a highly abstract and compressed manner, and indeed they relate quite closely to the progressions, cycles, and repetitions of formal fictional elements, which are clearly aesthetic devices. The framework, too, the three "horizontal" patterns, the four "representative" philosophical viewpoints explicitly raised in Part Two but implicit throughout, and the surrounding frame of the narrator's Olympian perspective, has a highly abstract and even geometric quality to it. The four "philosophies," represented by individual characters and presented in debate, while they are indicative of man's variety, are only a highly abstracted selection of human predilections, and they achieve a balance with respect to each other that would be hard to duplicate outside of an artistic framework. Geometry, like extrapolation in general, can only supply the outlines; artistry, feeling, and thought are evident in the shading between the lines, the people and their problems, the style and the wit, as we have observed.

Through everything, of course, as in the Poet's book, runs a kind of laughter, although it is not the same bitter, sardonic laughter as that which the Poet displays in Part Two, and which presumably causes Abbot Zerchi to dismiss the book of verse as little more than satire. Irony is a major tool of both writers, but the Poet's irony is more limited, more personal, more intent on destructive criticism, and related to a sense of outrage that the world should be as it is. The irony of Miller's narrator is to a great extent the irony of vast perspective, against which personal outrage would be rather out of place. Miller's humor involves more than irony, however; his style is witty, his characters are sympathetically treated for all their bumbling, and his approach is intellectual rather than sentimental. His people have little to be thankful for or to look forward to, but they find joy in simple tasks and meaning in greater ones, and they delight as much in contemplation as they do in playfulness. The author too appears to delight in little things, in puns and comic allusions, in episodes of slapstick, in dramatic effects of confrontation, discovery, and anticlimax.

Humor of any kind is relatively rare in science fiction, with the exception of what James Blish terms "the painful traveling-salesman banter which passes back and forth over real drawing-boards and spec sheets."[27] Perhaps because the scientist-author or the scientist-hero sees the world rigidly in terms of weights and measures and lines of force, perhaps because he is so busy seeking immediate solutions to mundane problems that he can't see himself from the perspective of anyone else, an even rarer occasion in science fiction is the evocation of the "comic spirit."[28] All the more to be appreciated, then, is the achievement of Walter M. Miller, Jr., for, in A Canticle for Leibowitz, he

[27]Blish (above, note 14), pp. 64-65. See also: L. Sprague de Camp, "Humor in Science Fiction," in Of Worlds Beyond: The Science of Science-Fiction Writing, ed. Lloyd Arthur Eschbach (Reading, Pennsylvania, 1957; reprinted Chicago, 1964), pp. 69-76; Martin Gardner, "Humorous Science Fiction," Writer, May, 1949, pp. 148-151.

[28]The book is, of course, "serious" or "high" comedy for the most part, although there are also pratfalls and slapstick, and throughout, there is the sense of "comic" perspective. See the essays by George Meredith, Henri Bergson, and Wylie Sypher in Comedy, ed. Wylie Sypher (Garden City, 1956). See also the discussions of "comedy," "irony," and "ironic comedy" in Northrop Frye, Anatomy of Criticism (Princeton, 1957), especially pp. 43-49, 177-181, 225-236.

has written a genuine comic novel. In doing so, however,
he has not written a work of "pure" science fiction; rather,
he has incorporated into his novel much of what is valuable
in science fiction and discarded much that is worthless for
his purposes. In other words, it would be more accurate to
say about A Canticle for Leibowitz that it uses science
fiction than to say that it is science fiction.

CHAPTER VII

ALGIS BUDRYS: ROGUE MOON (1960)

Author of well over one hundred stories and longer
works of science fiction since his first was published in
1952, Algis Budrys has also published other kinds of commercial fiction, and has, in addition, worked for several years
in the production and marketing areas of publishing.[1] Thus
it is not surprising that in his recent book review columns
for Galaxy he has emphasized the following facts: books are
products for sale, publishing is a business, rates of pay
are low, and writers need to be prolific and aware of the
market in order to make a living.[2] Making due allowance for
these conditions, however, Budrys has not accepted them as
excuses for inadequacy. And, although he has admitted the
impossibility of ever discovering absolute, objective

---

[1]See MIT Index and supplements (above, Chapter I,
note 35) for bibliographical data. Some biographical data
are available in Contemporary Authors, II (1963), and passing mention of some is made in Damon Knight, In Search of
Wonder: Essays on Modern Science Fiction, rev. ed.
(Chicago, 1967), pp. 199-203.

[2]Algis Budrys, "Galaxy Bookshelf," Galaxy, every
issue since February, 1965 (bimonthly to June, 1968, monthly
since then). See especially February, 1966, pp. 131-133.

criteria for quality in literature, Budrys has nevertheless maintained certain definite standards for the books he reviews. Giving credit to Damon Knight and to James Blish for the positive results of their essentially "destructive" criticism, Budrys has attempted, rather successfully, to continue in their tradition.[3]

Aware of the necessity for the writer of commercial fiction to create a "pocket universe" (in the words of Murray Leinster) in which the world is or gives promise of becoming comprehensible, Budrys demands that it be created with style, intelligence, and a feeling for both life and structure.[4] Not the least necessary of the parts, "good prose," he sees as an element which limits the author's audience and tends to become itself an object of worship by overly "literary" writers, yet he expects it and differentiates between those who can and cannot write "as writing is understood by three main types of literary specialists-- teachers of composition, literary critics and the other working professional writers who provide the day-in, day-out reading matter for the fiction audience."[5] On the other hand, in science fiction, he is aware of the necessary factors which distinguish it from other kinds of writing:

---

[3]On Blish, see Galaxy, June, 1965, pp. 168-169; on Knight, see Galaxy, December, 1967, pp. 187-189.

[4]On the "pocket universe," see Galaxy, June, 1966, pp. 141-142.

[5]Galaxy, August, 1965, p. 186.

"ingenuity"; "hard thought about a thing"; and the need, prior to writing, "to have created and resolved a speculative situation in his head."[6] In addition, there are the major qualities he can praise in a rather mediocre novel: "there is the melding of actual science with an author's counter-hypothesis that amplifies and romanticizes it, and there is the reader's growing sense of grasping something grand."[7] Most of all, however, Budrys requests that a writer of science fiction be a "storyteller," a term which he defines at length:

> A storyteller is someone with the gift of involving his audience closely in an adventure with a beginning, middle and clear-cut ending which logically and satisfactorily fulfills the promise of the preceding parts. To be a storyteller, a writer must be able to not only pose a real-sounding problem involving people or things worth saving, he must also be able to solve it or show that there is no solution for very good reasons.
>
> By the rules played in these pages, neatness counts. The writer is not allowed to bring in moral judgments, what "everyone knows" about the condition of the world or dogma of any sort. His characters may of course believe in these things, or they would not seem like people; but no individual who sets out to create a pocket universe is allowed the luxury of evading his responsibility behind a bunch of mere words, no matter how skillfully spoken or how comforting their message. He is very definitely, as you can see, allowed to solve problems, and it is by this trait that he is most readily distinguishable from some of his cousins in the Word game.[8]

---

[6]Galaxy, October, 1968, p. 170.

[7]Galaxy, February, 1965, p. 159.

[8]Galaxy, August, 1966, pp. 190-191.

And, by his own criteria, Budrys sees a definite reflection
of progress or improvement in science fiction from its
earliest days as a commercial publishing field.[9] Even
measured against the whole of science fiction, not just
relative to any single year, he singles out for special
praise new writers--Roger Zelazny, Samuel Delany, Brian
Aldiss, J. G. Ballard--because they are more in touch with
the real world, and in love with words but not to the
exclusion of story and intelligence, although he gives
credit to their predecessors, too (most notably Philip K.
Dick, Walter Miller, and Fritz Leiber).[10] Delany
especially, Budry claims, "operates on a plane which Robert
Heinlein never dreamed of, nor John W. Campbell, Jr., nor--
take a deep breath--Ted Sturgeon, Ray Bradbury or anyone
else we could have put forward as being a poet a mere five
or six years ago."[11]

Budrys' judgments may or may not be vindicated,
eventually, but they are certainly of value in dealing with
the man's own writings. Although they follow by at least
thirteen years his first published fiction, they can't be
too far from the opinions he had in the 1950s when his
stories were frequently rated poorly in the monthly reader
poll conducted by Astounding, to some extent perhaps because

---

[9]Galaxy, October, 1966, p. 158.

[10]Galaxy, October, 1967, pp. 192-194.

[11]Galaxy, October, 1967, p. 193.

they were too literary.[12]

Besides over a hundred stories (some of them published under the pseudonyms Ivan Janiver, Paul Janvier, William Scarff, John A. Sentry, and Albert Stroud), Algis Budrys has written at least seven science fiction novels which have seen magazine and paperback publication.[13] In each case, he has attempted to center his science and fiction on some human problem, frequently posed in psychological or sociological terms and handled somewhat melodramatically. Some Will Not Die (1961; published in part 1953 and 1954) sets up a dialectical opposition between absolute individualism and social restraint or cooperation on an earth devastated by plague. Man of Earth (1958; revised from a 1956 magazine version) concerns the process of psychological change in a man given a new, stronger body,

---

[12]Of twenty-eight stories published in Astounding/ Analog from November, 1952, to September, 1959, only two were ever ranked as high as second-best by readers' votes: "Citadel," February, 1955, the vote tabulation being given in "The Analytical Laboratory," June, 1955, p. 103; "The Executioner," January, 1956, reported on in "The Analytical Laboratory," April, 1956, p. 144. A large number of Budrys' stories finished last, and one possible reason is that they tended to deal with personal and emotional ramifications of individual, already established science fictions. "The Analytical Laboratory," appearing as close to monthly as publication space permits, is compiled by the editor, John W. Campbell, Jr.; winners of first and second places each month receive bonus payments, a policy first announced in the April, 1953, issue, p. 147.

[13]Stories listed under these names in the MIT Index (above, Chapter I, note 35) also appear in collections of Budrys' stories: The Unexpected Dimension (New York, 1960); Budrys' Inferno (New York, 1963).

set against a melodramatic plot in a background of war and
space exploration. Who? (1958) takes a scientist "repaired"
with metal parts and probably brainwashed by the Soviets,
and makes of him a symbol of loss of identity, in a kind of
satirical tirade against the Cold War. The Falling Torch
(1962; published in part 1958 and 1959) seems to be an
allegory of Budrys' own dream-wish of going back to rescue
his native Lithuania, disguised as Earth conquered by the
"Invaders." His latest, The Amsirs and the Iron Thorn
(1967; Budrys prefers the title, The Iron Thorn, given the
1966-67 magazine serial), is about "growing up" and losing
contact with one's past training and prejudices except as
reminiscences, but the story seems a confused melange of
adventure, rites of passage, accidental heroism on one world
(apparently Mars, settled and then forgotten), and dystopian
disappointment on another (Earth, somewhat as Wells imagined
it in The Time Machine).

His most complex and ambitious novel, generally
regarded as his best, is Rogue Moon (1960), a book about a
"hero" and a "scientist" who conquer an alien artifact on
the moon, with the help of a machine which itself subtly
destroys the conquerors. Published in paperback only, it
was highly praised in the few places where it was
reviewed.[14] Analog's P. Schuyler Miller called it "one of

[14]A shorter version of the novel also appeared,
just before the book publication: Algis Budrys, "Rogue
Moon," F&SF, December, 1960, pp. 5-38, 78-125.

the best science-fiction novels of 1961, [sic] and a sign-
post to where the field may be going," and referred back to
it in 1968 as "unforgettable."[15] Galaxy's Floyd C. Gale,
brusque with paperbacks, summed up Rogue Moon in five words:
"Spectacular invention, plot and characterization."[16] F&SF,
which had published the magazine version, gave the book two
reviews. Critic-in-residence Alfred Bester wrote that "Mr.
Budrys has come very close to realizing our ideal of science
fiction, the story of how human beings may be affected by
the science of the future."[17] Guest reviewer James Blish
was quite thorough and technical in his appreciation, offering numerous insights and complimenting Budrys for his
ability to learn and grow in his writing as well as for
"writing a work which epitomizes everything he has ever had
to offer us."[18] Five years after publication, the novel
was given notice by Kingsley Amis, in a survey of recent
science fiction for Holiday. Amid praise for Ballard,
Miller, Frederik Pohl and Poul Anderson, Amis commends
Budrys for being able "to move between different levels,"

---

[15]Review by P. Schuyler Miller, Analog, June, 1961,
p. 164. See also Miller's review of The Amsirs and the
Iron Thorn, Analog, October, 1968, pp. 164-165.

[16]Review by Floyd C. Gale, Galaxy, February, 1962,
p. 194.

[17]Review by Alfred Bester, F&SF, June, 1961,
pp. 104-105.

[18]Review by James Blish, F&SF, June, 1961,
pp. 105-109.

specifically referring to the book's three themes: adventure and exploration, the nature of courage, and the relationship of death and human identity.[19] For the most part, however, the novel was ignored outside the science fiction media, a situation predictable because of the low esteem in which science fiction as such is held by the literary public but a situation unfortunate since this is an honest attempt at writing a novel specifically science-fictional in form, and an attempt which largely succeeds, on its own terms.

Rogue Moon is a novel of about 55,000 words, divided into nine chapters, alternately long and short, the long ones being still further subdivided.[20] These breaks are fairly important, since it is partly through juxtaposition, parallels, and contrasts that Budrys attempts to integrate three separate stories, and to give different meanings to a scientific effort at overcoming death.

The central plot concerns an attempt by the Navy in 1959 to explore, on the dark side of the moon, a mysterious structure in which several men have lost their lives. In the absence of spaceships sophisticated enough for a major supply maneuver, they have taken advantage of a machine,

---

[19]Kingsley Amis, "Science Fiction: A Practical Nightmare," Holiday, February, 1965, p. 15.

[20]Algis Budrys, Rogue Moon (Greenwich, Connecticut, 1960). All page references in text refer to this paperback edition.

not yet perfected, which can duplicate and transmit elec-
tronically even men and complicated machinery. By means of
an apparent telepathic contact between the human duplicates
here and on the moon, Dr. Edward Hawks, the machine's inventor, hopes to make it possible for the "twin" on earth to
retain memories of his alternate's exploration of the
structure before the latter's death. Once a man has been
found who can stand to "die" again and again without going
mad, Hawks's technique works. The structure proves to be
explorable and sufficient descriptive detail is amassed that
subsequent exploration teams may be able to survive the
ordeal, but not the slightest understanding of the structure
is achieved.

Sharing the odd-numbered chapters with the main
story, the secondary plot revolves around Al Barker, the
compulsive daredevil who accomplishes this conquest of
death, and it is aimed at showing the kind of man who would
volunteer for, and survive repeated subjective death, and
what effect this experience might have on such a man. One
answer, or set of data, is offered by the man himself, whose
cocky self-appraisals and histrionic capabilities fail to
cover an increasingly fanatical preoccupation with the quest
and his success. Additional data emerge from Hawks's
contact with Barker's personal life, a tangle of love-hate
relationships fit for a "true romances" novelette. Barker,
his mistress, Claire Pack, and his pander, Vincent

Connington, have achieved a precarious balance in their social relationship. By introducing the inscrutable Hawks as a new factor, Connington upsets this balance, and Barker, partly because of the physiological and psychological effects of his new job, can neither restore the old, nor achieve a new equilibrium. Eventually Connington takes Claire away, resulting in Barker's transferring the focus of his energies to Hawks and the project, and to some extent in upon himself.

The third "plot" is a sentimental love-story involving Hawks and Elizabeth Cummings, a girl he meets by chance, who happens to like listening to him as much as he likes to talk. Their romance, the beginning of which is Platonic and the consummation of which lies beyond the confines of the novel, exists primarily to show the kind of man Hawks is, and why he is the kind of man who would send other men to death or insanity in quest of a phantom. Disconnected from the main narratives, since it is described only in the even-numbered chapters, this sequence offers an equally adolescent alternative to the devouring love of Barker and Claire, and it also provides an idyllic perspective of more or less normal human experience, against which to measure the whole project and Hawks's involvement in it.

As the science fiction plot supplies the novel with a center, without which the other stories would have no justification for existence, so the science fictions of the novel, both as surface realities and as symbolic constructs, predominate over all other aspects. Plots and characters are manipulated to achieve symbolic acts, poses, and confrontations suggested by the basic conceptions of the exploration and the two men who accomplish it. Style and characterization seldom, however, rise above the minimal clichés needed to propel the science fiction reader from incident to loaded incident; the reader may be asked to solve some intellectual puzzles, but he is rarely led to respond emotionally to the persons engaged in the action, including the featureless narrator. Where concessions are made to aesthetic form and artistic sensibility, a mechanical design is intimated; the intricate structure, the occasional snatches of style approaching poetry, the occasional references to art and the "whole man," suggest the geometrical sketch or outline of an artwork that might emerge from a mind totally trained in the sciences. Yet the novel has a sense of coherence, and even a sort of power, partly because of the bare bones of its construction, partly because of the unemotional pseudo-intellectualism of its scientist-hero, and partly because of the awe accorded its central symbolic construct, the alien artifact on the moon.

Each of the novel's three basic science fictions has a long history in the field. The treatment of telepathy has ranged from relatively realistic appraisals of its limitations, assuming its existence, to utopian and dystopian explorations of its ultimate potential. Fantasies of wish-fulfillment seem to have dominated, although practical speculation has not been lacking, and the whole area of e.s.p. has been overused perhaps in recent years. The matter transmitter or duplicator, which in real life may, like e.s.p., be simulated by illusionists and charlatans, has also assumed the status of a reality in science fiction, frequently functioning as the ultimate in transportation. Its use and misuse, its functioning and malfunctioning have been assumed as mere background, examined analytically, and employed for various effects from melodrama to black humor. The alien artifact found on the moon, the earth, or another planet is another hoary convention, signifying at least the existence at some time of an alien intelligence whose remains Earthmen have finally come upon. Frequently the device must be dealt with, because it is dangerous, or perhaps because it is a challenge, even a test for man, but occasionally it is regarded merely as a sign, or an object for contemplation. In each case, Budrys seems to take cognizance of the convention's history and connotations, even as he deals with its surface reality within his story, and exploits its symbolic possibilities on two levels, that of the characters and that of the reader.

Least developed of the science fictional motifs is the concept of identical minds in contact across the space between the earth and the moon. An accidental side-effect of the simultaneous recreation of a man in two separate machines receiving the same electronic signals, this contact bears little similarity to the usual dream-fantasy of e.s.p. as a perfectible "talent." Indeed, Hawks maintains that the word "telepathy" with its connotations of interpersonal communication is inapplicable to this phenomenon: "To be able to read a man's mind is to be able to be that man--to be where he is, to live whatever he is living. Even in this special case of ours, the two men could only, for one decaying moment, seem to be of one mind" (p. 94). To persuade us of the possibility of this special case, Budrys reinforces Hawks's skepticism about telepathy in general, by showing what elaborate precautions are necessary, to deprive the man on earth of any sensory experience of his own, in order to extend the duration of his contact with his alter ego on the moon. The most important evidence, however, is subjective, the memories of the volunteers who have experienced this contact. All of them except Barker have been driven mad, apparently by the illusion of their own deaths, so that Barker himself is the primary source for information about this modified telepathy. And Barker's testimony in support of this contact is unintentional: he seems unable to believe that he is not the same man as the many "Barkers" who die on the moon, so vivid and personal are the memories of the telepathic union.

The device which makes this contact possible,
Hawks's matter transmitter, or more precisely matter duplicator, is the major piece of futuristic technological
hardware in the novel. Physically, its most imposing
feature is its size. It occupies "tens of thousands of
square feet" (p. 7) and rises three stories; since the
floors have been removed and replaced by catwalks and
galleries, the transmitter seems almost to _be_ the entire
building. Apparently composed of many different kinds of
electronic equipment, it calls to mind similar laboratories
existing today for work with rockets, missiles, atomic
weapons, and the like, which, like Hawks's laboratory, also
share a quasi-military status. Its complexity, beyond that
of present-day computers, is called for by the need to store
information relating to every significant part of a human
being; such gigantic size is required because, in a contemporary setting, the desired complexity could be attained
only, if at all, by means of adding more equipment, not by
shortcuts or miniaturization beyond that which is already
available. Dozens, perhaps hundreds of men, kept busy
tending the transmitter, are dwarfed by it, engulfed in it,
dependent on it; if Hawks, and his chief assistants, Sam
Latourette and Ted Gersten, are representative of these
workers, they hardly exist except in the service of the
machine.

The fact of the transmitter's functioning is
attested to by the experiences of those who have been sent
by it to the moon, for whom it is little more than a means
of transportation, the understanding of which is relatively
unimportant. The manner in which it functions is important,
however, for Budrys and for Hawks; Hawks's explanations to
Barker of the technological process involved makes clear as
well the symbolic meaning which that process has for Budrys.
"Banks of amplifiers" measure, record, and store the "information" necessary to reconstruct a man out of "a local
supply of atoms." At the time of "transmission," the subject is disintegrated, and the "signals" that represent him
are sent to one or more "receivers," in each of which an
apparently identical individual is constructed to fit the
transmitted specifications. This individual will apparently
have all the characteristics, responses, and memories of the
original person on whom he is modeled, but if he doesn't, he
won't know, being the reproduction and not the original.
Each man who enters the transmitter undergoes death and
rebirth, but only that which the machine can perceive,
measure, and transmit will exist in the copy or copies.
A man can never know for sure that he is the same person he
was at some past time--his appearance, his actions, his
storehouse of memories all change with time and experience;
even the cells of which he is composed all die and are
replaced within a certain number of years--but in Hawks's

transmitter, the process is immeasurably speeded up. Thus Budrys raises, but does not answer categorically, a number of questions: what is it like to die, to know you have died and been reborn, how much of a man can we change or replace before we have a different man altogether, or something that is not quite the same as a man?

Although the transmitter enables the Navy's lunar project to succeed in the novel, that project is not the sole, or even the most important purpose for which it was intended. The transmitter enables human beings to get to the lunar surface at a time when space travel is not adequate, it enables the United States Navy to explore the mysterious structure before the "enemy" can get to the thing, and it makes it possible for the "explorer" himself to describe his passage in detail despite the fact that he has been "killed" while obtaining that information. The transmitter could also be used for other purposes, however, such as duplicating products at a much cheaper rate than manufacturing can offer; on this particular project, however, where a human being is being transmitted, the possibility of duplicating some of the transmitter's own equipment is ruled out because it would increase the margin of error. Neither transportation, exploration, nor manufacture, however, was apparently in Hawks's mind when he first began work on his transmitter, nor are they of any great importance to him now. His intention, he confides to

Elizabeth indirectly in Chapter Four, was to save lives; speaking of an "X-ray camera," the films of which could be brought to life with healthy tissue where a malignancy was, he seems to be referring guardedly to his own top secret work. The "test pattern" on the transmitter is the electronic description of Sam Latourette, the friend with terminal cancer whom he has to relieve as second in command on the moon project, and whom he hopes to reconstruct some day when the disease can be cured. Thus the moon project, itself, can be seen from Hawks's standpoint as, in one sense, a series of "experiments," testing the reliability of the transmitter, so as to be sure that the "real" Sam Latourette will be able to live again.

Ambiguous as the transmitter and its functions may be, it is at least amenable to and comprehensible in terms of human aims. The structure on the moon, the third major science fictional configuration of the novel, is even more ambiguous in that it and its function or functions cannot be resolved adequately in human terms. Whereas the transmitter is analogous to other, more familiar laboratory devices, the structure on the moon is analogous to other things in human experience only in terms of what it does: it kills people. It does not appear to be alive or to be native to the moon; it may be a trap or a test for man; it may be that its challenge is unintended, that it does not regard in any way the humans who enter it, that "regard" has nothing to do with its nature. It has a real existence, covering a measurable amount of space in a definite location, and it kills people; anything else that is said about it is subject to misinterpretation. Its physical appearance inside and outside seems to differ with time and with the observer: photographs of it are said to be unreliable; the charts drawn up by the Navy technicians from the reports of Barker can only pinpoint locations of dangers; the visual description Budrys gives us of Hawks's passage through it, following Barker on the final day, represents only Hawks's impressions, which differ from Barker's. Its incomprehensibility is further suggested by the fact that the various observers cannot even agree on a name for it; it is called an artifact, a device, a living organism, a machine, a formation, and a place, but no one can be quite sure that any of these appellations is correct, since they all refer to things in human experience.

By its very existence, and the fact that people die inside it, apparently killed by it, the structure evokes comparisons with other things man takes to be challenges. James Blish sees it as an analogue of a battlefield in war, on which, in order to "win," we must subject ourselves to a "weapons technology" that kills us before the enemy does, and more subtly, but he acknowledges that the book can also be read as a fable pitting man against nature.[21] Our space

---

[21]Blish (above, note 18), pp. 106-107.

program, too, is a struggle with nature, in which we use
armor, weapons, and strategy much as in war, and from which
the military hopes to gain still more knowledge and technique; but the space program is more than an analogy, since
the laboratory procedures in the novel are conceived of as
part of the United States' space program. The major difference between the space program's goals and destinations in
life and those in the novel is that in the latter case all
the unknowns and enigmas which may face future astronauts
are concentrated in a single object which seems to cause the
two results man fears the most from his explorations into
the unknown: death and madness. Perhaps only a man who is
already mad, or who is in love with death or the fear of
death, can withstand such pressure, and for Al Barker, who
apparently is such a man, the structure on the moon seems
to sum up his whole life of struggling, with mountains and
oceans, with machines and speed records, and with human
beings both en masse and individually, in sports, in love,
in every aspect of human life where competition can result
in a kind of victory. Hawks's observation that the thing
on the moon represents for Barker a "rite of passage" may
be partly correct, but if Barker has to prove himself even
to a machine, the machine must be regarded as internalized
in Barker, as the darker self in man which all men must try
to conquer. In the science fiction tradition from which
the structure on the moon descends, such an artifact is

normally presented as a more or less deliberate creation of some alien race, left behind as a riddle, test, threat, challenge, or trap by means of which to examine or prove the worthiness of mankind. The thing with which Barker does battle is obviously alien and seems to have been constructed for a purpose, but the conventional aftermath of confrontation with the maker of the thing is lacking, as the novel focuses mainly on the battle and its results for those involved in it. Finally, the fact that all impressions of the thing are different and inadequate suggests that really nothing has been gained, objectively, from the entire project, forcing the reader back even more into a confrontation with the motivations that surround such an undertaking.

As in most of his writings, Budrys seems to be quite concerned with human beings, but mainly with their perceptions of and reactions toward the central science fictional phenomena. Thus, although his characters may be more human than those of many other science fiction writers, they are still extremely limited in their psychology, being reduced pretty much to the one dimension necessary for the action of the science fiction story. This limitation in their psychology is further accentuated by the manner in which Budrys presents his characters' inner lives: either the character himself, or a central raisonneur, generally states explicitly, and explains, the causes, motivations, and

mental processes behind his acts, attitudes, and behavior in
general. Thus the reader is made aware that the author
knows something about psychology, and about his characters,
but not that he is capable of dramatizing his knowledge in
terms of fictional acts and situations, or that he is
capable of drawing characters who, like normal human beings,
are less conscious of and articulate about their own inner
workings. Whether the cause is the limitations on wordage
imposed by a publisher, a distrust in the reader's willing-
ness to put up with less action and more characterization,
a failure to imagine the necessary behavior, or an inability
to surpass the usual level of pulp characterization, the
results are that the reader is lectured to rather than
shown, and that some characters appear to be walking ency-
clopaedias.

In _Rogue Moon_, the _raisonneur_ is Edward Hawks,
D.Sc., who is also one of the two heroes, and the central
figure in the narrative, as well. As Research Director for
"Continental Electronics," developer of the matter transmitter, and chief of the moon project, he has status, power,
and creative ability many a reader engaged in the sciences
might envy. Engaged in a single-minded pursuit for a way to
overcome death, he could be regarded as obsessed if not
actually a "mad scientist." Wishing to save lives, yet
forced by the logic of his position in charge of the project
to send men to death or insanity, he should be under a

severe strain. And, indeed, as Budrys portrays him, we see
a man who might be regarded as only "functionally" sane,
i.e. capable of doing his job as long as he does not question its worth. Hawks seems to be almost totally involved
in his work, so much so that he is unable to relate emotionally to others; he says he would like to "get to know" his
new assistant better, he closes off the friendship he apparently had with his old assistant, and he plays at hate with
Barker, but every move seems to be rationally planned, and
partly aimed at keeping himself and his research team
functioning smoothly. The intensity of his self-control is
relaxed only slightly when he is in the company of Elizabeth
Cummings, with whom he "falls in love" because she is willing to listen to him talk. Even with her, however, he
observes the rules of security and does not talk about his
work directly, rather about his background, his curiosity
about how things work, his fear of death, and his dreams of
overcoming death.

Three of these characteristics, his self-control,
his fascination with machines, and his fear of death, seem
sufficient to sum up Hawks's behavior in general and,
although they may not be enough to make a believably rounded
person of him, they are given fictional reality by being
embodied in actions. His self-control is most obvious in
his confrontations with Barker and his friends, with whom he
refuses to become emotionally involved; his rational

analysis of things, including his own and Barker's reactions, is characteristically delivered in lectures. In the laboratory, where he is more sure of himself, speaking in terms of the process by which he has damaged people, these speeches are relatively objective and neutral; at Barker's home, where Hawks must react without rehearsing his material, where he is dealing with the alien specialty of psychology, and where he himself is involved as an actor, not merely as an experimenter, his monologues seem more pedantic, more driven, and more obviously tinged with a kind of intellectual sneer. That he has a need for self-control is indicated by the existence of the other two basic drives in him, shown in his less guarded moments alone or with Elizabeth, and less explicitly in other actions. His fascination with machines is shown by his comfortability in explaining things in terms of how they work, but also by his apparent compulsion to stare at and touch the matter transmitter, even when he is in conversation with others. His fear of death is seen in his memories of Rogan, driven mad by telepathic contact with death at the beginning of the book, in his following Barker through the lunar structure when the breakthrough is imminent (to prove he is not a mere procurer for his experiments, or for the death-machine on the moon), and in symbolic acts by both Hawks L (on the moon) and Hawks M (on earth) after the passage is effected and the telepathic contact broken. The lunar copy faces the

fact that the other Hawks is still on earth, continuing to
lead the life that both remember, and lets himself die of
oxygen starvation. The other Hawks insists on being
released from his spacesuit first, in order to have the
psychological advantage of watching Barker, who led the way
throughout the adventure, emerge after him.

Hawks is not only an actor in the novel, however;
he is also a spectator, a self-conscious observer of everything that is narrated. Although the narrator seldom
penetrates Hawks's consciousness, he adheres strictly to
Hawks's point-of-view, even to the extent of describing the
interior of the structure on the moon only when Hawks passes
through it, resulting in the existence of two independent
versions of Hawks. The outcome is that Hawks is not only
the central unifying device for the events of the book, but
also a kind of filtering agent responsible for the way
things are seen and the manner in which they are described.
Thus Hawks's participation in them determines the existence
of the two sub-plots, balanced in their pull on him, and
Hawks's way of seeing and relating to the world (simplistic,
mechanistic, perhaps emotionally retarded) may be held at
least partly responsible for the close approximation of the
other characters and their actions to the banal stereotypes
of pulp fiction. In this way Budrys can almost turn a
liability into a triumph, his apparent inability to draw
believable characters becoming a means of characterizing

the observing consciousness as well as a way of expressing artistic economy and restrictive discipline.

Thus a reason is apparent, if not fully satisfactory, for the extremely limited characterization given all the other persons in the novel except Barker. Lacking background or antecedents, they all seem suspended in mid-air, important not in themselves but in how they affect or relate to Barker or Hawks. Most of the people connected with Hawks are purely business associates, practically machines for getting certain jobs done; the Navy's zombies on the moon, whose duplicates on earth are now living the lives they remember, are the most explicit statement of this theme, but the scientists in the laboratory are no more emotionally alive, with the possible exception of Sam Latourette, who gets removed from his job because of emotional involvement. He idolizes Hawks, dislikes Barker, and is perhaps the only man in the laboratory who could understand the unconscious irony in Hawks's description of Ted Gersten, who is to take over Latourette's position: "He's a hard man to understand. He never shows more than he has to. It's very hard to accommodate yourself to a man like that" (p. 68).

Elizabeth Cummings, Hawks's girl-friend, is a bloodless bundle of apparently compassionate clichés, an adolescent's dream of pure love uncomplicated by the realities of physical, psychological, social, and economic existence; their first meeting is not only impossibly coincidental, but

also obtrusively engineered to allow Hawks to play the role
of a hero rescuing a damsel in distress; their subsequent
encounters, neatly punctuating the novel's structure,
exhibit little reason for the apparent romantic involvement
which develops.

The characters connected with Barker are more interesting, perhaps, if not more pleasant. As Hawks dampens
emotions, Barker quickens them, attracting, almost demanding
what he calls "assassins" for his entourage. As a _femme_
fatale, Claire Pack is rather disappointing, seen by Hawks
as rather repulsively sexual, thin, long-legged, a compulsive toucher of flesh (Hawks likes to touch machines, which
are clean), a woman whose eyes are "flat calm" when she is
flirting or trying to seduce, and whose breasts, used as
weapons, have no trace of femininity. Apparently attractive
to others, she is cast in the role of a vampire to Barker
(nibbling at him, raising a purple bruise on his neck) and
an alley cat to Vincent Connington (whom she despises, but
for whom she leaves Barker, after Barker shows he can fear
like any other man, and Connie shows his own abilities at
manipulating people). But to Hawks she is only a tramp, a
fallen woman whose attempts to seduce him (she tries simple
physical flirtation, challenging him to take her away from
Barker, commanding him to make love to her, and appealing to
his sympathy for someone lost and misunderstood) he fends
off with no apparent regrets.

Connington is the closest approximation to a villain in this book, a pudgy, loud-mouthed braggart who drives a big car, wears cowboy boots, smokes green cigars, and drinks too much. Like Claire, he is a caricature, of the glad-hander, the public relations man as seen by his enemies, or by those who have no use for professional or amateur public relations. Jealous of Hawks and Barker, whom he sees as "movers," he shows his ability to manipulate people by bringing them together as, in his analogy, a chemist pre-pares a chemical reaction. Even when he drunkenly announces to them his belief that Hawks and Barker will destroy each other, neither is dissuaded from the coming partnership. But he can only predict that some kind of fireworks will go off, not how or what kind, and he has no control over his experiment; he seems as surprised as anyone else when, as a side reaction, Claire leaves Barker for him. A would-be manipulator, he is pathetically easy to manipulate; like Hawks, Barker, and Claire, he is a victim of his needs and desires but, unlike them, he doesn't know what those needs and desires are.

The only other character whose complexity, such as it is, approaches that of Hawks is Al Barker, the nominal hero of the adventure if not of the novel. Although Barker, too, is seen through the eyes of Hawks, he is seen in terms of his relationships with adventure and death, and with Claire and Connie, as well as in his continual confrontation

with Hawks. Representatively important as an adventurer and
an experimental object or guinea pig, he is also employed by
Budrys as a counterweight to the figure of Hawks in the
overall balanced pattern of the novel.

As an adventurer, Barker appears to be obsessed with
death and overcoming it physically by escaping from it
(whereas Hawks hopes to outwit death, or to overcome it
mechanically). He sees himself as a warrior (Mimbreno
Apache by birth, OSS assassin in World War II by experience,
Sir Lancelot by analogy in a mock-Arthurian dialogue with a
naval ensign preparing him for the matter transmitter) whose
time has passed (the Indian wars are over, Indians don't
fight distinctively in modern mechanized warfare, Sir
Lancelot is a myth). Besides providing a spectacle for
other men (mountain-climbing, skin-diving, auto-racing, and
boat-racing), Barker has competed successfully on other
levels (an Ivy League graduate, he boasts of being a "whole
man," affects an English accent, and has hobnobbed with the
rich). Yet everything he has fought to obtain (his woman,
his wealth, his reputation, his veneer of culture) he risks
daily, not merely against physical perils (symbolized by his
speeding around a hairpin curve on the ocean cliff near his
home) but also against psychologically dangerous human
beings (Claire and Connie, whom he considers "old, familiar
assassins").

For this man, the chance to die again and again is a challenge to prove himself against death in a new and different way, not merely to escape it but to experience it and yet to continue to live. The compulsive need to prove himself forces Barker to accept the job before he even knows what it is, and requires him to continue in it, despite the terror of it, when he is taunted with implicit charges of cowardice by Hawks, a man whom Barker feels to be the real coward, staying safely behind the lines while others do his dirty work. This need to prove himself enables Barker to retain his sanity, that is, to continue to function as a tool for Hawks and the Navy to use in their exploration of the moon formation, but the multiple experiences of death do have an effect on him.

Between the sheer fatigue of the adventure, the psychological jolt of death, the confrontation with his "murderer," and the strain of maintaining security when he wants to exult in his "victories," Barker seems to lose his control over his everyday existence. This change is most explicitly dramatized by the events of the night after his first "death," which produce a new alignment in his relations with Claire and Connie. Having perhaps matured a bit as a result of his conquest of death and fear, Barker can no longer view Connington as a mere source of amusement, an object for psychological torture. Partly out of jealousy for a rival heretofore rightly considered impotent, partly

out of fear of death and vindictiveness toward Hawks who has
exposed this fear, Barker has to prove himself once more,
this time by beating up the drunken Connington who has dared
to pass out on Claire's bed. Sensing Barker's panic, and
smarting under Hawks's rejection of her, Claire sides with
Connie, and Barker, unable to cope, banishes her for what
he calls "eating carrion." As the days and deaths pass on,
Barker, alone with only Hawks to hate (Claire and Connie
have left, smashing up Barker's house to punish him), aban-
dons the cliffside house (symbol of his worldly accomplish-
ments) and moves to the city, his life becoming more and
more exclusively bound up with the conquest of the thing on
the moon.

Another force at work on Barker, which may be what
ultimately tips the balance against him, is the matter
transmitter. Whatever subtle changes occur when he is
continually reconstructed according to the machine's electronic memory, he could not know, even if he were able to
admit to himself that he is not the same man after each
transmission. Since the pattern in the memory banks is
supposed to be constant, such changes should be random and
slight. The example suggested in the novel is the memory
of the color of his first schoolbook; he insists that it was
"orange, with blue printing," but since he never said this
before transmission, no one can know if it is true. In
fact, his insistence on one particular story and

illustration in the book seems as much an act of faith as of memory. The three goldfish, leaping out of their bowl onto a bookcase, then back again, are analogues for Barker himself, one of nature's experiments like the first sea-creature that learned to live on land (p. 98). The changes after the first one could be cumulatively regressive, however, reproducing a Barker closer to the one originally scanned than is the Barker just wheeled into the transmitter, whose newer memories were not in the original pattern. This could explain, in part, Barker's problems in coping with his social environment at the same time that his work within the formation and his understanding of himself are improving. The culmination of this development is seen in the last chapter, where the Barker on the moon is forced to choose between two actions, either of which denies him survival. Useless to those who live on the moon, he must either choose death, as Hawks does, or take a chance on being scrambled by the moon's inadequate transmitter if he chooses to compete with the Barker already reconstructed on earth. Budrys, understandably, does not tell the reader which of the choices Barker makes.

By implication, of course, Budrys is showing the reader how a man is inevitably changed in his struggles, by his enemy, by himself, by the tools he employs to confront his adversary. And Hawks, like Barker, is also a representative man, also changed by the tools and methods he

employs, however much the two may appear to differ in their
basic outlooks on life.

Barker, who has tried to see and do everything worth
doing, who has money and contacts and an Ivy League education, considers himself truly cultured: "'Would you care to
discuss art with me, Doctor? Western or Oriental. Or
music? Pick your slice of civilized culture. I know 'em
all. I'm a whole man, Hawks--' Barker got clumsily up to
his feet. 'A better man than anybody else I know'" (p. 28).
In this passage and elsewhere, however, both Barker and
Budrys seem intent on disproving the assertion that Barker
is "a whole man." Physically, he is missing a leg and wears
a wooden one in place of it. Psychologically, he is lacking
awareness of the actual existence of other people except as
they please or anger him. As a "whole man," culturally,
Barker glibly spouts literary allusions (a trite one from
Byron, an irrelevant one from Chaucer, an imaginary one from
a pseudo-Arthurian drama), but seems unaware of his own
parallels in literature (his wooden leg recalls Captain
Ahab, his Friday crucifixion Jesus Christ, and through them
the archetypes of defiant and reborn heroes and gods). His
veneer of culture is in conflict with his claim to be a
warrior, and both are romantic poses, but defensive, almost
paranoiac violence, physical and verbal, does seem more
characteristic of him than the admiration of the fine arts,
knowledge about which he seems to possess largely as he

would a weapon. Even what he does have he continually sacrifices in the experiment, to be born again of different atoms and perhaps different memories, making his claim to "wholeness" even more hollow by his failure to recognize what is happening to him.

Hawks does not claim to be cultured, although he does reply to Barker's taunts one time by replying, "I've also read a book" (p. 47). Physically whole, he is as psychologically limited as Barker, able to get people to do what he wants not so much by threats or force of personality as by virtue of his superior knowledge which others trust as they might that of a magician. Barker, in fact, indirectly calls him a magician, Merlin, whose role to Lancelot in the imaginary playlet is that of an armorer to a knight. As a scientist or technician, Hawks is indeed an armorer, unable himself to go off into the battle until it has already been won. Where Barker deals with things in terms of glory, Hawks considers jobs to be done; whereas Barker sees those beneath him as animals, Hawks sees those under him as cogs in a machine; if Barker can summon up quotations from great literature, Hawks can summon up allusions to scientific inventions and discoveries.

Within his own area, Hawks is more "whole" than Barker, more capable than anyone else in the novel in fact in terms of predicting and controlling the phenomena with which he comes in contact. As a theoretical scientist, and as a technician on a specific project, he finds it extremely useful to assume that events can be interpreted in terms of empiricism, relativism, and determinism. The mere existence of the matter transmitter would seem to indicate that the theory is correct that man is nothing more than his measurable parts. Despite the subjectivity of each man's experience within the lunar formation, it, too, can be measured and explored _as_ _if_ it were what the measurements declare it to be, regardless of what it _really_ is. Any body will trigger the reactions of the lunar formation, and it was thought that any man could learn to find his way around in there. If it takes a special kind of man to survive the shock of apparent death, this does not invalidate relativism as much as it suggests that most men take subjective experience too seriously. Dealing with something like the structure on the moon (and perhaps all of nature is like that), one has to follow the same rules that it does, to be aware that if he does this, it will do that (and kill him, in all probability). In order to gain control over nature, in any of its aspects, a scientist has to be willing to forego his desires and mere subjective impressions, to observe carefully what actually happens in order to predict what may happen next. And in order to defeat the thing on the moon, Barker has to give up the idea that the wishes of a strong man will be respected for themselves, and to learn the methods and attitudes of science, which Hawks has long been familiar with, and which he uses to make Barker a part of his attack on the lunar formation.

To be sure, the scientific viewpoint is also limited; useful though it is in some cases, it is perhaps less effective in terms of people, and in terms of subjective phenomena than is a species of romanticism, such as that of Barker. If charisma does not work on nature, it does tend to impress people, and both Barker and Hawks employ it in their relations with others. Hawks, too, is aware of subjective areas of his experience which are important to him, and which he definitely does not want to lose, however unscientific such an attachment may be.

Oddly enough, it is Connington, rather early in the book, who makes explicit the thesis that neither way of seeing things is adequate:

> "A technician--like you, Hawks--sees the whole world as cause an' effect. And the world's consistent, explained that way, so why look any further? Man like you, Barker, sees the world moved by deeds of strong men. And your way of lookin' at it works out, too.
>
> "But the world's big. Complicated. Part-answer can look like the whole answer and act like the whole answer for a long time. For instance, Hawks can think of himself as manipulating causes an' producing effects he wants. 'N you, Barker, you can think of Hawks and you as s'perior, Overman types. Hawks can think of you as specified factor t' be inserted in new environment, so Hawks can solve new 'vironment. You can think of yourself as indomitable figure slugging it out with th' unknown. And so it goes, roun' and roun', an' who's right? Both of you? Maybe. Maybe. But can you stan' to be on the same job together?" (p. 29)

Drunken, and inflated with his apparent success, Connington sees himself as the prime mover, and seems to interpret the world in a third way, in terms of the relationships between people. In his inept mastery, in his role as a would-be god gifted with neither omniscience nor omnipotence, Connington seems calculated to provide an ironic commentary on his own creator; Budrys also seems to bring his characters together in hopes of confrontation and conflict, and then to let them work things out themselves. But Connington is also important in that he does act as a spokesman for this third ingredient in story-telling. Besides having an active hero and a scientific raisonneur, a science fiction novel can also use some measure of dramatic conflict.

Nevertheless, Hawks is the most obvious spokesman for Budrys throughout the novel. If Hawks is satirized, in terms of his obsessions and his one-sidedness, so are the other characters in the book. If he is, as James Blish suggests, "demonstrably, clinically, incurably insane," so are the others and, as Blish continues, so are we, so is contemporary Western civilized man.[22] For Hawks's insanity is at least partly that of a specialized sort of intelligence which our civilization has encouraged the growth and refinement of for centuries. Functionally, and within his

---

[22]Blish (above, note 18), p. 107.

discipline, Hawks is taken to be a genius; even outside his specialty, he seems to stand for awareness. He is the most aware of forces manipulating him as well as of the reverse. His is the novel's central experiencing consciousness. And it is Hawks who makes the speech which most nearly counter-balances the ultimate futility of the project itself. Trying, almost incoherently, to declare himself to Elizabeth the night before he, too, goes through the matter transmitter, Hawks hits on, among other things, the subject of entropy, or the tendency of all of the energy in the universe to run downhill:

> "The thing is, the universe is dying! . . . Only one thing in the entire universe grows fuller, and richer, and forces its way uphill. Intelligence--human lives--we're the only things there are that don't obey the universal law. The universe kills our bodies; . . . And in that way, in the end, it kills our brains.
>
> "But our minds . . . [sic] There's the precious thing; there's the phenomenon that has nothing to do with time and space except to use them--to describe to itself the lives our bodies live in the physical Universe." (pp. 153-154)

Thus Budrys appears to be saying that the scientific world-view is the best we've achieved so far, that insanity may be just another name for intelligence, and that intelligence may be no more than a basic drive which we can hardly resist, but that the glory of man is that he pursues intelligence voluntarily, as much because he can as because he must.

Insofar as Budrys was trying to create an artwork, not just to make a symbolic comment on the noble insanity

of man as exhibited in institutionalized science, the whole
does not seem to be fully integrated. The structure of the
novel has a kind of geometric balance, and the patterns
apparent have some aesthetic justification, but there is
not enough density or weight, in terms of characterization
and superficial realistic detail, to make the patterns come
to life. The style, with all due allowances for Hawks's
cultural inadequacies as narrator-surrogate, seldom achieves
a level consonant with the significance imposed on things
and people in the novel. And, largely because of the inadequacy of structure and style, the symbolic shadows of both
the characters and the science fictions seem far greater
than the objects that are supposed to cast those shadows.

The structure of the novel is extraordinarily complex, especially considering its length (A Canticle for
Leibowitz is hardly this involved, and it is twice as long
as Rogue Moon). In about 55,000 words, Budrys attempts to
balance the three viewpoints just discussed, two distinct
groupings of characters, three plots, and a number of
different settings. In nine chapters, he continuously
alternates and juxtaposes parallel and antithetical events,
persons, and locales, widening his canvas far beyond the
confines of the laboratory at the center, suggesting by
implication certain comments on the subjectivity of place
and time. Repetition with variation is employed in a number
of ways, the most significant of which is probably the

symbolic recapitulation of the action in the passage of
Barker and Hawks through the mysterious formation on the
moon.

The relations between the two groups of characters
can almost be diagrammed like a chemical reaction. At first
we find three groups, Elizabeth alone, Barker and his satellites, and the complex arrangement around Hawks, including
his personal relationship with Latourette, his contacts with
the Navy over the head of his nominal boss, his employer,
and the sense of direct responsibility toward him felt by
his staff. With the coming of Barker, the two complex
groups become connected at two points: Hawks gets swept up
somewhat in the Barker-Connington-Pack love triangle, and
Hawks's staff gets involved, negatively as far as emotions
are concerned, with Barker. Balancing this top-heavy,
unstable arrangement is Hawks's private relationship with
Elizabeth, still very tentative. The first casualty of the
reaction is Sam Latourette, replaced by Ted Gersten, who is
not as concerned for Hawks or himself, nor as excitable by
Barker. The next spin-off finds Claire and Connie deserting
Barker and Hawks, while Hawks's bond with Elizabeth grows
stronger. With the conquest of the lunar formation,
Barker's usefulness is gone, and the complex of relations
within the company will begin to dissolve, since it existed
only for the duration of the project. Strongest of all now
is the attachment between Hawks and Elizabeth. This diagram

is complicated still more, of course, by the fact that
"Barker" is really Barker, $Barker_1$, $Barker_2$, $Barker_3$, etc.,
and that Hawks becomes $Hawks_1$ with the final moon shot.

Of the three plots, one is kept almost entirely
distinct from the other two. The love-story of Hawks and
Elizabeth Cummings is handled mainly in the even chapters,
with only occasional brief allusions to it being made
elsewhere. Besides being convenient interludes between
important blocks of action in the main part of the book,
these chapters chart the growth of a romance which begins
with an accidental meeting on the road and climaxes with a
declaration of love on a seaside promontory. The time
intervening between these two events is spent almost
entirely in talk, during which Elizabeth (and the reader)
gets to know Hawks a little better, and the couple's
progressive interest in each other is barely suggested.

The other chapters seem to represent a five-act
drama in which the dominance shifts from Barker's love-life
to the conquest of the lunar structure (simultaneous with
the growth of Hawks's romance). Chapter I introduces the
characters and sets the scene. Chapter III contains an
exposition of the novel's science fictions and the beginning
of the central action. Chapter V presents the first shot
and its aftermath, climactic events in both the exploration
plot and the Barker "love"-plot. Chapter VII features
rising action for the moon exploration and dénouements for

Barker's love-life and Sam Latourette's life as a whole.
Chapter IX features the final climax and anticlimax of the
major plot, the minor plot having ceased to exist.

Each chapter is a discrete unit within the structure
of the novel, in terms of time as well as of action. Each
even-numbered chapter occupies a single evening between the
events of the surrounding chapters. Four of the five odd-
numbered chapters cover events taking place in a single day.
Chapter VII, however, although it also functions structurally as a single day, has seven sections strung out over a
considerable length of time. Unlike the sections in the
other daytime chapters, they are not identified by cardinal
numbers; instead, they are set apart by "time-signatures,"
ranging from 4:38 to 9:30, indicating the number of minutes
Barker has so far managed to survive within the lunar
structure. A number of days may pass between any two
sections, setting up a third time-scale for the chapter, but
the number is usually unspecified, and Barker's time-scale
is apparently the one to which everyone connected with the
project is most closely tied.

Each section within a chapter is also a complete
unit, with its own beginning, climax, and ending, other
standard features as well: a confrontation between two
characters; a setting different from those in surrounding
sections; a single significant image, sometimes enforcing a
distinct philosophical point. Some of these dramatic

vignettes are quite effective. Chapter I, section i, for example, sets the scene in the laboratory, shows the volunteer, Rogan, driven mad, and reveals the need for a man in love with death. Chapter III, section ii presents the mock-Arthuriad and Chapter IX, section iii is the trip through the lunar formation. The last two sections are both conclusions for Hawks and both are handled for startling, if sentimental effects. In IX, v, he reminds Barker that they are both duplicates and he clings to his resolve to die, by letting his oxygen run out:

Hawks clambered over the rocks until he began to pant. Then he stood, wedged in place. He turned his face up, and stars glinted on the glass. He took one shallow breath after another, more and more quickly. His eyes watered. Then he blinked sharply, viciously, repeatedly. "No," he said. "No, I'm not going to fall for that." He blinked again and again. "I'm not afraid of you," he said. "Someday I, or another man, will hold you in his hand." (p. 174)

The "you" is apparently Death, but it is also the moon, the earth, the death-machine, life in general, and Elizabeth. In IX, vi, the ending is unambiguous. After emerging from his suit, knowing he is not the same man, Hawks opens a note held in his hand and reads the message he knows is there: "Remember me to her" (p. 176). In Chapter VII, the sections have other functions, too: via its characters, each section there relates back to an earlier event in the book; via its time-signature, each section relates ahead to the passage through the lunar formation in Chapter IX.

The passage through the lunar structure, which we

experience with Hawks for the first time in Chapter IX, is
measured off by his watch, which he apparently looks at
whenever something in particular catches his eye. Some of
his visions relate only to the artifact, itself, but most
are related to sights of Barker's space-suited bodies. In
only one case is a time-signature exactly repeated: at
6:39 in the formation, Hawks and Barker have just passed a
spot littered with Barker's corpses; at 6:39 in Chapter VII,
Barker reports that Connington and Claire have just smashed
up his house, in leaving him, and he announces his plans to
move into the city. Thus it is suggested that Barker's
experiences on earth affected those on the moon, as well as
vice versa, and we are reminded then, as throughout the
passage, of the subjectivity of experience, of time, even of
life. At 9:19, and again a few seconds later, the passage
through the formation almost has a serious effect on Hawks's
earthly life, as Barker stops for a moment, looking
desperate. He acknowledges later that he almost didn't want
to leave, apparently because the job would then be over, but
possibly because he knew that he could stand it, while the
experience of death would punish Hawks, permanently.

If Rogue Moon were merely a story of exploration, of
man's meeting the challenge of nature, much of this complexity would be superfluous. But the novel also seems intended
to be a portrait of a scientist, and as such, an essay on
the differences between scientists and other men. Although

Hawks is measured against others as well, he is contrasted
mainly with Barker, who, for the sake of artistic economy,
is drawn as differently from Hawks as possible. Thus the
need to contrast these two kinds of heroes, their outlooks,
and their life styles requires Budrys to present each one in
a more or less "natural" habitat, as well as in the enclosed
situation where they match themselves against the thing on
the moon, the machine which takes them there, and each
other. In addition, Budrys seems to be trying to say something about the nature of art, and about the ways in which
art can try to deal with science. But in cramming all this
into such a small space, he has sacrificed the detail and
density which might have made it more believable. And,
whether accidentally or deliberately, he has sacrificed a
great deal more by his reliance upon pulp shortcuts in style
and characterization.

The setting, for example, is quite indefinite. The
season is indeterminate, and the only day named is a
symbolic "good" Friday when Barker first "dies," yet the
year is clearly given as 1959, already past when the novel
appeared, suggesting perhaps that the book is more a fantasy
than a prediction, but suggesting as well some reliance upon
the details of contemporary reality. The place is never
specified, either, leaving Los Angeles the most likely area,
for reasons of symbolism rather than of local coloring. The
region has a coastline, it is in a time-zone differing from

Washington, D.C., it has at least one major electronics firm
involved in the space program, and it apparently is inhabited by a number of idiosyncratic characters. The western
coast is preferable, presumably, because it is the end of
the American frontier, and its ocean is more future-
oriented, less involved with historic ties and associations,
but none of this is stated by Budrys. Los Angeles or
Southern California is indicated because of its relative
freedom for living styles, its involvement with the space
program, its stable weather, and not least, its identification with the fantasy world of Hollywood, but this also is
left unexplained. Even the locales are left shadowy and
vague: the laboratory, Barker's cliffside house, and
Elizabeth's studio are not exactly suffused with local
color; the moon base is also indistinct, and located on the
dark side of the moon, the side never seen from earth; the
only thing, in fact, that Budrys describes in any detail is
the lunar artifact, which is still left rather enigmatic.

The characters, for the most part, are imagined less
as real people than as symbolic constructs, who can almost
be summed up entirely, in terms of their names. Hawks, the
scientist-as-hero, is high-flying and rapacious. Barker,
the adventurer-hero, is aggressive and sharp-tongued and
perhaps somewhat of a "con-man" (like a circus barker).
Connington is even more obviously a "con-artist," making a
living out of manipulating people, and he sees himself as

"cunning," whereas others see him as fat ("ton") and ineffectual. Claire Pack is a kind of glorified camp-follower, whose intentions are always clear ("clair"), and who is accused by Barker of "eating carrion." Elizabeth Cummings may be imagined by Hawks to be regal, but her last name is an ironic comment on his adolescent conception of "pure" love. The other characters, some of whom are also symbolically named, are even less developed than these.

When characters are described, it is often in terms of bodily movements, such as empty smiles and gestures, which may be intended to represent frustrated violence or to invest the characters with a thingness like that of machinery. But the device is employed so frequently as to seem almost a tic on the part of Budrys, or a pulp fiction device which keeps things moving and fills out the total number of words (science fiction magazines pay by the word). Hawks, Barker, and Claire are each referred to as "thin," as if this word could make them appear more "hungry" and in better "fighting" shape than the portly Connington. Touching things, especially machines, is a characteristic of Hawks, while touching people is representative of Claire. Barker is continually being related to images of war and competition, and shows his contempt for others by comparing them with animals. Some of these devices are effective, but they are practically all that Budrys relies on for characterization. Most of the action seems to be unconnected with

thought or motivation, and that which is explained is
handled in terms of speeches, mostly by Hawks, which seem
taken from a book on elementary psychology translated into
more or less colloquial speech. The final effect is of
stiffly jointed puppets, dabbed with paint, and dandled on
strings.

Much of what has been said can be said to be criticism of Budrys' style, and the impression it gives of the
narrator and/or Hawks as somewhat lacking in intelligence
and discrimination. But style is also a matter of specific
words, and sounds, and sentence structure, and here, perhaps
especially, Budrys reveals his training in pulp fiction.
He uses a distinctly limited vocabulary, avoiding even
science fictional jargon for the most part, concentrating
apparently on the fastest and most direct way of saying
things. Sentences and paragraphs are short, even choppy,
dominated by short, hard verbs, resulting in a staccato
rhythm that, at its best, has the compression of poetry, but
that often deteriorates into the hard-boiled manner of the
tough guy detective story. With such a rapid pace precipi-
tating the reader from event to event, presumably he will
not notice that the only flavor added to these direct
statements comes from cursory adverbial modifiers. A common
shortcut in the writing of pulp fiction, these adverbs and
adverbial phrases almost pass unnoticed, but they avoid the
necessity of writing dialogue or description which expresses

itself well enough not to need such additives. They are
most noticeable when, as in Rogue Moon, they are at their
most awkward or uninformative, as in clumsy sentences like
"Barker got clumsily up to his feet" (p. 28) and "Barker
came quietly upward out of his chair" (p. 116) or in
obtrusive speech tags like "drily," "huskily," "evenly,"
"uncertainly," and a myriad of others.[23]

The language does rise occasionally to the level of
minor poetry, as in the pseudo-Arthurian exchange of
dialogue between Barker and the Naval ensign preparing him
for his first test, and where Budrys puts words to relatively unusual usage: "the kitchen door of the house sighed
shut on its airspring" (p. 29), "his eyes were looking out
through the narrow mask of his lashes" (p. 110), "fluores-
cents tittered into light" (p. 126). But in such cases it
seems obviously contrived, in relationship to the flatness
of the whole. His use of images is frequently effective,
concrete in description, central to an action, suggestive of
relationships, and his description of the lunar artifact is
quite a tour de force, but the language involved is seldom
more than adequate. His command of tone seems particularly
weak; though there are occasional snatches of poetry, such

---

[23]For more detailed criticism of this kind of
proliferation of adverbs in science fiction, and the
related problem of strange verbs being substituted for
"said," see William Atheling, Jr. [James Blish], The Issue
at Hand: Studies in Contemporary Magazine Science Fiction,
ed. James Blish (Chicago, 1964), especially pp. 81-86,
109-112.

as the mad Rogan's babbled phrase, "an dark and nowhere starlights" (pp. 5, 119), to try to convey the awe of the adventure, the book as a whole seems to alternate between an aura of menace, suspense, and presumed but not demonstrated suppressed violent emotion and an aura of adolescent, oozing sentimentality, neither of which is particularly fitting to the author's apparent philosophical and artistic aims.

Thus the style seems inadequate to the content, the execution to the conception. Yet the failure is not absolute, rather it is suggestive of what might be accomplished under other circumstances. For a science fiction audience, style and characterization are non-essentials, length and development are secondary to immediate impact, clarity of structure, and original ideas and variations. Even from a literary standpoint, it can be seen that Budrys has tried to tell his story in terms of people, in terms of human needs and desires, and that, under certain restrictions, he has managed to compress a great deal, and to suggest much by an elaborate use of symbolism. An author with more sensitivity, with more regard for human realities and for words, might well have written a better novel, but without Budrys' science fictional vision, he probably would never have conceived of it.

CHAPTER VIII

J. G. BALLARD: THE CRYSTAL WORLD (1966)

The most controversial figure in science fiction in
the 1960's has been J[ames] G[raham] Ballard, whose stories
and novels since 1956 have bewildered and even infuriated
fans and readers accustomed to the old established conventions and unwilling to change their ways.[1] In a guest
editorial for the British science fiction magazine New
Worlds in 1962, Ballard made his attack quite explicit:
"Science fiction must jettison its present narrative forms
and plots. Most of these are far too explicit to express
any subtle interplay of character and theme. . . . I think,
most of the hard work will fall, not on the writer and
editor, but on the readers. The onus is on them to accept
a more oblique narrative style, understated themes, private
symbols and vocabularies."[2] He goes on to say that not only
are aliens and interstellar travel dispensable, but the

---

[1]See MIT Index and supplements (above, chapter I,
note 35) for bibliographical information. See Contemporary
Authors, VII-VIII (1963) for biographical information.

[2]J. G. Ballard, "Which Way to Inner Space?" New
Worlds, May, 1962, pp. 117-118.

whole emphasis on physical science and engineering should be abandoned in favor of the biological sciences (including psychology), because "the only truly alien planet is Earth."[3]

In "The Venus Hunters," a novelette published the following year, Ballard elaborated his position in both practice and precept.[4] Essentially a sketch of the personal relationship which develops between Ward, a new astronomer at a major observatory, and Kandinski, an apparent crackpot who claims to have seen and talked with aliens whose space-ship landed on Earth, this story is unusual for Ballard in that it does involve aliens and interstellar travel, both of which are real within the fictional context, but it is also unusual for science fiction before Ballard, because the aliens' existence is less important than what people think about it.

Ward insists at first on treating Kandinski's book on the landings as science fiction, which he brushes off as trivial: "Perhaps I'm too skeptical. I can't take it seriously." When Kandinski counters that Ward takes it too seriously, Ward shifts his ground: "It's not so much the sensationalism that puts me off as the psychological

---

[3]"Which Way," p. 117.

[4]J. G. Ballard, "The Venus Hunters," Terminal Beach (New York, 1964), pp. 85-115. Originally published as "The Encounter," Amazing, June, 1963, this story is not included in the British collection, confusingly titled The Terminal Beach, which was also published in 1964.

implications. Most of the themes in these stories come
straight out of the more unpleasant reaches of the unconscious." Kandinski sees through this gambit, also, and
voices another disclaimer: "That sounds rather dubious and,
if I may say so, second-hand. Take the best of these
stories for what they are: imaginative exercises on the
theme of tomorrow."[5] Another character, Professor Cameron,
also of the observatory, sees Kandinski's existence almost
as conclusive proof of Jung's thesis that the sighting of
flying saucers is a part of the mass hysteria accompanying
the end of a Platonic Great Year. Cameron, too, has something to say about science fiction and the unconscious:

"Most people regard Charles Kandinski as a lunatic,
but as a matter of fact he is performing one of the
most important roles in the world today, the role
of a prophet alerting people to this coming crisis.
The real significance of his fantasies, like that
of the ban-the-bomb movements, is to be found elsewhere than on the conscious plane, as an expression
of the immense psychic forces stirring below the
surface of rational life, like the isotactic movements of the continental tables which heralded the
major geological transformations. . . .

". . . It's unfortunate for Kandinski, and for
the writers of science fiction for that matter,
that they have to perform their task of describing
the symbols of transformation in a so-called
rationalist society, where a scientific, or at
least a pseudo-scientific explanation is required
a priori. And because the true prophet never deals
in what may be rationally deduced, people such as
Charles Kandinski are ignored or derided today."[6]

----

[5]"Venus," pp. 93-94.

[6]"Venus," pp. 107-108. See also C. G. Jung, Flying
Saucers: A Modern Myth of Things Seen in the Sky, trans.
R. F. C. Hull (New York, 1959).

Ward, however, comes to like and to believe
Kandinski, and even interrupts a major scientific conference to see the space-ship for himself when it lands again.
He even goes so far as to issue a joint communiqué on the
landing, but it does not lend credence to Kandinski, rather
opening Ward himself to derision. His reputation ruined
and his job lost, he is about to leave for Princeton (where
he will have the lowly task of teaching freshman physics),
when Kandinski stops him and tries to persuade him to continue the crusade:

> "Ward, you can't drop your responsibilities like
> this!"
>
> "Please, Charles," Ward said, feeling his temper
> rising. He pulled his hand away but Kandinski seized
> him by the shoulder and almost dragged him off the
> car.
>
> Ward wrenched himself away. "Leave me alone!"
> he snapped fiercely. "I saw your space-ship, didn't
> I?"[7]

Although aliens and spaceships exist in this story,
Ballard's concern is in the area where they, the "science
fictions" of the tale, intersect with reality, or where
fiction meets reality in general. In keeping with his
earlier manifesto, he emphasizes man and Earth, and the
reader is presented with, in Ballard's words, an "oblique
narrative style" and an "understated theme." In one sense,
the theme of the story is the nature of science fiction,
and the story is so constructed that all three spokesmen

---

[7] "Venus," p. 115.

are discredited by their obvious biases making their statements incomplete at best.

Yet each of the critiques offered can be applied to
science fiction, perhaps especially as Ballard writes it.
He exploits quite deliberately themes from "the more
unpleasant reaches of the unconscious." He prophesies of
unpleasantnesses likely to come. And he is also quite aware
that what he is writing is fiction, that its explanations
are window-dressing, and that its content should not be
taken "too seriously," but rather treated as an "imaginative
exercise on the theme of tomorrow."

Ballard has not been preaching anything new. Occasional science fiction stories have dealt with his themes
for over thirty years and only in the conservative reaches
of popular fiction could his style and narrative method be
considered innovative.[8] But his practice is consistent with
itself and with his precepts, and he provides a focal point
for the long-predicted intermingling of science fiction and
mainstream literature. Ballard's works are symptomatic of
the growing consciousness of science fiction writers, not

---

[8]In some of his more recent stories, however,
Ballard has been experimenting with a fragmented form in
which chronology and character become confused, although
there is unity of theme. See "The Assassination Weapon,"
in Best S. F. Stories from New Worlds, ed. Michael Moorcock
(London, 1967), about which Moorcock writes that it is "one
of a group of stories which explore the possibilities of a
form which is largely Mr. Ballard's own invention and which
is without doubt one of the most successful developments of
its kind since Joyce" (p. 7).

only that their themes and symbols are becoming common
property, but also that their literature has definite
connections with contemporary life and letters.

Ballard has so far published nine books in the
United States, including five collections of stories: The
Voices of Time (1962), Billennium (1962), Passport to
Eternity (1963), Terminal Beach (1964), and The Impossible
Man (1966). The majority of these stories were published
first in England, and almost all of them reflect his concentration on "inner space," a term popularized by J. B.
Priestley's 1953 diatribe against science fiction's stereotypes of outer space.[9] Most of them reflect a preoccupation
with time, especially time past and time made solid or
spatial by some symbol or monument, and with landscapes of
desolation, which correspond to the internal sense of empty
time and space in his protagonists, who are often beyond
action, beyond hope, even beyond communication. Shifting
sands and desolate seas are frequently sketched in his
stories, including a series set in the decaying artists'
colony of "Vermilion Sands," where old myths may be
re-enacted before powerless observers, and poets are known
by the style of type in their automatic writing machines.[10]

---

[9]J. B. Priestley, "Thoughts in the Wilderness:
They Come from Inner Space," New Statesman and Nation,
December 5, 1953, pp. 712, 714.

[10]The specific story referred to is "Studio 5, The
Stars," Billennium (New York, 1962). Others in the series
include: "Prima Belladonna," also in Billennium; "The

But whereas such devices can be used lightly in a short story, a novel based on similar material needs a good deal of depth and detail about the scene, the events, and the people. What can be a semisweet melancholy in a shorter form becomes an enervating, exhausting despair in the longer.

Ballard's first novel, The Wind from Nowhere (1961), traces the struggle of several survivors against a wind which inexplicably rises five miles per hour each day all over the world. They end up at a giant pyramid (without giant foundations) built by the multimillionaire Hardoon to withstand the wind and glorify himself. The wind wins, however, and then begins to die down, again for no known reason. The narrative conventionally shifts from character to character until the final group is assembled, and concentrates on the steadfastness of Britons in the face of adversity.

The Drowned World (1962) has an equally mysterious catastrophe, but it focuses on one man and his reactions. The biologist Robert Kerans gradually succumbs to the lure of the South, the sun, and the prehistoric past which, in waking dreams, dominate his meager existence in a world where only the polar regions are fit for human habitation.

Thousand Dreams of Stellavista," Passport to Eternity (New York, 1963); "The Screen Game," The Impossible Man (New York, 1966); "The Cloud-Sculptors of Coral D," F&SF, December, 1967.

The Burning World (1964) continues Ballard's journey through
the unconscious, this time of a Doctor Charles Ransom,
attempting to survive in a world where the oceans have
receded and the rains don't fall. Industrial pollution of
nature is blamed in part for the catastrophe, and human
penance seems mystically related to the rain's return at
the book's end.

In all three cases, there is a pointed contrast
between heroes and villains, both treated rather strangely,
and a clearly implied relationship between mental states
and physical environments. Least effective is the first
book, which has too many protagonists and too much reliance
on stereotyped human villainy: Hardoon and his paramilitary
henchmen are too obviously comic-book figures, not worth the
effort expended by either the wind or Ballard to get rid of
them. The isolated scapegoats of the latter two books,
dragging themselves along to survive in a fatal environment,
manage to achieve some human personality as they try to
understand themselves, others, and the mental landscapes
which imprison them as much as do the physical. The
villains, men who are wealthy despite or because of the
catastrophe, control other people and trained animals which
menace the protagonists, yet which seem to blend into the
landscape, and to resemble dark thoughts in a dream. And
both the good and evil seem to seek some symbolic act which
will restore the world to the way it was. The same sort of

situation exists in Ballard's latest, and perhaps best
novel, The Crystal World (1966), which seems to recapitulate
the themes of its predecessors, but also to complete them
and to add something new, in terms of the environment and of
the reaction to it.

The critical reaction to The Crystal World was
generally favorable. Martin Levin wrote in the New York
Times Book Review that Ballard had "effectively streamlined
the archetypal frame of the adventure story, which subsists
on sharp moral contrasts, with anti-matter cabalistics."[11]
B. A. Young, writing in Punch, observed that, despite the
absurdity of the catastrophe's explanation, "the story deals
exclusively with the reactions of men to the new phenomenon
and is exciting and literate."[12] Judith Merril expanded the
scope of her F&SF column to give a full-scale critique of
the Ballard canon.[13] Insisting that most of his works need
to be read in the context of the others, she describes at
one point the relations between the parts of this latest
trilogy:

> Where Drowned World examined time-past in terms of
> psychophysical and geophysical evolution--a return
> to the womb-of-the-world--and Drought [The Burning
> World] explored the drying-up of life in time-future

---

[11]Review by Martin Levin, New York Times Book
Review, May 15, 1966, p. 41.

[12]Review by B. A. Young, Punch, June 1, 1966,
p. 820.

[13]Review by Judith Merril, F&SF, August, 1966,
pp. 57-69.

> from the platform of the culture-complex of man's
> accomplishments till now, CW [sic] presents us with
> a (literally, physically) crystallized pattern of
> time-now--the frozen present, infinite moment, immor-
> tality in the instant of I am. In the first book,
> archetypal figures were moved by powerful blind
> biophysic forces to fulfill--or re-enact--their
> mythic roles; in the second, elaborately evolved and
> multi-faceted allegorical personae picked their way
> through an elegant/decadent choreography of desue-
> tude and devolution on a dying earth; the third book
> is actively inhabited by individuals entirely alive
> and aware in the only moment of reality we know at
> all--the eternally passing present we call now,
> where the focus in space expands as time narrows
> down, and action shots of life-in-process are not
> only possible, but inevitable.14

Because of its position in the trilogy and because, unlike

its predecessors, it is "a novel, and a good one," she

concludes that The Crystal World is his best work to date,

and a good sign for science fiction and for the literature

into which it and the main stream are merging. Miss

Merril's judgment of Ballard and of the present and future

meaning of "SF" are not shared throughout the science

fiction field, but even the reviewers for Analog and Galaxy,

although they did not review the novel, have given Ballard

some qualified approval, Miller somewhat quizzically, Budrys

despite a passionate dislike of the Ballard school of

"inertial science fiction."15

14Merril, p. 61.

15P. Schuyler Miller, "The Reference Library,"
Analog, January, 1967, p. 166; Algis Budrys, "Galaxy Book-
shelf," Galaxy, December, 1966, p. 128, but see also
August, 1966, pp. 188-189, and October, 1967, pp. 192-193.

The book itself, The Crystal World, is a novel of about 48,000 words, divided into two parts of roughly equal length.[16] The first six chapters show us Edward Sanders, a doctor from a leprosarium, finding his way to a crystallized forest in the heart of Africa, ostensibly in search of Suzanne Clair, the (married) woman he loves. On the way he meets a French newspaperwoman, Louise Peret, to whom he makes love and becomes somewhat attached, a mine-owner named Thorensen, a military physician by the name of Radek, a melancholy priest, Father Balthus, dressed in black, and a fussy little madman dressed in white, named Ventress.

The last eight chapters are told in retrospect, framed by a letter in which Sanders, two months later, resigns his hospital post and predicts his return to the forest. In the interim, he has twice gotten lost in and narrowly escaped from the forest. The first time he was caught in a running gun-battle, the focus of which, Ventress' tubercular young wife, Serena, Thorensen was trying to protect from her husband. Finding refuge with Suzanne and her husband Max, at their little hospital, Sanders found time, after Louise's arrival, to make love to both women. Later, looking for Suzanne, he fell asleep at the forest's edge, and woke to find his arm crystallized, presaging for him the living death from which he had earlier

---

[16] J. G. Ballard, The Crystal World (New York, 1966). All page references in text refer to this edition.

freed Radek. With the help of Ventress, who advised him to run, and Balthus, who gave him a jewelled cross, Sanders fled again. On his way out, he ran across Serena crystallized alive, Thorensen and his henchmen dead, Ventress running for survival, and Suzanne and some native lepers celebrating the coming of the universal crystallization. The last chapter concludes with Sanders, watched by Louise and Max, going up the river again in a speedboat.

As in the previous novels, the basic science fiction consists of the catastrophe and its explanation. Although flood myths are ancient, the science fictional catastrophe story is a modern variation involving four basic elements: an unprecedented world-wide catastrophe (atomic attack, alien visitation, natural cataclysm), a scientific explanation which may blame man and/or suggest solutions, a group of survivors (usually relatively random), and an attempt to do something constructive (escape with a whole skin, join with other refugees, overcome the menace, preserve something of civilization). The horrors of devastation and the primitive reaction of man to survive at all costs are usually stressed. Ballard, however, takes the catastrophe less for its own sake and more as a metaphor for the human condition, using the obligatory scientific explanation, if at all, partly to mollify the reader's desire for material causation and partly to heighten the symbolism, but not as a basis for a solution. His characters, for whom survival seems more a matter of reflex than of will, try as individuals to find in the devastation something to live for.

Like its predecessors, The Crystal World is set in the immediate future, insuring the treatment of science and technology at their present stage of development; very little is ever at all advanced over contemporary technological hardware. None of the usual props of science fiction make an appearance in this particular novel (the Echo satellite, mentioned twice, is of course already in existence); vehicles and machines are not evoked to impress us with marvels. An automobile, a boat, and a helicopter fall victim to the crystallization, recalling their ruined counterparts in the first two parts of the trilogy. In The Drowned World a helicopter is downed and boats are a major means of transport. In The Burning World, a houseboat aground in a drying river is the hero's hideaway, and cars become such useless hunks of metal that their parts are scavenged for pavilions, shacks, and other structures apparently viewed by Ballard as folk or "pop" art.

A scientist is again the protagonist but Dr. Sanders, like Kerans and Dr. Ransom before him, is not a savior or a hero, merely a lost soul trying to find some meaning in the contemporary world. The fact that he is a medical man, unable to cure himself, unwilling to practice his sacred profession, suggests how deep the contemporary malaise must be, but how extensive it is is uncertain,

since there are two other medical men in this book as well.
Suzanne's husband, Dr. Max Clair, is clearly on the side of
life as we know it, tending to his patients, refusing to
get involved in his wife's love affairs with Sanders and
the crystals, refusing even to treat the doomed native
lepers who gather outside his hospital, attracted by the
crystallized forest and attracting the attention of Sanders
and Suzanne. The French military doctor, Radek, becomes a
symbol of death, or the living death awaiting everyone from
the crystallization. Torn loose by Sanders and thrust into
the river's swift current, he later confronts his would-be
benefactor as a grotesque parody of a human being, no longer
encysted but marked by raw wounds from the forced separation, and seeking blindly to return to the forest of which
he had become a part, both physically and psychologically.
Thus Sanders is framed between life and death, his every
vacillation seen as tending toward the extremes symbolized
by Clair and Radek.

Even his occupation is ambiguous, especially in the
light of his behavior and attitude toward it. A medical
doctor, he is confused by the customs officials with a
physicist they are expecting, yet Radek later suggests,
ominously, that Sanders' experience with leprosy may be of
more value in dealing with the strange phenomena, which
Radek seems to regard as a kind of virus, than the physicist's theories can be. Ostensibly a healer and restorer

to life, Sanders has concentrated on leprosy, apparently
fascinated by its slow but visible development, which
Ventress compares to the progress of life toward death.
Partly by unconscious design, Sanders himself contracted
the malady, as did Suzanne, when she worked with him and
the natives. Their infection is revealed at a time of love-
making, which almost makes it seem a venereal disease,
passed on in the supposedly life-giving act of intercourse.

Although Sanders is the closest to a scientific
spokesman in The Crystal World, his attempt to understand
the crystallization is not undertaken in order that he may
help stop its advance, as Radek hoped, but for purely
personal reasons, as he indicates in the first part of his
letter of resignation:

> . . . what most surprised me, Paul, was the extent
> to which I was prepared for the transformation of
> the forest. . . . I accepted all these wonders as
> part of the natural order of things, part of the
> inward pattern of the universe. . . . I quickly
> came to understand it, knowing that its hazards
> were a small price to pay for its illumination of
> my life. . . .
>
> . . . the very absence of surprise confirms my
> belief that this illuminated forest in some way
> reflects an earlier period of our lives, perhaps
> an archaic memory we are born with of some ances-
> tral paradise where the unity of time and space is
> the signature of every leaf and flower. . . . In
> the forest life and death have a different meaning
> from that in our ordinary lack-lustre world. Here
> we have always associated movement with life and
> the passage of time, but from my experience within
> the forest near Mont Royal I know that all motion
> leads inevitably to death, and that time is its
> servant. (pp. 93-94)

Sanders' explanation, which follows immediately, is that the phenomenon is a "super-saturation" of matter which has lost its store of time because of collisions with anti-matter and anti-time. Depending on an interpretation of, or speculation on, anti-matter unorthodox in or out of science fiction, this explanation is logical only in a verbal sense, much as we can speak of a "green sun" or a "four-dimensional figure" without any concrete examples in the real world.[17] But Ballard is less interested in scientifically perceivable actuality than he is in a metaphor to embody his view of time as something solid or spatial. Science, or rather scientific knowledge, seems to serve Ballard mainly as a source of vocabulary, vocabulary open to vague and suggestive usage, unlike the precise and functional meanings assigned it in scientific research.

Pseudo-scientific jargon may be required by the conventions of science fiction, but for Ballard it really only deepens the mystery, rather than clearing it up. And in the context of Dr. Sanders' relationship with the crystal forest, even this much explanation is somewhat superfluous. It is motivated by the need for Sanders to communicate with the head of his hospital, from which he is resigning, and his desire to clarify the situation to this man who is

---

[17]"The green sun" is a figure used to demonstrate the difference between putting two words together and constructing a "realistic" fantasy-world, in J. R. R. Tolkien, "On Fairy-Stories," Tree and Leaf (London, 1964), p. 45.

totally unacquainted with the phenomena. Sanders' own

initial reaction, two months before, is shown by Ballard as

by no means that of a dispassionate observer, or seeker

after knowledge:

> For some reason he felt less concerned to find a
> so-called scientific explanation for the phenomenon
> he had just seen. The beauty of the spectacle had
> turned the keys of memory, and a thousand images of
> childhood, forgotten for nearly forty years, filled
> his mind, recalling the paradisal world when every-
> thing seemed illuminated by that prismatic light
> described so exactly by Wordsworth in his recollec-
> tion of childhood. The magical shore in front of
> him seemed to glow like that brief spring. (p. 77)

To such a poetic, quasi-mystical vision, a "scien-

tific explanation" is irrelevant, suggesting to many people

in science fiction that Ballard really does not belong.

Algis Budrys' attack on Ballard as "master of the inertial

science fiction novel" is representative:

> A story by J. G. Ballard, as you know, calls for
> people who don't think. One begins with characters
> who regard the physical universe as a mysterious
> and arbitrary place, and who would not dream of
> trying to understand its actual laws. Furthermore,
> in order to be the protagonist of a J. G. Ballard
> novel, or anything more than a very minor character
> therein, you must have cut yourself off from the
> entire body of scientific education. In this way,
> when the world disaster--be it wind or water--
> comes upon you, you are under no obligation to do
> anything about it but sit and worship.[18]

Viewed as science fiction, Ballard's novels and characters

may well seem inane, but Ballard's relationship to science

fiction is somewhat ambivalent. Although he depends on the

science fiction audience for his livelihood, he uses the

---

[18]Galaxy, December, 1966, p. 128.

science fiction cosmos as he sees fit, drawing from it
images, figures, conventions, and rationalizations subordinated to the "subtle interplay of character and theme."[19]

The crystal forest is such a science fiction, in
the sense that its physical, concrete reality in the world
of the novel may be explainable only in terms borrowed or
adapted from the discoveries of modern science, but science
apparently can do nothing about it, except to observe and
theorize. The crystallization is real, empirically, in
that it can be seen and felt, but it cannot be trapped for
analysis: photography fails to reproduce more than a dark
glistening; centrifuging a crystallized object, although
the movement removes the crystallization, reveals no physical or chemical additive. Normally, one would expect a
residue of matter or release of energy, but apparently the
agglutinating agent is time, which we cannot stop and
really measure. How the scientists know that time is the
cause Ballard does not indicate, but time is obviously
involved in the continued growth of the phenomenon.
Whatever the mechanism responsible, it appears also to be
manifesting itself elsewhere on Earth, and in outer space
as well. If it continues to grow, these scientists (and
Sanders, apparently the only character in the novel convinced of their findings) believe it will not stop until

---

[19]"Which Way" (above, note 2), p. 117.

the end of time in a startlingly literal sense. Although science can assign it a material cause and can predict its future course, prediction and analysis in this case do not mean control, any more than they do in the parallel, slower process by which energy declines and entropy increases, as is predicted by the Second Law of Thermodynamics.[20]

Two things only seem to resist the crystallization, both of which are explained pseudo-scientifically, but interpreted symbolically. Movement, especially rapid movement, not only prevents matter from expanding, because it forces the three spatial co-ordinates into continual change, but it can also undo crystallization which has already begun, apparently because the object is returned to normal space-time where movement is a part of life. The parallel with life is obvious: growth, decay, change, movement all distinguish living from non-living things, and man's search for cultural growth and progress is undertaken in the face of the inevitable stasis of complete entropy assumed by our modern cosmology. Thus movement and action are seen as intrinsically important, in making life what it is, however absurd they may seem in terms of accomplishing goals which, by definition, are worthless measured against the eternal and universal. The other remedy is precious stones, which supposedly have stored up a large supply of time. Jewels,

---

[20]But see the discussion of entropy in Alan Isaacs, The Survival of God in the Scientific Age (Baltimore, 1966), pp. 31-34.

of course, are even more obviously symbolic, representing
art, beauty, and values of a strictly cultural nature; here,
as traditionally, they serve as talismans offering escape
from danger, and one particularly effective helper for
Sanders is the large cross given him by Father Balthus,
which adds a suggestion of religious aid as well.

Like Ray Bradbury then, Ballard gives aid and comfort to the enemies of science by suggesting magical
relations and causation. Like Bradbury, he refuses to
believe that science can solve everything, and even suggests
that science cannot solve anything that is really important
for human beings. But whereas Bradbury writes little
morality plays about man's potential for good or evil
determining his use of science, Ballard tells of spiritual
odysseys for which science is irrelevant, except as a curious human attitude, or an indirect force far behind the
scenes that turns out objects to balance those of nature in
man's physical environment.[21] Science and science fictions,
like other things and attitudes, are merely counters on the
board where Sanders and his predecessors, Kerans and Ransom,
play the "game" of life in the face of death.

---

[21]See Miller (above, note 14). On Bradbury, see
Sam Moskowitz, Seekers of Tomorrow: Masters of Modern
Science Fiction (Cleveland and New York, 1966), pp. 352-
373, and Damon Knight, In Search of Wonder: Essays on
Modern Science Fiction, rev. ed. (Chicago, 1967), pp. 108-
113. Compare Knight's denigration of Bradbury in the latter
volume with the role Knight has played in introducing
Ballard to American audiences, according to Algis Budrys,
Galaxy, December, 1966, pp. 128-129.

The shape of the book as a whole indicates its
focus on Sanders. It is his voyage inward, geographically
and psychologically, that we are following. What he sees,
experiences, and thinks becomes the subject of the novel,
outlined by the subtitles of the book's subdivisions.
Unnumbered, each chapter bears a title which refers, in
telegraphic, suspense-novel style, to an object or tableau
with symbolic as well as melodramatic significance at the
climax of the chapter. "The dark river" (each subtitle has
only one capitalized letter), for example, describes the
menacing appearance to Sanders in the first chapter of the
river by which he gets to Port Matarre and will late get
to the forest, but it also suggests time, and perhaps blood.
"The prismatic sun" at the end refers explicitly to the
apparent beginnings of crystallization in the sun, but it
also reminds us of the sun's appearance within the forest,
of the appearance of the forest itself, and of Sanders'
final rejection of black and white and gray, in favor of
the fantastic colors of the crystal world.

The first half of the book, describing Sanders'
approach to and first entrance into the forest, is entitled
"Equinox." The title refers first of all to the date,
March 21, and also to the condition of light and shadow, of
extreme white and black, at Port Matarre, near to but not
quite at the forest. The balance of day and night suggests
to Sanders the need to act, to commit himself in some way.

By making love to Louise, for all that she seems to resemble Suzanne, he tips the balance, revealing to himself that Suzanne is not his real reason for going to Mont Royal, and foreshadowing the headlong attraction the forest itself will have on him. The equality of day and night is parallelled by the black and white figures of Father Balthus and Ventress, who travelled upriver with him, who seem to menace him, yet who as yet mean nothing to him.

The second half, concerning Sanders' adventures in and around the forest, bears the title "The Illuminated Man," a phrase which appears in the epigraph and in the conclusion of Sanders' letter: "by night the illuminated man races among the trees, his arms like golden cartwheels and his head like a spectral crown" (p. 203). In the context of the letter, written after the doctor's second escape from the forest, the reference is apparently to the figure of Ventress which Sanders visualizes still running through the forest to avoid crystallization, as if the time elapsed where Sanders is, outside the forest, had not affected anything within the forest. But Sanders himself has been forced to run the same way when he was inside the area of crystallization, and "illumination" also suggests light and color, contrasting with the black and white of others' appearances and moral values, which Sanders now seems to feel he has transcended. The actions of others, whether they are trying to use him (as are Ventress and Thorensen) or he is attempting to make use of them (Louise, Suzanne, and Max), hardly touch him beyond the surface, where they are seen as tending toward irrelevance and absurdity. "The illuminated man" should then be Sanders himself in his "enlightenment," which he considers a kind of mystical peace, but which may also be seen as an obsession. By extension, the phrase may refer to man in general, or to any man who has achieved peace and acceptance of death, whether by chemical or mechanical, mystical or rational means.

Although the narrative is in third person, the narrator is limited to Sanders' point-of-view. Thus we see everything and everyone else as he does, but we do not really see Sanders from outside. Occasional philosophical asides, sketchy explanations, and statements about other characters' motivations, although presented in third person, seem to be meant as Sanders' observations, since they are in keeping with his oversimplified view of anything outside himself. In the novelette, "The Illuminated Man," which contains this novel in embryo, the protagonist and the narrator are the same, a professional journalist named, appropriately, James B.--, and the observations are obviously those of the man who is being overcome by the forest.[22] The second part of the novel maintains this

---

[22] J. G. Ballard, "The Illuminated Man," F&SF, May, 1964, pp. 5-31.

relationship somewhat, since the events are reviewed within the context of Sanders' letter, but the narrator has a separate existence beyond that. The separation of narrator and protagonist is incomplete, however, and the apparent overlapping of consciousness contributes to the reader's unsureness as to just what is the real world of the novel.

From Sanders' viewpoint, then, the actions and intrigues of others, even where they involve himself, are all melodramatic and pointless, the other characters are all rather like silhouettes, posturing and ambiguous, with ominous names and behavior, and only the setting is solid and detailed, something to which he can relate.

As he gets more and more deeply involved with the crystal world, Sanders becomes superficially involved with other people and their relationships with him, with each other, and with the forest, but not enough that it changes him, or that it allows any of them to become a solid character. He is one of the principles in a romantic quadrangle which appears to be rather low-key, raising no great amount of passion or jealousy in any of the participants. Max and Louise both accept with relative equanimity Sanders' relationship with Suzanne. Sanders' love-making with Louise and Suzanne in succeeding chapters seems to rouse him only to a dispassionate comparison: Louise, taken outside the affected zone, is sunny, warm, and alive; Suzanne, in the outskirts of the forest, is shadowed, cold,

and dead, marked with the leonine mask of the leprosy that
he and she share. In the end, he rejects Louise's plea
that he return to civilization, choosing instead the crystal
forest of which Suzanne by now has presumably become a part,
but the choice hardly involves either woman as a person.

The mere idea that people had sexual intercourse was
seldom allowed in science fiction a few years ago, and Harry
Harrison could still complain about sexual prohibitions and
inhibitions in 1964.[23] But Ballard and others have broken
through those taboos to some extent, and not for the sake of
sheer exhibitionism: there is no clinical detail involved,
and the scenes are not obligatory, not included merely to
show that the author is following a trend. Sex is a part of
life for Edward Sanders, for Louise, and for Suzanne, and it
is in a sense a refuge from the fears aroused by the strange
phenomena. And love, in this situation, seems as meaningless as death, the kind of death offered Sanders by the guns
of Ventress and Thorensen, whose love triangle contrasts
sharply with Sanders' own.

Ventress, Thorensen, and Serena have no meaning, no
connection, no relationship to Sanders, yet he is continually swept up by the blood feud which pits the white-clad
eccentric against the hulking mine-owner and his black

---

[23]Harry Harrison, "We Are Sitting on Our . . .
[sic]" S. F. Horizons, 1 (Spring, 1964), 39-42. As early
as 1952, however, sex was included in a science fiction
novel by an outsider: Bernard Wolfe, Limbo (New York,
1952).

assistants. Both parties threaten Sanders' life, both use
him as bait to attract the other, both let him go for no
more reason than the apparent madness which sets them
against each other. Both want to possess and to hide the
pitiful, tubercular Serena, a young girl who looks ancient,
a sexless creature each claims as his wife, a dying goddess
they attempt to save from crystallization by means of gifts
of jewels. A spark of the doctor in Sanders revives when
he sees her, but his advice, that she be removed from the
forest, would only prolong her agony; the forest offers her
eternity, as it does later for Balthus, for Suzanne, and
for Sanders himself. The feud is finally won by Ventress,
who kills Thorensen's men one by one and then kills
Thorensen himself. But Thorensen, dead, shares the bed of
the serene, immortal Serena, and Ventress, alive, is forced
to run forever to avoid the fate, alone, which he had sought
to share with her. The whole intrigue is rendered even more
absurd by the fact, later known to Sanders, that they will
all, living or dead, be caught up eventually in the
universal crystallization.

None of these characters seems to have any real
existence except in relation to Sanders. Persons have
meaning and value only insofar as they embody his situation
symbolically, lead him toward his final solution, or try to
bring him back to the outside world. They frequently seem
to be posing, like static figures in a frieze, unreal,

vague, and, to use a favorite word of Ballard's, "ambiguous." No doubt it is partly because they are such puppets, their motivations hidden from the unimaginative, unempathic Sanders, that the novel has such an aura of mystery. Where they do take part in the action, it is often with the growls, snaps, twitches, grimaces, and other meaningless gestures so common in pulp fiction. Much of what dialogue there is allows of little hesitation, circumlocution, even thought. Short and direct, as in a conventional suspense-novel, such speeches imply total communication, which is certainly not the case here. Except where the situation is simple and functional, as in giving directions, Ballard's characters tend to commune with themselves (and with the reader), their remarks only partly, and almost accidentally, register with each other, since no one is really listening.[24] Sanders, particularly, sees and hears and understands only what he wants or needs to, in order to get along, until he can achieve his mystical union with the world of crystal.

Dialogue and interpersonal communication play a rather minor role, actually, the description of things taking up the major share of the book. Ballard seems highly interested in what effects he can achieve by balancing light

---

[24]This non-communication, too, could be viewed as just another convention, at least since Chekhov, one which is basic to the theater of Samuel Beckett, Harold Pinter, and others, but it is a convention seldom exploited in science fiction.

and shadow, forms and shapes, landscapes and objects,
animals and people, in and out of the area of crystallization. Light and color are rampant in the forest, whose
brightness seems to make the outside world drab and dark by
contrast. Even at night, the moonlight suffices to trigger
the prismatic effect that the crystals have on light, but
by day the crystal world is a "maze of rainbows" and a
"blaze of colors." Repetitive use of such words as
"crystal," "prism," "glass," "jewels," and "ice," rather
than specific naming of individual colors, serves to remind
the reader of the kaleidoscope of color within the affected
area, while "black" and "white," "light" and "dark" emphasize the drabness of the surroundings. Jewels and ice
serve also to evoke contrast of temperature, ice being associated with the coolness within the forest and the waves of
cold that accompany each advance of the crystallization,
jewels preserving some time and life in opposition to the
crystal growth, even as they give up their color and luster.
Trees and plants and stones, rivers and roads, houses and
furnishings, machines, costumes, are all described in more
detail within the zone than outside it, their weird shapes
and colors attracting Sanders' attention. From outside,
figures inside, moving or still, appear ghostly white or
blazing with color, and Sanders himself, on his emergence,
is said to glow in the dark. And it is only against this
fantastic background that the actions and movements of the

characters, relatively senseless in themselves, are given some meaning.

Movement resists the crystallization and is in turn resisted by it. Sanders and Ventress run to escape the crystals and they, as well as Thorensen and his men, are seen to participate in a grotesque ballet, running toward and away from each other, as knives and bullets and cannon-balls fly through the air. Crocodiles stumble about, one of them dead and hollowed out for one of Thorensen's hench-men who, gunning for Ventress, almost succeeds in shooting Sanders. Crystallized birds are seen occasionally, one of them even flying from his branch in apparent violation of the crystal world's natural laws (Radek and Sanders suffer severe wounds after being torn away from crystals of which they have begun to be a part). Cars on the road and boats on the river are stopped from moving; even a helicopter that stayed too long on the ground is brought to earth with a crash when its crystallized rotors jam in mid-air. The one vehicle started again is Thorensen's boat, which advances only a little as a result of the firing of its cannon (the speed of the movement and the vibration appar-ently overcoming the crystals for a moment, as do the rivals' hand-guns and rifles).

Things are prominent in the identification of characters: Ventress and Balthus are known by the color of their clothing, Louise by her sunglasses' covering half of

her face, Serena by her jewels, Suzanne by her face which to
Sanders is "a pale lantern." The characters' actions, too,
are given meaning largely by virtue of their association
with things. Thus the jewels, with their "stored-up time,"
not only give warmth and life of a sort to Serena, but also
give meaning to the character of Father Balthus. In the
first part of the book, he is enraged by the sight of a
crucifix which, along with plants and stones and the like,
was left by a native on the forest's outskirts, so that it
could become crystallized into an item for sale to tourists.
Calling it obscene, Balthus shakes it angrily, making the
crystals disappear, "light pouring from them as from a
burning taper" (p. 33). In the second part, when Sanders
stumbles on him, playing the organ in his forest-surrounded
chapel, Balthus is a changed man, having given in to the
heresy which had so angered him earlier. After giving
Sanders a few days' sanctuary, he thrusts into the doctor's
arms a large jewelled cross, and assumes a crucifixion
position in anticipation of his martyrdom. The cross
enables Sanders to escape, and also to perform another
godlike but futile act of resurrection, freeing a young
native child who has begun to crystallize. With fitting
irony, Sanders is charged with grand theft when the jewels
are seen to be missing from the cross; he is saved by the
living, Max and Louise, at whose suggestion soldiers test
out his defense, invading the forest for a short time, as

if exorcising its evil spirit with more jewelled crosses.

Sanders, perhaps the only one to whom the news has really penetrated that the crystallization is universal and inevitable, is well aware that his escape can only be temporary. One reason for his emergence may have been a desire to say good-bye, to life, to the outside world, to Max and Louise and his colleague at the hospital. But he knows now that the only sane attitude to take toward the forest is to avoid not only struggles and intrigue (the response of Ventress and Thorensen) but also love and attachments (the response of Max and Louise), and to welcome the coming of the crystallization by becoming a part of it. This is what Radek and others have done, involuntarily perhaps, but any later separation is even more involuntary. This is what Father Balthus does, believing that he and the Church have outlived their usefulness when "divinity can be seen to exist in every leaf and flower" (p. 193). This is what the hopeless native lepers do, when Max and Sanders reject them, and what Suzanne does, when she joins the natives to lead them in their ceremonial dances of welcome. In each voluntary case, the final step is a gesture of acceptance, not merely of death, but of a kind of immortality, a kind of life in death repugnant at first but ultimately desirable. And finally, this is what Sanders must do, partly to escape the world of action and decision-making, partly to rejoin Suzanne, partly to become immortalized in a kind of jewelled setting which ultimately no one will be able to see and appreciate, since they will all have joined him.

The theme of immortality is underscored by reference to a painting, "Island of the Dead," by Arnold Böcklin. This is a familiar gambit of Ballard's, used also in his previous two novels:

> Over the mantelpiece was a huge painting by the early 20th century surrealist Delvaux, in which ashen-faced women danced naked to the waist with dandified skeletons in tuxedos against a spectral bone-like landscape. On another wall one of Max Ernst's self-devouring phantasmagoric jungles screamed silently to itself, like the sump of some insane unconscious.[25]

> On the right . . . was a reproduction of a small painting by Tanguy, "Jours de Lenteur." [sic] With its smooth pebble-like objects, drained of all associations, suspended on a washed tidal floor, this painting above all others had helped to isolate him from the tiresome repetitions of everyday life.[26]

But where these books explore landscapes somewhat similar to those of the paintings, The Crystal World uses the Böcklin, only briefly alluded to, as a jumping-off point. It is Port Matarre, with its darkness and shadow, which is compared to the painting, so the world of crystal which is beyond Port Matarre is symbolically beyond or transcending death and the

---

[25]J. G. Ballard, The Drowned World (New York, 1962), p. 27.

[26]J. G. Ballard, The Burning World (New York, 1964), p. 12.

dead worlds of the earlier volumes in the trilogy.[27]

As is perhaps too often the case with Ballard,
however, this reference stands out obviously as a symbol.
Father Balthus, described as trying not to reveal himself,
suggests the allusion to Sanders, whom he does not know,
as they wait to land and disembark in the novel's opening
pages:

> "The light at Port Matarre is always like this, very
> heavy and penumbral--do you know Böcklin's painting,
> 'Island of the Dead,' where cypresses stand guard
> above a cliff pierced by a hypogeum, while a storm
> hovers over the sea? It's in the Kunstmuseum in my
> native Basel--" He broke off as the steamer's
> engines drummed into life. "We're moving. At last."
> (p. 6)

After this, he barely says two sentences to Sanders before
their later encounter in the crystallized forest. Even
here, the symbolic nature of things is left pretty much to
speak for itself, but Ballard frequently spells out his
implications with excruciating thoroughness, as if not
trusting the average science fiction reader to get the
point. For example, after Ventress has smuggled a pistol
through customs in Sanders' suitcase, taking advantage of
the perfunctory inspection given a "leper-doctor," Sanders
is outraged at the ruse: "The smuggling of this pistol
unknown to himself seemed to symbolize, in sexual terms as
well, all his hidden motives for coming to Port Matarre"

---

[27]A painting more analogous to Ballard's crystal
forest, Max Ernst's Eye of Silence, was chosen for the
dust-jacket of the hard-cover edition of The Crystal World
(above, note 15).

(p. 21). Again, after Sanders' first escape from the forest
to the Clairs' hospital, the doctor muses to Louise over
the strange goings-on, in order for the reader to be told
explicitly of Ballard's manipulations: "Looking back, they
all seem to pair off--Ventress with his white suit and the
mine-owner Thorensen with his black gang. . . . Then there
are Suzanne and yourself--you haven't met her but she's your
exact opposite, very elusive and shadowy. When you arrived
this morning, Louise, it was as if you'd stepped out of the
sun. Again, there's Balthus, that priest, with his death-
mask face, though God alone knows who his twin is" (p. 161).
The fact, soon to be revealed, that Sanders also has a
"death-mask," that of the leper, is apparently insufficient
to answer the implied question Sanders ends with, so Ballard
sees to it that Louise clarifies things for us, as she
replies immediately, "Perhaps you, Edward" (p. 161).

Such obviousness may be explainable on the grounds
that he is trying to reach unsubtle readers, but it is out
of keeping with his own demands that readers learn to accept
obliqueness and subtlety. And clumsiness is evident in
other ways as well. The flying crystallized bird is one.
Another is the fact that Louise finds her way to Mont Royal
apparently after the way is blocked. Stylistically, Ballard
often inverts normal word order by starting off a paragraph
with a long descriptive clause, delaying the subject and
main verb to the middle of the sentence. These semi-

periodic sentences may add something to the sense of predominance of things over people and their actions, but they
may also be a kind of stylistic tic, an attempt at evoking
elegance.

The fact that these slow, almost meandering
sentences make the reader decrease his pace, and often mark
off paragraphs as conceptual units probably indicates that
they are deliberate attempts at increasing aesthetic
distance. By distancing the reader, however, they also call
attention to themselves, and their own sound and shape is
not always an aesthetic delight, as a couple of random
examples may illustrate:

> The sergeant smiled amiably. His relaxed good humor,
> uncharacteristic of the military in its dealings
> with civilians, suggested to Sanders that perhaps
> the events in the forest near by for once had made
> these soldiers only too glad to see their fellow men,
> whether in uniform or out. (p. 67)

> High above, the cupola over the staircase had fallen
> through and Sanders could see a cluster of stars,
> but the light from the forest below cast the hall
> into almost complete darkness. (p. 167)

Not only are these sentences awkward, but they are vaguely
dishonest as well: Are soldiers always uncomfortable with
civilians? Is it the light from below that produces the
darkness? Wouldn't the outside light reduce the visibility
of stars? If not, why the "but"? On the other hand,
Ballard's style is frequently quite appropriate to his
content: "After many delays, the small passenger steamer
was at last approaching the line of jetties, but although

it was ten o'clock the surface of the water was still gray
and sluggish, leaching away the somber tinctures of the
collapsing vegetation along the banks" (p. 3). Although
the "but" again seems irrelevant, the "slowness" of the
steamer, the "sluggishness" of the water, and the "collapse"
of the vegetation are emphasized by the diction and word
order.

The everyday vocabulary in the above excerpts is not
exceptionable, exhibiting a precision and freshness rare in
science fiction, but it is not really typical of Ballard
either. As Brian Aldiss notes in an article on Ballard and
two other British writers, "He enjoys encrusting his
sentences with adjective and rare words until, like the
transformations in 'The Illuminated Man,' they hand [sic.
"stand"?] in 'huge pieces of opalescent candy, whose countless reflections glowed like giant chimeras in the cut-glass
walls.'"[28] Ballard's vocabulary in the second part of the
sixth chapter, when Sanders has just entered the forest for
the first time, includes in the span of five pages (84-89)
the following relatively uncommon terms: palisade, minaret,
jasper, mandalas, glacé, basalt, panoply, lattices, enclave,
fleur-de-lis, bifurcated, aureoles, iridescent, pilasters,
friezes, annealed, lapis lazuli, vestigial, cuirass, and
armorial. Such ornateness is not out of keeping with the

---

[28]Brian Aldiss, "British Science Fiction Now,"
S F Horizons, 2 (Winter, 1965), 31-32.

context of the description of the crystal world, but it is
not reserved only for that, nor is it always used with precision even within that specialized context. And once it is
realized that much of the strangeness of the crystal world
is due to the exotic nature of the words describing it, the
sense of awe and wonder momentarily aroused begins to seem a
bit mechanically contrived. Yet the discerning reader can
also appreciate the author's technique, which does not rely
only on ornate vocabulary; relatively simple images, like
the crystallized plant, and the appropriate combination of
sound and sense are also quite effective.

The paragraph where the sentence quoted by Aldiss,
slightly revised, now appears, does offer a good example of
Ballard's style:

> Dr. Sanders brushed the frost off his suit, picking
> at the crystal splinters embedded like needles in
> his hands. The air in the house was cold and
> motionless, but as the storm subsided, moving away
> across the forest, the process of vitrification
> seemed to diminish. Everything in the high-ceilinged
> room had been transformed by the frost. Several
> plate-glass windows appeared to have been fractured
> and then fused together above the carpet, and the
> ornate Persian patterns swam below the surface like
> the floor of some perfumed pool in the Arabian
> Nights. All the furniture was covered by the same
> glacé sheath, the arms and legs of the straight-
> backed chairs against the walls embellished by
> exquisite curlicues and helixes. The imitation
> Louis XV pieces had been transformed into huge frag-
> ments of opalescent candy, whose multiple reflections
> glowed like giant chimeras in the cut-glass walls.
> (pp. 97-98)

Here we have the exotic vocabulary, allusions to fragments
of culture, the mingling of distancing words like "seemed"

and "appeared" (almost epidemic with Ballard) with literal
metaphors, signifying direct transformations. Sense impressions begin with Sanders, his pain and his coldness, the
shift spatially to sight, embodying his view of the room
around him. The coldness introduced with the consonants
"f" and "k" seems to remain as they are repeated again and
again, and the "arms and legs" of the chairs suggest not
only Sanders' cold and pain ("needles in his hands") but
also the crystallization of human beings. "Plate-glass"
and "fracture" strike me as subtly onomatopoetic, as do
the quick pronunciations required in reading aloud the
phrases "fused together" and "swam below the surface."
The whole mysterious picture almost demands a culminating
metaphor, which Ballard supplies in double measure, evoking
the images of rock candy and chimeras.

   To the exotic vocabulary and the profusion of metaphors, Ballard adds still a third deliberate mechanism to
evoke the strange and distant: allusion to works of art,
sometimes employed for incongruity (as is the reference to
Louis XV furniture in a context where style and ostentation
are absurd), sometimes to re-inforce the novel's themes of
art and immortality. Böcklin's painting and Wordsworth's
"Immortality Ode," already mentioned, are smoothly integrated into the story. The obvious quotation from Shelley--
"Life, like a dome of many-colored glass, stains the white
radiance of eternity" (p. 148)--seems stilted, uttered by

Suzanne in conversation with Sanders, just after his first
emergence from the forest. In context, however, it can be
seen either as a device to put him off, so that he does not
come close enough to see the signs of her infection (she is
sitting distant from him and in shadow), or as an indication
of her preoccupation (which Sanders, at this time, might
regard as morbid or deranged) with the crystal forest as an
alternative to deterioration and death. Still, color in the
novel is generally applied to the crystals in sunlight, and
neither light nor crystal is regarded as symbolizing life.

Allusions to Conrad's Heart of Darkness are implicit
in the geographical setting, in the purgatory of the book's
second half, and perhaps in the filtering consciousness of
Sanders' letter; the situation of Serena and her lovers,
too, may owe something to Conrad's sentimental short story,
"The Lagoon." And behind the scenes there seems to lurk the
inspired madness of Coleridge's "Kubla Khan."

Like the pulp melodrama and stereotypes, the bits
and pieces of modern technology and the science fictions
associated with them, the allusions and quotations serve
Ballard as raw materials for a collage, which Brian Aldiss
has pointed out is a key term for Ballard's art.[29] Scraps
of electrical and automotive equipment become works of art
in The Burning World. Draining the "pool" in The Drowned
World reveals old buildings transformed by seaweed and

[29]Aldiss, p. 33.

barnacles. The crystallization, too, works changes on
ordinary things like houses, cars, and boats, revealing
strange, quasi-magical shapes. And the net effect is to
produce tableaus of marvels out of ordinary objects and
landscapes.

But these tableaus and landscapes are not only
arresting in themselves, in their strangeness, but also in
terms of their familiarity, their psychological significance. The ubiquitous waters of the first book in the
trilogy carry Kerans back to the primeval womb of man's
prehistory. The wasteland of burning sands in the second
volume makes Ransom struggle for survival, fighting for
precious drops of water, only to find rain where he has
finally given himself up (as "ransom"?) to the dried lake
where he began his journey, and to the desert of his mind
(he does not notice, perhaps because he is dead or mad,
when the rain begins). The crystal forest, represented as
a present-day phenomenon, is a symbol of infantile regres-
sion (like the womb) and of approaching death (like the
desert), but it also represents the immortality offered by
art. The play of black and white, light and shadow, life
and life-in-death, the figures running back and forth across
a strange landscape, the tableaus of posturing men and
frozen plants and animals, the desire of characters to
become crystalline shapes and thus to avoid disfiguring
decay and death, the allusions to the Romantic "religion"

of art, all seem to add up to a quest by the author for artistic immortality. Yet at the same time, his use of bits and pieces from modern life, cultural and technological, seems to undercut that aim, reminding us that everything but death is transitory.

On the level of novelistic realism, The Crystal World is not wholly successful. Besides being counters in a game or notes in counterpoint, the characters could have been more developed, more consistent, more believable, their actions better motivated, even granting Sanders' inability to perceive their depths. Even their function in the novel could have been more organic, less obviously intended for symbolic purposes. As a work of literary art, the book suffers from some problems of style and language, which are also not excused by Sanders' role in the narration. To be sure, Ballard does not offer the same faults we see in most writers of pulp fiction, but he, too, is hampered by many of the same restrictions. And the fact that he has so humanized some old conventions, creating a fictional world in which old dreams and images come true and man's ambiguous and contradictory desires can be embodied, is a genuine, if minor, artistic accomplishment.

CONCLUSION

Clearly, these six novels are works of science
fiction. Each presents fantasy as reality, bridging the gap
in part by "scientific" means, telling a story the style and
format of which are determined by the requirements of popular, or pulp fiction. But these works are not merely
elaborations of formulas, whether of science or of popular
fiction. Each author obviously takes part in the contemporary "cosmology" of science fiction, borrowing from it
adding to it, subscribing to its basic values. Each author
obviously is aiming his story at an audience habituated to
action, adventure, and wonder, in a "pocket universe" where,
as Algis Budrys has written, "the essential conflict is
between comfortable ignorance and pitiless intelligence."[1]
But each book succeeds to some extent in making its "scientific" content meaningful in human terms, in making its
pulp form viable, and in making its comment on the world.

---

[1]Algis Budrys, "Galaxy Bookshelf," Galaxy, June,
1965, p. 164. Budrys' remark is partly in jest, but others
have made similar observations: "The conflict is not
between boy and girl or virtue and vice. It is between
Enlightenment, represented by idealistic scientists, and
Stupidity," Stanley Frank, "Out of this World," Nation's
Business, March, 1952, p. 81. See also Kingsley Amis, New
Maps of Hell: A Survey of Science Fiction (London, 1961),
pp. 79-81.

we live in now. And each author has succeeded to some
extent in creating his own unique variation on a number of
themes, in developing his own aesthetic construct, and in
determining his own distinguishable voice, thus making
himself liable for judgment on his own literary vices and
virtues.

All six authors make use of traditional patterns of
fantasy in their novels. Clarke's novel features a utopia,
an extraordinary voyage, contact with the "supernatural,"
and the end of the world. Asimov seems mainly concerned
with the pattern of dystopia, but there are also suggestions
of utopia and of the extraordinary voyage in his book
(suggestions intended for further development in subsequent
volumes of a trilogy). Sturgeon approaches the ideals of
utopia and divinity in terms of his homo gestalt, and relies
to some extent on the machinery of the fairy tale in showing
how his gestalt grows up. Miller's novel employs the motifs
of dystopia, the marvelous journey, and a world-catastrophe,
and suggests as well the concepts of utopia (the cloistered
life) and contact with the supernatural. Budrys' book is
primarily based on the extraordinary voyage and its
adventures, but it also has overtones of dystopia and the
supernatural, and stresses a novel approach to the mytho-
logical motif of death and rebirth. Finally, J. G. Ballard
presents us with an extraordinary journey, a conception of
the end of the world, and suggestions of a kind of utopia or

immortality within, dystopia beyond, and the supernatural above his crystallized forest (all five motifs being invoked in a third variation in his trilogy).

The traditional dreams that lie behind these conventions are given science-fictional twists, however, aimed at anchoring them more solidly in reality. The setting and action indicate an outward thrust in space and time, which should loosen the reader's prejudices concerning contemporary actualities. The presence of technological marvels conceivable, if not yet realized, today is intended to help him accept the hypothetical possibility of the fictional world. And the important role played by one or more spokesmen for the scientific world-view is at least partly intended to reinforce belief in the marvelous phenomena: in overcoming his professional skepticism, the scientist sets an example for the reader; in making explanatory pronouncements, the scientist acts as a figure of authority, whose knowledge is to be trusted.

The earth is the physical setting for most of the action in all six books, and three of them take place in the present, but the thrust of the fiction tends to be outward in space and forward in time. In the novels by Clarke, Asimov, and Miller, the time is the future and civilization on other worlds is a reality. Budrys' book is bound to the present, but its characters' major accomplishment, taking place on the moon, points toward future

developments. Even in Sturgeon's More than Human, limited
to the here and now, the development of the gestalt is
outward, from person to group to race, and the achievement
of maturity points toward the future. Of the six authors,
Ballard is most involved in an inward, psychological journey, but even he takes care to make plain that the crystallization is spreading throughout the galaxy, and that the
stopping of time is equivalent to the approach of eternity.

Continuity, from the present to the future, from
the earth into space, is provided primarily by the mind of
man, treated both socially and individually. The cultural
storehouse of man, his "group mind," can only accumulate
information and misinformation, but without it, a man's
sense of continuity could not exist. Culture, it would
appear, must be preserved, not so much because it is valuable in itself, as it is from the standpoint of humanism,
but because it may contain something practical and useful
for somebody at a future time and place. The literal "group
minds" of Clarke and Sturgeon, the automated libraries of
Clarke, Asimov, and Miller, Asimov's robots, Budrys' matter-
recreating machine, and Miller's Order of Leibowitz all
share this "caretaker" function. So do individuals,
however, such as: Asimov's amateur historian, Lije Baley;
Clarke's Overlords; Sturgeon's psychiatrist; the abbots of
Miller's monastery; Al Barker, Budrys' caricature of the
"whole man"; and Dr. Edward Sanders, the "anti-hero" of

Ballard's novel. Although the individual intellect is
limited in its storage capacity, it is capable of grasping
far more than its personal isolation in time and space; it
can face and deal with changes in its world, however much
they may fill it with fear and anxiety; confronted with
death, even annihilation, it can visualize, and dream of,
and work to bring about immortality. And in each book there
is at least one character who dares to go a little farther
than he knows that others have done: Jan Rodricks, who gets
to see another world, despite the Overlords' restrictions;
Lije Baley, who considers emigration from a stagnant earth
(and eventually overcomes his culture's psychological
restrictions); Gerry and Hip, who strive to find themselves,
and find homo gestalt; Thon Taddeo, Brother Francis, Brother
Kornhoer, and Brother Joshua in A Canticle for Leibowitz;
Barker and Dr. Edward Hawks, each of whom dares death and
the moon in his own way; and a number of Ballard's characters who seem to welcome eternal living death.

Technological hardware, besides providing a thread
of continuity, a bridge from the present into the future,
is used to suggest an equivocal attitude toward the kind of
achievement that it represents. Futuristic and contemporary
machines and devices are featured rather extensively in five
of these books, and parapsychological phenomena function
similarly in the other, seeming to suggest not only the
promise but also the limit of man's inventiveness,

ingenuity, and ability to cope with his total environment.
Asimov is the most affirmative of these six authors in his
attitude towards man's achievement, but he makes it clear
that technology creates new problems as well as solving new
ones, and he seems to suggest that human incentive is more
important to technological advance than vice versa. Ballard
is probably the least affirmative toward technology (perhaps
of all science fiction writers, not just these six), but
even he has some use for machines, if only as temporary
means of escape and as geometric figures for ornamentation.

The figure of the scientist, too, is subjected to
some degree of ambivalence in these works. While his
presence, his discoveries, and his explanations help
solidify the author's fictional world, the spokesman for
science is also subjected to critical scrutiny within that
world, and in terms of his relationship to that world.
Clarke's major scientist-figures, the Overlords, have an
advanced material civilization, but they are also parallelled in several ways with devils, and visualized as
trapped in their intellect, an evolutionary cul de sac.
The technicians of Asimov's City are unimpressive as
persons, and of the leading spokesmen for the science of
the Spacers, one is a robot and the other almost equally
mechanical in his unemotional, mechanical approach to human
beings and human problems. In Sturgeon's novel, the
psychiatrist is extremely limited in his activity, both

"central controls" of the gestalt are crippled (Lone mentally and Gerry emotionally), and the voice of conscience, Hip, wins the final struggle less because of his ability to manipulate than because of his resentment at being manipulated. Miller's Thon Taddeo is an honorable man, but as a scientist he is as amoral as the euthanasia doctor who is his spiritual successor, while the monks, even those who have a mixed calling, are all willing to sacrifice science for religion. Budrys' Hawks is impressive as an inventor and a technician, but less so as a man and an administrator; however high his ideals, he is a manipulator, and a dangerous one, sending men to death and insanity, holding tremendous power because of his understanding of things beyond other men. And Ballard's medical men, however much they may differ in terms of acceptance or rejection of the crystallization, are rather "ambiguous" and somewhat detached from that part of their training which we call scientific. Thus each novelist suggests that we examine his "scientist" both as a scientist and as a human being; by implication, too, we are being asked to consider the place and role of science in our own culture, as well as in the civilizations of the future.

Unfortunately, perhaps, the author does not offer us much of a character to examine in such a thorough manner. The shallowness with which these characters (and others in the books) are drawn may be partly the result of their

diagrammatic roles. Characters who are primarily spokesmen
for a particular, limited point of view, puppets manipulated
to show a specific projection or extrapolation coming true,
or devices enabling the reader to see a world or background
more important to the writer than is the experiencing consciousness itself, can hardly aspire to the complexity and
ambiguity of the human condition (itself a literary convention, to some extent) which the great characters of fiction
exhibit. Indeed, where the backgrounds and the science
fictions, in short, the extrapolations, are so important, it
may be that characters should only be one element in the
fictional world, of no preponderant importance, and that the
traditional emphasis on character is out of place. A more
severe criticism is the observation that, when characters in
science fiction are placed in situations where their human
characteristics should be visible, where their reactions
should parallel those of living, breathing persons, they
tend instead to resemble countless other characters of pulp
fiction, indistinguishable from one another in their obtuse-
ness, their reliance on physical action, and their utter
lack of imagination. Aside from Miller's characters and
Ballard's protagonist (to some extent), the only characters
in these six books who rise at all above the standard level
of pulp characterization are Clarke's Karellen (an alien),
Asimov's Daneel (a robot), and Sturgeon's Lone (an idiot).

A relatively frequent reliance on melodrama and sentimentality in these novels can also be traced to the influence of pulp fiction. If the novel is short, as commercial considerations tend to make most science fiction novels, if the philosophical content predominates over considerations of aesthetic form and the action is primarily a means to maintain reader interest and continuity, as is usually the case in science fiction, an oversimplification of human impulse and motivation is not unlikely, and melodrama and sentimentality may be to an extent the products of such an oversimplification. But where they are not just the results of a necessary shorthand method, or where they are indulged in at some length, a model in conventional pulp fiction should not be hard to find. The deliberate withholding of information necessary to a fuller understanding of the situation, a traditional gambit of both the detective story and the horror story, is quite evident in the novels by Clarke, Asimov, and Sturgeon. The sentimental value of small children is exploited by Clarke and Sturgeon, that of young or at least innocent love by Sturgeon and Budrys, and that of the stereotyped "suburban" family by Clarke and Asimov. The melodrama of the chase plays a significant role for Clarke, Asimov, and Ballard, and that which is implicit in the confrontation of adversaries is made explicit by Asimov, Sturgeon, Miller, Budrys, and Ballard. In some cases the author, directly or through one

of his characters, tries to rationalize the characters'
behavior, but only in Miller's novel is the behavior or the
rationalization convincing.

In style, too, the influence of pulp fiction is
quite noticeable. Superfluous modifiers, dialogue which
carries an unconscionably large amount of information, a
preponderance of "telling" over "showing," mannerisms of
speech and behavior used not only to identify a character
but practically as a matter of reflex, and numerous other
devices help the pulp writer turn out a maximum of wordage
in a minimum of time. And although science fiction writers,
relative to other commercial authors, may write more for
love and less for money, they are still subject to financial
needs and deadline pressures, they are not likely to receive
meticulous editing as regards style, and they may even
develop a taste for the kind of sloppy writing encouraged by
commercial considerations and conventionally accepted within
the field.

But the problems with style in science fiction go
deeper than mere sloppy habits that higher rates of pay and
more careful editing could reduce or eliminate. There seems
to be a basic fear of style as something debilitating to an
exciting story or idea, or at least an avoidance of style as
something which may be attractive when added on, but which
is strictly unnecessary. The difference between this attitude and that of "literary" people has been pointed out by

Algis Budrys, in a recent review of an anthology of stories
culled from science fiction's "literary" magazine:

> This collection from F&SF contains two kinds of
> stories, really, although the standards of writing
> are uniform, and high, and the grasp of facts
> appears to occupy an acceptably even range no
> matter . . . whose story we're considering. One
> kind of story is by people who are engaged with
> life and use facts to grapple with it and explain
> it; people like Delany, Leiber, Aldiss, and Davidson,
> for example and for all they do it in strikingly
> different ways. Another kind of story is by people
> who are engaged in some kind of professional contem-
> plation, be it as educators, poets, philosophers or
> whatever. Those people tend to grapple with words
> and other symbols not as tools but as things in
> themselves.[2]

Budrys may be overstating the difference slightly--indeed,
he has just recently acknowledged that "grappling with life"
in science fiction is fairly new--but then in other science
fiction magazines words are taken even more lightly than in
F&SF.[3]

This attitude of opposition toward style is, I
believe, responsible for a lot of bad writing in science
fiction, and thus acts as a major obstacle to its literary
acceptance. Yet it is based on a misconception, on the
belief that there is a necessary opposition between words

---

[2]Algis Budrys, "Galaxy Bookshelf," Galaxy, October,
1968, p. 169.

[3]For all that it has a rather low circulation (see
above, chapter I, note 65), F&SF is the one science fiction
magazine which gets some attention from the literati. See,
for example: C. S. Lewis, "On Science Fiction," Of Other
Worlds (New York, 1966), p. 67; James Yaffe, "The Modern
Trend Toward Meaningful Martians," Saturday Review, April
23, 1960, pp. 22-23.

"as tools" and words "as things in themselves" and that the former is somehow better than the latter. To be sure, the pace of adventure may be more important to the average reader of science fiction than is the cadence of the prose, but that does not necessarily mean that he is totally tone-deaf. And to more critical readers, the failure of the style may preclude any interest in the book as a whole. Furthermore, to say that the aim of the science fiction writer is the communication of concepts rather than the communication of style is to beg the question, since a writer cannot choose not to have a style, of some sort. Even the barest scientific or technical prose requires a style of precision and authority, and the avoidance of a good (i.e., appropriate) style in any context results inevitably in a bad (i.e., inappropriate) style. And where the human complexity of the characters is so underplayed, as it usually is in science fiction, the experience of the reader could be made more vivid and meaningful by the presence of a fully aware, experiencing consciousness as narrator, revealing itself largely in terms of style. The possibility is largely unexplored, perhaps because science fiction writers see themselves as technicians, putting together patterns of ideas and motifs with little regard to what it all means, perhaps because most people who are drawn to science fiction are themselves not whole as individuals, and are hence incapable of creating a persona who is fully aware of the implications of his story.[4]

Of our six writers, Miller seems most in command of his style and his persona, dignified, reserved, yet wryly humorous, sympathetic but ironic, and even Miller seems somewhat self-restricted, involved to an extent in ideas but not in persons, and not emotionally to any great degree. In a novel of comparable scope, Clarke exhibits much less self-assurance and comprehension of the whole, his essentially flat and even banal style and his inconsistent persona being countered by the emotional effect of a predominantly elegiac tone. Sturgeon's book is more tightly woven than either of these, and unified in part by a consistent tone of wonder and discovery, which adapts itself chameleon-like to different characters and situations, but its very intensity within the limits of language he has set for himself results in some rather gauche sentimentality and melodrama, and what is almost a denial of human complexity. Asimov, Ballard, and Budrys all suffer, to some extent, from the awkward use in their books of the device of the limited point-of-view, which Sturgeon uses admirably in the middle section of his novel. While the limitation to a single consciousness, slightly amplified beyond the first person narration of

---

[4]In surveys aimed at defining the average reader, "there is nothing to contradict the hypothesis that he is an intellectualized, somewhat detached individual who has severely repressed his sexual interests." Ednita P. Bernabev, "Science Fiction: A New Mythos," The Psycho-analytic Quarterly, XXVI, 4 (1957), 527-535.

experience, successfully unifies all three books, the
intellectual and psychological limitations of those
characters are such that their awareness of themselves and
of their environments is far from complete, and the promise
of life and meaning implicit in their situations is not
fulfilled in these novels. The tendency of Lije Baley, a
simple, conventional bureaucrat, to see only the obvious
is captured by Asimov's plain, lucid, sometimes ponderous
style. The quick, nervous, even jumpy style that Budrys
affects is at least partly responsible for the flatness of
his minor characters and the impression that his protagonist
is blind to any but clichéd action and behavior. The
ornate, almost langorous style of Ballard coincides with the
dreamy behavior of his "hero," for whom other people are
little more than silhouettes. The characterization resulting from this restriction may be deliberate, and barely
adequate, but the impression of the fiction as a whole is
badly cramped, except perhaps in the case of Ballard, where
the hero's impressions of phenomena are so obviously more
important than his thoughts about people.

But the pulp tradition has not been merely a debilitating influence on these authors. The need for clarity and
relative simplicity in commercial markets makes for a
directness of style and impression, unmarred by irrelevan-
cies (if also unmarred by literary niceties). The need for
story eliminates or at least reduces the interminable

digressions and lengthy theoretical descriptions which make
so much straight utopian writing all but unreadable. The
sense of adventure and discovery which goes so well with
adolescent psychology and stories of growing up is admirably
suited to a medium which stresses the wonders of the universe and the excitement of scientific discovery, although
it may make any sense of mature emotional involvement
extremely difficult to achieve. The need for scientific
rationalizing tends to anchor one's fantasy, so as not to
let it go too far beyond the bounds of verisimilitude, but
an absolute obeisance to contemporary scientific method,
theory, and knowledge, resulting in thinly disguised propaganda for a particular set of values, is not thereby
demanded. The continuity provided by the science fiction
community of fans, editors, and other writers is responsible
not only for a reservoir of motifs and concepts, but also
for a sense of audience, which in turn offers encouragement,
financially as well as emotionally, to a writer interested
in experimenting and developing science fictional ideas.
And the commercial need for compression and word economy
can help a writer develop a sense of craftsmanship, an
ability to work within limits, and a capacity for effective
use of symbolism, suggesting by word and image much that
the average fan's lack of patience with philosophizing and
literary "difficulties" will not allow him fully, and
perhaps laboriously, to develop. In other words, it should

be recognized that the style and traditions of pulp science fiction, although clearly different from those of great literature, are alive and functional, and even open to change.

Each of the six authors is clearly conscious of his audience's taste for the simplicity and obviousness of pulp fiction conventions and where he takes them beyond the boundaries of their prejudices is not in the area of style. Like all good science fiction, and unlike much other popular art, these books present their readers with something to think about. Love and death, art and religion, progress and sterility, as well as the promise and threat of science are frequently important considerations, even in the worst science fiction. Although they are often treated in the abstract, and the thinking is sometimes rather fuzzy, at least thought is conspicuous by its presence, and there is usually some attempt at translating the abstractions into the concrete particularities of fiction.

In these six novels, scientific abstractions and philosophical ideas, along with archetypal fears and desires, are given concrete form fairly successfully, in an attempt to make clear their human meaning, i.e., their importance for humanity, for Western civilization, for the individual human characters who inhabit these worlds of fiction, and to some extent for the individual reader. For Clarke, for example, God and Satan are reduced to extraterrestrial intelligent beings, utopia comes about only because justice is administered painlessly from above, and man is both puny and great from the perspective of the universe, puny in intellect by comparison with the Over-lords, great in escaping the intellect and joining the Overmind. And against the background of cataclysmic changes in man's world and his conception of it, individual men and women pursue their individual dreams. For Asimov, the population explosion ends with the City, the space race with the confederation of the Outer Planets, the advance of technology with the creation of the perfect robot, and the clash of cultures and philosophies is shown in the confron-tation between a single man and a single machine, whose partnership symbolizes a way out of cultural stagnation. Lije Baley, too, is just an ordinary man, for whom this fictional world and the changes in it are real and impor-tant for him in terms of his daily activities, his preju-dices, his self-image. The ideal of partnership and cooperation within the human race as it is now constituted, and without a complete metamorphosis and loss of identity as demanded by Clarke's Overmind, is explored by Sturgeon in terms of parapsychological talents and the overcoming of personal emotional barriers. The potential for good or evil in such a superman is really only hinted at in this novel, which concentrates mainly on the individual loneli-ness and insecurity which must be overcome to achieve community. The traditional paradox of the Tree of Knowledge is Miller's theme, given body by spokesmen for various competing ways of knowledge, of which the scientific way receives the most vivid and flashy presentation. Other theological problems are also propounded, inconclusively, but the protagonists, the abbots and monks of the Order of Leibowitz, are also pictured as very much in this world, and having to deal with practical as well as theoretical knowledge, daily living as well as the vision of eternal life, and allegiance to an earthly ideal (preservation of human culture) in fulfillment of a heavenly one (coming to terms with God). Immortality of the flesh is achieved by machine in Budrys' fiction, in a quest which ultimately seems to reflect man's total involvement with his natural environment. These two goals are given concrete shape in the alien artifact on the moon and in Hawks's gigantic device for transmitting signals and recreating matter, while the adventure of exploration is balanced on earth by interpersonal episodes revolving around the question of and quest for personal identity. Finally, Ballard's nonsentient crystallizing process makes time itself concrete for his characters whose posturings and melodramatic conflicts, whose choices of one "living death" over another are fundamentally irrelevant in the face of slow, but irresistible time, except insofar as these poses and decisions define their characters to their own satisfaction.

Each of these novels, then, achieves a unique variation on a number of traditional forms and ideas, satisfies to some extent the desire for aesthetic form and balance as well as the desire for eventful action and adventure, and pays some attention to the need for verisimilitude and an appropriate style, all within the limitations of pulp or popular fiction. If none of them is a masterpiece, none of them is exactly a negligible accomplishment, either; even the Asimov book is a striking <u>tour de force</u>, and Miller's novel is a solid literary achievement.

As far as the progress of science fiction in general is concerned, of course, these six studies are only suggestive, not a thorough and complete survey of the field. Such a study would probably be voluminous, going into much more depth as regards the science in science fiction, the psychological aspects of fantasy, and the relationship of science fiction to "popular" literature in general and to the mass media. It would also have to include numerous other authors of some importance, historically, intellectually, and aesthetically. Besides Verne, Wells, and the other authors of the turn of the century, it would have to cover some utopian and Gothic fantasy before them and such pioneers in the pulp field as H. P. Lovecraft, E. E. Smith, John Taine, and John W. Campbell, Jr. Outside the pulp field since the

Twenties, such a project would have to include consideration

of the anti-utopians and of such recent writers as Gore

Vidal, William Golding, Anthony Burgess, Bernard Wolfe,

Kurt Vonnegut, Jr., and George R. Stewart. Inside the pulp

field a number of writers come to mind who have written

books roughly as good as the six examined here, including

(in alphabetical order) Brian Aldiss, Alfred Bester, James

Blish, Ray Bradbury, Hal Clement, Samuel Delany, Philip K.

Dick, Robert A. Heinlein, Edgar Pangborn, Cordwainer Smith,

A. E. Van Vogt, John Wyndham, and Roger Zelazny. In addi-

tion, it would have to consider contemporary writers in

other countries and languages.

As far as the prospects of science fiction (and

science fiction studies) are concerned, it is possible that

studies such as this one, Alexei Panshin's critical volume

on Heinlein, and to some extent Sam Moskowitz's series,

will help general and specialized readers to see science

fiction more in terms of individual works and writers, and

less in terms of a conglomerate or corporate image.[5] If,

as I suspect, the science fictional way of seeing (specula-

tive, planning, taking science and technology into account

---

[5]Alexei Panshin, Heinlein in Dimension: A Critical
Analysis (Chicago, 1968). Sam Moskowitz, Explorers of the
Infinite: Shapers of Science Fiction (Cleveland and New
York, 1963), Seekers of Tomorrow: Masters of Modern Science
Fiction (Cleveland and New York, 1966), and the companion
anthologies, Masterpieces of Science Fiction (Cleveland and
New York, 1966), and Modern Masterpieces of Science Fiction
(Cleveland and New York, 1965).

as part of the real world) is gaining, interest in reading and writing science fiction should increase, thereby increasing the remuneration and probably improving the competition and the criticism.[6] Perhaps, as Kingsley Amis has suggested, "serious writers as yet unborn or still at school will soon regard science fiction as a natural way of writing."[7] At present, however, there are still significant obstacles in the way of "great science fiction" being written. Writers inside the science fiction community are hampered perhaps by being too close to the body of tradition to break away, and by being paid too little to allow them- selves the luxury of time in thinking over carefully, feel- ing at length, and rewriting.[8] And writers outside the pulp field are perhaps too close to the anti-scientific tradition that C. P. Snow identifies with the subculture of

---

[6]Concerning literature's acknowledgment of science and technology, see, for example: Geoffrey Barraclough, An Introduction to Contemporary History (Baltimore, 1967), pp. 233-268; Stephen Spender, The Struggle of the Modern (Berkeley and Los Angeles, 1965), passim.

[7]From a taped conversation between Amis, Brian Aldiss, and C. S. Lewis, "Unreal Estates," in C. S. Lewis, Of Other Worlds (New York, 1966), p. 94.

[8]Regarding the science fiction tradition, James Blish maintains that most science fiction writers are capa- ble of writing other things, but afraid of it, too: William Atheling, Jr. [James Blish], The Issue at Hand: Studies in Contemporary Magazine Science Fiction, ed. James Blish (Chicago, 1964), pp. 121-130. Concerning the problems of making a living, see Algis Budrys, "Galaxy Bookshelf," Galaxy, December, 1965, p. 151, and June, 1966, p. 148.

the "humanists" (although humanism, logically, should
embrace whatever is human, including science), and too
little concerned with scientific accuracy and the logic of
extrapolation.[9] There is also the fact that precious
little great literature is ever written at any one time, a
principle which applies to the main stream as well as to
science fiction. But Amis' suggestion is an interesting
one, posed in a truly science fictional manner.

---

[9]C. P. Snow, The Two Cultures and the Scientific
Revolution (New York, 1959).

BIBLIOGRAPHIES

BIBLIOGRAPHIES

Prefatory Notes

1. <u>Division</u>. Bibliography A: Primary Works is subdivided into three categories: I. Works by Authors Studied; II. Anthologies of Science Fiction Stories Cited in Text; III. Other Science Fictional Novels, Plays, and Stories. Bibliography B: Secondary Works Cited in Text is subdivided into six categories: I. Books and Essays in Books; II. Magazine Articles; III. Book Reviews of Novels Studied; IV. Continuing Magazine Features; V. Handbooks and Bibliographical Guides; VI. Miscellaneous Published and Unpublished Materials.

2. <u>Comprehensiveness</u>. Even a full accounting of useful works consulted would require twice as many entries. To avoid making the bibliographical part of this study too long and unwieldy, only works cited in the text have been included, except in two sections. Section I in Bibliography A includes all known books of fiction written by Clarke, Asimov, Sturgeon, Miller, Budrys, and Ballard. Section III in Bibliography A includes at least one work by every author cited in the text.

3. <u>Abbreviations</u>. Science fiction magazines are identified, as in the text, by their short names or abbreviations. Astounding stands for Astounding Science Fiction (March, 1938, through January, 1960) and Astounding Science Fact and Fiction (February, 1960, through September, 1960). Analog stands for Analog Science Fact and Fiction (October, 1960, through November, 1961), Analog Science Fact--Science Fiction (December, 1961, through March, 1965), and Analog Science Fiction--Science Fact (April, 1965, through January, 1969). F&SF stands for The Magazine of Fantasy and Science Fiction (Winter-Spring, 1950, through January, 1969). Galaxy stands for Galaxy Science Fiction (January, 1951, through September 1958), and Galaxy Magazine (October, 1958, through January, 1969). IF is also called IF, Worlds of Science Fiction, although the subtitle is not included in the publishing data at the bottom of the title page (March, 1952, through January, 1969). New Worlds stands for New Worlds Science Fiction (March, 1953, through April, 1964)

and New Worlds S F (May, 1964, through December, 1967).
Venture stands for Venture Science Fiction (January, 1957,
through July, 1958).

    4. Pseudonyms. With few exceptions, well-known
pseudonyms have been left intact. In the following alpha-
betical listing of those pseudonyms known to me, the
author's real name is in parentheses: Anthony Boucher
(William Anthony Parker White), Anthony Burgess (John
Anthony Burgess Wilson), John Christopher (Christopher
Youd), Hal Clement (Harry C. Stubbs), Edmund Crispin (R. B.
Montgomery), George Eliot (Mary Ann Evans), H. H. Holmes
(William Anthony Parker White), Murray Leinster (Will F.
Jenkins), George Orwell (Eric Blair), J. H. Rosny aîné
(Joseph Henri Honoré Boëx), Nevil Shute (Nevil Shute
Norway), Cordwainer Smith (Paul A. Linebarger), Fyodor
Sologub (Fedor Kuzmich Teternikov), John Taine (Eric Temple
Bell), William Tenn (Phillip Klass), Mark Twain (Samuel
Langhorne Clemens), John Wyndham (John Beynon Harris).
Edward Hamilton Waldo is the name Theodore Sturgeon was born
with, but the latter is now his legal name, according to
Sam Moskowitz, Seekers of Tomorrow: Masters of Modern
Science Fiction (Cleveland and New York, 1966), p. 232.

BIBLIOGRAPHY A: PRIMARY WORKS

I. Works by Authors Studied

Listing for each author includes all books of fiction published through December 31, 1968, arranged according to date of first appearance in book form. Date of novels' prior magazine appearance given in parentheses unless both dates are the same. Magazine pieces cited above in text, including original appearance of the specific novels analyzed, listed according to date of first publication.

a. Arthur C. Clarke (chapter III)

1950   "Guardian Angel," Famous Fantastic Mysteries, April, pp. 98ff. Also in New Worlds, Winter, pp. 2ff.

1951   Prelude to Space. New York.
Sands of Mars. New York.

1952   Islands in the Sky (juvenile). New York.

1953   Against the Fall of Night (1948). New York.
Childhood's End. New York.
Expedition to Earth (stories). New York.

1955   Earthlight (1951). New York.

1956   The City and the Stars (revision of Against the Fall of Night). New York.
Reach for Tomorrow (stories). New York.

1957   The Deep Range. New York.
Tales from the White Hart (stories). New York.

1958   The Other Side of the Sky (stories). New York.

1959   Across the Sea of Stars (omnibus, including Childhood's End--edition cited above in text--, Earthlight, and 18 stories from previous collections). New York.

1961   A Fall of Moondust. New York.
From the Ocean, From the Stars (omnibus, including The City and the Stars, The Deep Range, and all 24 stories from The Other Side of the Sky). New York.

1962   Tales of Ten Worlds (stories). New York.

1963   Dolphin Island (juvenile). New York.
        Glide Path (non-science fiction). New York.

1964   Prelude to Mars (omnibus, including Prelude to Space,
            Sands of Mars, and 16 stories from previous
            collections). New York.

1968   2001: A Space Odyssey. New York.

                b. Isaac Asimov (chapter IV)

1950   I, Robot (stories). New York.
        Pebble in the Sky. Garden City.

1951   Foundation (1942-45). New York.
        The Stars, Like Dust. Garden City.

1952   The Currents of Space. Garden City.
        David Starr: Space Ranger (juvenile, published under
            pseudonym of "Paul French"). Garden City.
        Foundation and Empire (1945-46). New York.

1953   "The Caves of Steel," Galaxy, October, pp. 4-66;
            November, pp. 98-159; December, pp. 108-159.
        Lucky Starr and the Pirates of the Asteroids (juve-
            nile, published under pseudonym of "Paul French").
            Garden City.
        Second Foundation (1948-49). New York.

1954   The Caves of Steel. Garden City.
        Lucky Starr and the Oceans of Venus (juvenile, pub-
            lished under pseudonym of "Paul French"). Garden
            City.

1955   The End of Eternity. Garden City.
        The Martian Way and Other Stories. Garden City.

1956   Lucky Starr and the Big Sun of Mercury (juvenile,
            published under pseudonym of "Paul French").
            Garden City.

1957   Earth is Room Enough (stories). Garden City.
        Lucky Starr and the Moons of Jupiter (juvenile,
            published under pseudonym of "Paul French").
            Garden City.
        The Naked Sun (1956). Garden City.

1958   The Death Dealers (non-science fiction). New York.
Lucky Starr and the Rings of Saturn (juvenile,
     published under pseudonym of "Paul French").
Garden City.

1959   Nine Tomorrows (stories). Garden City.

1964   The Rest of the Robots (omnibus, including The Caves
     of Steel--edition cited above in text--, The
     Naked Sun, and 8 stories not contained in previ-
     ous collections). Garden City.

1966   Fantastic Voyage. New York.
The Foundation Trilogy (omnibus, including Foundation,
     Foundation and Empire, Second Foundation).
Garden City.

1967   Asimov's Mysteries (stories, some non-science
     fiction). Garden City.
Through a Glass, Clearly (stories). London.

          c. Theodore Sturgeon (chapter V)

1948   Without Sorcery (stories). New York.

1950   The Dreaming Jewels. New York.

1952   "Baby is Three," Galaxy, October, pp. 4-62.

1953   E Pluribus Unicorn (stories). New York.
More than Human (edition cited above in text).
     New York.

1955   A Way Home (stories). New York.
Caviar (stories). New York.

1956   I, Libertine (non-science fiction, published under
     pseudonym of "Frederick R. Ewing"). New York.

1958   The Cosmic Rape. New York.
A Touch of Strange (stories). New York.

1959   Aliens Four (stories). New York.

1960   Beyond (stories). New York.
Venus Plus X. New York.

1961   Some of Your Blood. New York.
Voyage to the Bottom of the Sea. New York.

1964   Sturgeon in Orbit (stories). New York.

1966   Starshine (stories). New York.

        d. Walter M. Miller, Jr. (chapter VI)

1955   "A Canticle for Leibowitz," F&SF, April, pp. 93-111.
        "The Darfsteller," Astounding, January, pp. 10-65.

1956   "And the Light is Risen," F&SF, August, pp. 3-80.

1957   "The Last Canticle," F&SF, February, pp. 3-50.

1960   A Canticle for Leibowitz (edition cited above in
            text). Philadelphia.

1962   Conditionally Human (stories). New York.

1964   The View from the Stars (stories). New York.

        e. Algis Budrys (chapter VII)

1954   False Night. New York.

1955   "Citadel," Astounding, February, pp. 70-92.

1956   "The Executioner," Astounding, January, pp. 8-38.

1958   Man of Earth (1956). New York.
        Who? New York.

1960   "Rogue Moon," F&SF, December, pp. 5-38, 78-125.
        Rogue Moon (edition cited above in text). Greenwich,
            Connecticut.
        The Unexpected Dimension (stories). New York.

1961   Some Will Not Die (revision of False Night).
            Evanston, Illinois.

1962   Budrys' Inferno (stories). New York.
        The Falling Torch (1958-59). New York.

1967   The Amsirs and the Iron Thorn (1966-67). Greenwich,
            Connecticut.

f. J. G. Ballard (chapter VIII)

1962 Billennium (stories). New York.
The Drowned World. New York.
The Voices of Time (stories). New York.
The Wind from Nowhere. New York.

1963 Passport to Eternity (stories). New York.

1964 The Burning World. New York.
"The Illuminated Man," F&SF, May, pp. 5-31.
Terminal Beach (stories). New York.
The Terminal Beach (stories). London.

1966 "The Assassination Weapon," New Worlds, April,
pp. 4-12.
The Crystal World (edition cited above in text).
New York.
The Impossible Man (stories). New York.

1967 "The Cloud-Sculptors of Coral D," F&SF, December,
pp. 113-127.

II. Anthologies of Science Fiction Stories
Cited in Text

Alphabetical listing by editors, including all
anthologies cited above in text. Anthologies appearing
in series are grouped together as a single item.

Asimov, Isaac, ed. The Hugo Winners. New York, 1962.

Bleiler, Everett, and Dikty, T. E., eds. The Best Science-
Fiction Stories: 1949 through --1954. 6 vols.
New York, 1949-1954.

Crispin, Edmund, ed. Best S F through Best S F Five:
Science Fiction Stories. 5 vols. London, 1955, 1956,
1958, 1961, 1964.

Franklin, H. Bruce. Future Perfect: American Science
Fiction of the Nineteenth Century. New York, 1966.

Healy, Raymond J., and McComas, J. Francis, eds.
Adventures in Time and Space. New York, 1946.

Merril, Judith, ed. S F: The Year's Greatest Science-
     Fiction and Fantasy through Fourth Annual Edition,
     changed to The Year's Best S-F, Fifth through Eleventh
     Annual Editions, changed to S F 12. 12 vols.
     New York, 1956-1966, 1968.

Moorcock, Michael, ed. Best S. F. Stories from "New
     Worlds." London, 1967.

Moskowitz, Sam, ed. Masterpieces of Science Fiction.
     Cleveland and New York, 1966.

_____. Modern Masterpieces of Science Fiction.
     Cleveland and New York, 1965.

_____. Science Fiction by Gaslight: A History and
     Anthology of Science Fiction in the Popular Magazines,
     1891-1911. Cleveland and New York, 1968.

The "Playboy" Book of Science Fiction and Fantasy. Chicago,
     1966.

The "Post" Reader of Fantasy and Science Fiction. Garden
     City, 1964.

Pratt, Fletcher, ed. World of Wonder. New York, 1951.

Tenn, William, ed. Children of Wonder. New York, 1953.

III. Other Science Fictional Novels,

Plays, and Stories

     Alphabetical listing of authors referred to in text,
including at least one work representative of his science
fictional or utopian writing. Place and date given indicate edition available. Unless otherwise indicated, one
date in parentheses indicates first publication in book
form; a second date indicates earlier magazine publication.

Aldiss, Brian. Graybeard. New York, 1965 (1964).

_____. The Long Afternoon of Earth (story-cycle).
     New York, 1962 (1961).

_____. Starship. New York, 1960 (1958).

Andrae, Johann Valentin. Christianopolis, trans. Felix
     Emil Held. New York, 1916 (1619).

Bacon, Francis. "New Atlantis," Essays and New Atlantis. New York, 1942 (1627).

Balzac, Honoré de. Le Médecin de campagne, in v. 13 of Oeuvres complètes, ed. Jean A. Ducourneau. Paris, 1965 (1833).

_____. La Recherche de l'absolu, in v. 14 of Oeuvres complètes, ed. Jean A. Ducourneau. Paris, 1965 (1834).

Bellamy, Edward. The Blindman's World and Other Stories. Boston, 1898.

_____. Doctor Heidenhoff's Process. New York, 1880.

_____. Equality. Toronto, 1897.

_____. Looking Backward: 2000-1887. New York, 1962 (1888).

Bester, Alfred. The Demolished Man. Chicago, 1953.

_____. The Stars My Destination. New York, 1956.

Blish, James. A Case of Conscience. London, 1960 (1958).

Bradbury, Ray. Fahrenheit 451. London, 1954.

_____. The Martian Chronicles (story-cycle). Garden City, 1950.

Briussov, Valeriy. "The Republic of the Southern Cross," The Republic of the Southern Cross and Other Stories, trans. unknown. New York, 1919 (before 1908, date of German translation).

Brown, Charles Brockden. Wieland. New York, 1926 (1798).

Brown, Fredric. The Lights in the Sky are Stars. New York, 1953.

_____. What Mad Universe. Chicago, 1948.

Bulgakov, Mikhail. "The Fatal Eggs," The Fatal Eggs: Soviet Satire, trans. Mirra Ginsburg. New York, 1965 (1925).

_____. The Heart of a Dog, trans. Michael Glenny. New York, 1968 (written 1925).

Bulgakov, Mikhail. The Master and Margarita, trans. Mirra Ginsburg. New York, 1967 (written 1925-1940).

Burgess, Anthony. A Clockwork Orange. London, 1964 (1962).

_____. The Wanting Seed. London, 1965 (1962).

Burroughs, Edgar Rice. A Princess of Mars. New York, 1963 (1917; 1912).

Butler, Samuel. Erewhon and Erewhon Revisited. London and New York, 1962 (1872 and 1901).

Caidin, Martin. Marooned. New York, 1965 (1964).

Campanella, Tommasso. City of the Sun, trans. unknown, in Famous Utopias, ed. unknown, introduction by Charles B. Andrews. New York, n.d. (1637; written 1623).

Campbell, John W., Jr. Who Goes There? and Other Stories. Chicago, 1955.

Čapek, Karel. The Absolute at Large, trans. unknown. New York, 1927.

_____. Krakatit, trans. Lawrence Hyde. London, 1925 (1924).

_____. R. U. R., trans. Paul Selver, in R. U. R. and the Insect Play, by the Brothers Čapek. London, New York, and Toronto, 1964 (1921).

_____. War with the Newts, trans. M. and R. Weatherall. New York, 1964 (1936).

Christopher, John. No Blade of Grass. New York, 1967 (1956).

Clement, Hal. Mission of Gravity. Garden City, 1954.

Collier, John. Fancies and Goodnights (stories). New York, 1961 (1951).

Cummings, Ray. The Girl in the Golden Atom. New York, 1923 (original magazine publication, 1919).

Cyrano de Bergerac, Saavinien. Histoire comique des états et empires de la lune et du soleil, ed. P. L. Jacob [Paul Lacroix]. Paris, 1858 (1650, 1656).

Davidson, Avram. Or All the Seas with Oysters (stories). New York, 1962.

DeCamp, L. Sprague. Lest Darkness Fall. New York, 1941 (1939).

Delany, Samuel R. _Babel-17_. New York, 1966.

_____. _The Ballad of Beta-II_. New York, 1965.

_____. _The Einstein Intersection_. New York, 1967.

_____. _Nova_. Garden City, 1968.

del Rey, Lester. _Nerves_. New York, 1956.

Dennis, Nigel. _Cards of Identity_. New York, 1960 (1955).

Dick, Philip K. _Eye in the Sky_. New York, 1957.

_____. _The Man in the High Castle_. New York, 1964 (1962).

_____. _Solar Lottery_. New York, 1955.

_____. _The Three Stigmata of Palmer Eldritch_. Garden City, 1965.

Döblin, Alexander. _Berg, Meere, und Giganten_. Berlin, 1924.

_____. _Giganten_ (revision of _Berg, Meere, und Giganten_). Berlin, 1932.

Dominik, Hans. _Atomgewicht 500_. Berlin, 1935.

_____. _Das Erbe der Uraniden_. Berlin, 1928.

Doyle, Arthur Conan. _The Complete Professor Challenger Stories_ (omnibus, including _The Lost World_, _The Poison Belt_, _The Land of Mist_, "The Disintegration Machine," and "When the World Screamed.") London, 1963 (1912, 1913, 1926, 1928, 1929).

Eliot, George. _Middlemarch_, ed. Gordon S. Haight. Cambridge, Massachusetts, 1956 (1871-72).

Ely, David. _Seconds_. New York, 1964 (1963).

Farmer, Philip José. _The Alley God_ (stories). New York, 1959.

_____. _The Lovers_. New York, 1962 (1959).

_____. _Strange Relations_ (stories). New York, 1960.

Fast, Howard. _The Edge of Tomorrow_ (stories). New York, 1961.

Flaubert, Gustave. Madame Bovary, ed. Christian Gauss. New York, 1958 (1857).

Forster, E. M. "The Machine Stops," Collected Short Stories of E. M. Forster. London, 1965 (1909).

Frank, Pat. Alas, Babylon. New York, 1960 (1959).

_____. Forbidden Area. Philadelphia, 1956.

_____. Mr. Adam. Philadelphia and New York, 1946.

Gail, Otto Willi. Der Schuss ins All. Breslau, 1925.

_____. "The Shot into Infinity," trans. Francis Currier, Wonder Stories Quarterly, Fall, 1929, pp. 6ff.

_____. Der Stein vom Mond. Breslau, 1926.

_____. "The Stone from the Moon," trans. Francis Currier, Wonder Stories Quarterly, March, 1930, pp. 294ff.

Gernsback, Hugo. Ralph 124C 41+, 2nd ed. New York, 1958 (1925; 1911).

Gillon, Diana and Meir. The Unsleep. New York, 1962 (1961).

Goethe, Johann Wolfgang von. Faust, parts one and two, ed. Erich Trunz. Hamburg, 1963.

Golding, William. The Brass Butterfly (play). London, 1958.

_____. "Envoy Extraordinary," in Sometime, Never: Three Tales of Imagination by William Golding, John Wyndham, Mervyn Peake. New York, 1957.

_____. The Inheritors. New York, 1963 (1955).

_____. Lord of the Flies. New York, 1964 (1954).

Graves, Robert. Watch the Northwind Rise. New York, 1949.

Hamilton, Edmond. Captain Future series. 15 of 17 novels in Captain Future magazine, 1941-1944; 4 stories and 2 of 3 novels in Startling Stories, 1945-1950.

Hanstein, Otfrid von. "Between Earth and Moon," trans. Francis Currier, Wonder Stories Quarterly, Fall, 1930, pp. 6ff.

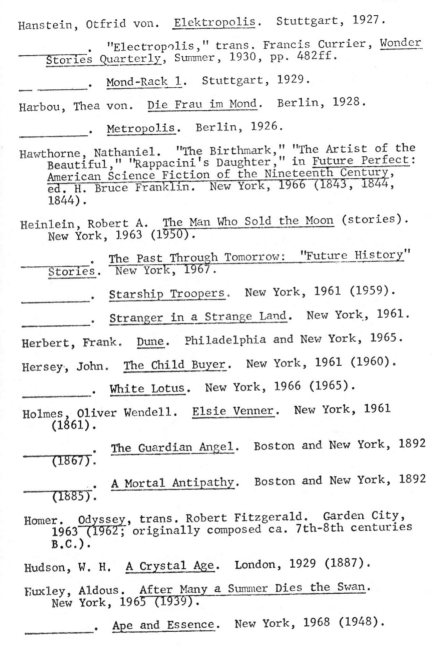

Hanstein, Otfrid von. Elektropolis. Stuttgart, 1927.

_____. "Electropolis," trans. Francis Currier, Wonder Stories Quarterly, Summer, 1930, pp. 482ff.

_____. Mond-Rack 1. Stuttgart, 1929.

Harbou, Thea von. Die Frau im Mond. Berlin, 1928.

_____. Metropolis. Berlin, 1926.

Hawthorne, Nathaniel. "The Birthmark," "The Artist of the Beautiful," "Rappacini's Daughter," in Future Perfect: American Science Fiction of the Nineteenth Century, ed. H. Bruce Franklin. New York, 1966 (1843, 1844, 1844).

Heinlein, Robert A. The Man Who Sold the Moon (stories). New York, 1963 (1950).

_____. The Past Through Tomorrow: "Future History" Stories. New York, 1967.

_____. Starship Troopers. New York, 1961 (1959).

_____. Stranger in a Strange Land. New York, 1961.

Herbert, Frank. Dune. Philadelphia and New York, 1965.

Hersey, John. The Child Buyer. New York, 1961 (1960).

_____. White Lotus. New York, 1966 (1965).

Holmes, Oliver Wendell. Elsie Venner. New York, 1961 (1861).

_____. The Guardian Angel. Boston and New York, 1892 (1867).

_____. A Mortal Antipathy. Boston and New York, 1892 (1885).

Homer. Odyssey, trans. Robert Fitzgerald. Garden City, 1963 (1962; originally composed ca. 7th-8th centuries B.C.).

Hudson, W. H. A Crystal Age. London, 1929 (1887).

Huxley, Aldous. After Many a Summer Dies the Swan. New York, 1965 (1939).

_____. Ape and Essence. New York, 1968 (1948).

Huxley, Aldous. Brave New World. New York, 1962 (1932).

_____. Island. New York, 1962.

Jackson, Shirley. The Haunting of Hill House. New York, 1962 (1959).

Jünger, Ernst. Gläserne Bienen. Stuttgart, 1957.

_____. Heliopolis. Tübingen, 1949.

Kellermann, Bernhard. Der Tunnel. Frankfurt a. M., 1952 (1913).

Kline, Otis Adalbert. The Outlaws of Mars. New York, 1961 (magazine version, 1933).

Kornbluth, C. M. Not This August. Garden City, 1955.

_____. The Syndic. Garden City, 1953.

Kuttner, Henry. Bypass to Otherness (stories). New York, 1961.

_____. Return to Otherness (stories). New York, 1962.

_____, and Moore, C. L. No Boundaries (stories). New York, 1955.

Lasswitz, Kurd. Auf Zwei Planeten. Leipzig, 1897.

_____. Nie und Immer (stories). 2 vols. Leipzig, 1902.

Leiber, Fritz. The Big Time. New York, 1961.

_____. Gather, Darkness. New York, 1950.

_____. The Wanderer. New York, 1964.

Leinster, Murray. Colonial Survey (stories). New York, 1956.

Lewis, C. S. Out of the Silent Planet. New York, 1962 (1938).

_____. Perelandra. New York, 1962 (1943).

_____. That Hideous Strength. New York, 1962 (1945).

Lewis, Matthew G. The Monk, ed. Louis F. Peck. New York, 1959 (1796).

Lewis, Percy Wyndham. The Childermass, Section I.
London, 1928.

_____. The Human Age: Book Two, Monstre Gai; Book
Three, Malign Fiesta. London, 1955.

London, Jack. The Iron Heel. Chicago and New York, 1913
(1907).

Lovecraft, H. P. The Case of Charles Dexter Ward.
New York, 1965 (1952; 1941).

_____. "The Colour Out of Space" and "The Shadow Out
of Time," in The Outsider and Others (stories), ed.
August Derleth and Donald Wandrei. Sauk City,
Wisconsin, 1939 (original magazine publications, 1927,
1936).

Lucian of Samosata. "A True Story," Selected Satires of
Lucian, ed. and trans. Lionel Casson. Garden City,
1962 (originally written 2nd century A.D.).

MacDonald, John D. Ballroom of the Skies. Greenwich,
Connecticut, 1968 (1952).

_____. The Girl, the Gold Watch, and Everything.
Greenwich, Connecticut, 1965 (1962).

_____. Wine of the Dreamers. Greenwich, Connecticut,
1968 (1951).

Maurois, André. Le Chapître suivant. Paris, 1927.

_____. La Machine à lire les pensées. Paris, 1937.

_____. Le Peseur d'âmes. Paris, 1931.

_____. Voyage au pays des Articoles. Paris, 1928.

Melville, Herman. "The Bell-Tower," in Future Perfect:
American Science Fiction of the Nineteenth Century,
ed. H. Bruce Franklin. New York, 1966 (1855).

_____. Moby-Dick. New York, 1961 (1851).

Mercier, Sebastien. L'An deux mille quatre cent quarante;
reve s'il fût jamais. London, 1775 (1770).

Merritt, A. The Moon Pool. New York, 1966 (original
magazine version, 1919).

Merritt, A. The Ship of Ishtar. New York, 1966 (original magazine version, 1924).

Meyrink, Gustave. Der Golem. Leipzig and Berlin, 1915.

Miller, Warren. Looking for the General. New York, 1964.

_____. The Siege of Harlem. New York, 1965 (1964).

Moore, C. L. Judgment Night. New York, 1965 (1952; 1943).

Moore, Ward. Bring the Jubilee. New York, 1953 (1952).

More, Thomas. Utopia, trans. unknown, ed. Edward Surtz. New Haven and London, 1964.

Morris, William. News from Nowhere. Chicago, n.d. (1890).

Orwell, George. 1984. New York, 1949.

Pangborn, Edgar. Davy. New York, 1964.

_____. The Judgment of Eve. New York, 1966.

_____. A Mirror for Observers. Garden City, 1954.

_____. West of the Sun. Garden City, 1953.

Plato. Republic, "Timaeus," and "Critias," in v. 3 of The Dialogues of Plato, trans. Benjamin Jowett. London, 1931 (originally written 4th century B.C.).

Poe, Edgar Allan. "Descent into the Maelstrom," "The Facts in the Case of M. Valdemar," "The Murders in the Rue Morgue," "The Mystery of Arthur Gordon Pym," "The Mystery of Marie Roget," "The Purloined Letter," and "A Tale of the Ragged Mountains," The Complete Tales and Poems of Edgar Allan Poe. New York, 1938 (1841, 1845, 1841, 1837, 1842, 1844, 1844).

_____. "The Facts in the Case of M. Valdemar" and "A Tale of the Ragged Mountains" also in Future Perfect: American Science Fiction of the Nineteenth Century, ed. H. Bruce Franklin. New York, 1966.

Pohl, Frederik. Alternating Currents (stories). New York, 1956.

_____. The Case Against Tomorrow (stories). New York, 1956.

_____. Tomorrow Times 7 (stories). New York, 1959.

Pohl, Frederik, and Kornbluth, C. M. <u>The Space Merchants</u>.
New York, 1960 (1953).

Rand, Ayn. <u>Anthem</u>. New York, 1961 (1946).

_____. <u>Atlas Shrugged</u>. New York, 1960 (1957).

Rosny, J. H., <u>aîné</u>. <u>Eyrimah</u>. Paris, 1895.

_____. <u>Le Félin géant</u>. Paris, 1920.

_____. <u>La Force mystérieuse</u>. Paris, 1914.

_____. <u>La Guerre de feu</u>. Paris, 1911.

_____. <u>La Mort de la terre</u>. Paris, 1912.

_____. <u>Vamireh</u>. Paris, 1892.

Russell, Eric Frank. <u>Dreadful Sanctuary</u>. New York, 1963
(1951; 1948).

_____. <u>Dreadful Sanctuary</u>, rev. ed. London, 1967
(1953).

_____. <u>Sentinels from Space</u>. New York, 1960 (1951).

Scheerbart, Paul. <u>Astrale Noveletten</u> (stories). Munich,
1912.

_____. <u>Die grosse Revolution: Ein Mondroman</u>.
Leipzig, 1902.

_____. <u>Lesabèndio: Ein Asteroïden-Roman</u>. Munich,
1913.

_____. <u>Das Perpetuum Mobile; Die Geschichte einer
Erfindung</u>. Leipzig, 1909.

Shaw, Bernard. <u>Back to Methusaleh</u> (play). Baltimore, 1961
(1921).

Shelley, Mary. <u>Frankenstein: Or, The Modern Prometheus</u>.
New York, n.d. (1817).

_____. <u>The Last Man</u>. Lincoln, Nebraska, 1965 (1826).

Shute, Nevil. <u>On the Beach</u>. New York, 1960 (1957).

Simak, Clifford. <u>City</u> (story-cycle). New York, 1952.

_____. <u>Way Station</u>. New York, 1964 (1963).

Siodmak, Kurt. Donovan's Brain. New York, 1961 (1942).

_____. Die Macht im Dunkeln. Zürich and Leipzig, 1937.

_____. Rache im Äther. Berlin, 1932.

Skinner, B. F. Walden Two. New York, 1966 (1948).

Smith, Cordwainer. You Will Never Be the Same (story-cycle). Evanston, Illinois, 1963.

Smith, E. E. Children of the Lens. New York, 1966 (1954; 1947-48).

_____. First Lensman. New York, 1964 (1950).

_____. Galactic Patrol. New York, 1966 (1950; 1937-38).

_____. Gray Lensmen. New York, 1965 (1951; 1939-40).

_____. Second Stage Lensmen. New York, 1965 (1953; 1941-42).

_____. Skylark Duquesne. New York, 1966 (1965).

_____. The Skylark of Space. New York, 1966 (1946; 1928).

_____. Skylark of Valeron. New York, 1963 (1949; 1934-35).

_____. Skylark Three. New York, 1963 (1948; 1930).

_____. Triplanetary. New York, 1965 (1948; 1934).

Sologub, Fyodor. The Created Legend, v. 1 trans. John Cournos. New York, 1916 (trilogy, original publication in 5 parts: 3 parts in Russian, 1907-11; 2 parts in German, 1912-13).

Stapledon, W. Olaf. Last and First Men. Harmondsworth, England, 1963 (1930).

_____. Odd John. New York, 1965 (1935).

_____. Sirius. Harmondsworth, England, 1964 (1944).

_____. Star Maker. New York, 1961 (1937).

Stewart, George R. Earth Abides. New York, 1949.

Swift, Johnathan. Gulliver's Travels, in The Portable Swift, ed. Carl Van Doren. New York, 1960 (1948; original publication, 1726).

Taine, John. Before the Dawn. New York, 1934.

_____. Seeds of Life and White Lily. New York, 1966 (1931; 1931 and 1934; 1930).

Tolkien, J. R. R. Lord of the Rings. 3 vols. New York, 1965 (1955).

Tolstoi, Alexei. Aelita, trans. Lucy Flaxman. Moscow, n.d. (1922).

_____. The Garin Death-Ray, trans. George Hanna. Moscow, 1955 (1927).

Turgenev, Ivan. Fathers and Sons, ed. and trans. Ralph E. Matlaw. New York, 1966 (1862).

Twain, Mark. A Connecticut Yankee in King Arthur's Court. New York, 1949 (1889).

Van Vogt, A. E. Triad (omnibus, including Slan, The World of Null-A, and The Voyage of the Space Beagle). New York, n.d. (1940, 1945, 1950).

Verne, Jules. De la terre à la lune. Paris, 1945 (1865).

_____. The Sphinx of the Ice-Fields, trans. unknown, in Edgar Allan Poe and Jules Verne, The Mystery of Arthur Gordon Pym, ed. Basil Ashmore. London, 1964 (1960; original French publication, 1897).

_____. Vingt mille lieues sous les mers. Paris, 1871 (1870).

_____. Voyage au centre de la terre. Paris, 1945 (1864).

Vidal, Gore. Messiah. New York, 1954.

_____. Visit to a Small Planet (play). New York, 1956.

Villiers de l'Isle-Adam. L'Ève future. Paris, 1887.

Vonnegut, Kurt, Jr. Cat's Cradle. Harmondsworth, England, 1965 (1963).

_____. Player Piano. London, 1954 (1953).

Vonnegut, Kurt, Jr. The Sirens of Titan. New York, 1959.

Waugh, Evelyn. Love Among the Ruins. New York, 1953.

Wells, H. G. A Modern Utopia. Lincoln, Nebraska, 1967 (1905).

_____. The Time Machine, in Seven Science Fiction Novels of H. G. Wells. New York, 1951 (1895; 1888).

Werfel, Franz. Stern der Ungeboren. Frankfurt a. M., 1946.

Wibberley, Leonard. The Mouse on the Moon. New York, 1963 (1962).

_____. The Mouse that Roared. New York, 1959 (1955).

Williamson, Jack. The Humanoids. New York, 1963 (1949).

Wilson, Angus. The Old Men at the Zoo. Harmondsworth, England, 1964 (1961).

Wolfe, Bernard. Limbo. New York, 1952.

Wyndham, John. The John Wyndham Omnibus (including The Day of the Triffids, The Kraken Wakes [originally titled Out of the Deeps in U.S.A.], and The Chrysalids [originally titled Re-Birth in U.S.A.]. New York, 1964 (1951, 1953, 1955).

Zamiatin, Eugene. We, trans. Gregory Zilboorg. New York, 1959 (1924).

Zelazny, Roger. This Immortal. New York, 1966.

Zola, Emile. Le Docteur Pascal, in v. 6 of Oeuvres complètes, ed. Henri Mitterand. Lausanne, 1968 (1893).

BIBLIOGRAPHY B: SECONDARY WORKS

I. Books, and Essays in Books

Alphabetical listing by authors, except for anthologies or collections of essays listed by editor or first
author on title page. Single essays in collections or
anthologies otherwise not directly relevant to this study
are listed by author. Anthologies of science fiction
stories with critical comment and/or apparatus may be found
in Bibliography A: Primary Works, section II: Anthologies.

Albérès, R.-M. "Merveilleux et fantastique: de la féerie
à la 'fiction scientifique,'" chapter XXI, Histoire du
roman moderne. Paris, 1962.

Allott, Kenneth. Jules Verne. New York, 1967.

Amis, Kingsley. New Maps of Hell: A Survey of Science
Fiction. London, 1961.

Anderson, Bernhard. Understanding the Old Testament.
Englewood Cliffs, New Jersey, 1957.

Asimov, Isaac. Is Anyone There? Garden City, 1967.

Atheling, William, Jr. [James Blish]. The Issue at Hand:
Studies in Contemporary Magazine Science Fiction,
ed. James Blish. Chicago, 1964.

Auden, W. H. "The Guilty Vicarage," pp. 146-158 in The
Dyer's Hand. New York, 1962.

Bailey, J. O. Pilgrims Through Space and Time: Trends and
Patterns in Scientific and Utopian Fiction. New York,
1947.

Bamberger, Bernard J. Fallen Angels. Philadelphia, 1952.

Barraclough, Geoffrey. An Introduction to Contemporary
History. Baltimore, 1967.

Barzun, Jacques. Classic, Romantic and Modern, rev. ed.
Garden City, 1961.

Bergier, Jacques. "La science-fiction," in Histoire des
littératures, ed. Raymond Queneau, Encyclopédie de la
Pléiade, III. Paris, 1958.

Bettelheim, Bruno. The Informed Heart: Autonomy in a Mass
Age. Glencoe, Illinois, 1960.

Bloch, Robert. The Eighth Stage of Fandom: Selections from 25 Years of Fan Writing, ed. Earl Kemp. Chicago, 1962.

Boisdeffre, Pierre de. "La 'Science-Fiction,'" pp. 439-440 in Une Histoire vivante de la littérature d'aujourd'hui (1938-1958). Paris, 1958.

Bowman, Sylvia E., et al. Edward Bellamy Abroad: An American Prophet's Influence. New York, 1962.

Bretnor, Reginald, ed. Modern Science Fiction: Its Meaning and Its Future. New York, 1953.

Bridenne, Jean-Jacques. La Littérature française d'imagination scientifique. Dassonville, 1950-51.

Brunetière, Ferdinand. Le Roman naturaliste, rev. ed. Paris, 1892.

Buck, Philo M. The World's Great Age. New York, 1930.

Butler, E[liza] M[arian]. The Myth of the Magus. Cambridge, England, and New York, 1948.

Campbell, John W. Collected Editorials from "Analog," ed. Harry Harrison. Garden City, 1966.

_____. "The Value of Science Fiction," in Science Marches On, ed. James Stokley. New York, 1951.

Clarke, Arthur C. Profiles of the Future: An Inquiry into the Limits of the Possible. New York, Toronto, and London, 1965.

_____. Voices from the Sky: Previews of the Coming Space Age. New York, 1967.

Davenport, Basil. Inquiry into Science Fiction. New York, London, and Toronto, 1955.

_____, et al. The Science Fiction Novel: Imagination and Social Criticism, 2nd ed. Chicago, 1964.

Dedeyan, Charles. Le Thème de Faust dans la littérature européene. 4 vols. Paris, 1954-62.

Durant, Will. The Story of Philosophy. New York, 1953.

Elmgren, John. Gestalt Psychology: A Survey and Some Contributions. Göteborgs Högskoles Årsskrift, 44. Göteborg, 1938.

Eschbach, Lloyd Arthur, ed. Of Worlds Beyond: The Science of Science Fiction Writing. Reading, Pennsylvania, 1947; reprinted Chicago, 1964.

Eurich, Nell. Science in Utopia: A Mighty Design. Cambridge, Massachusetts, 1967.

Evans, I. O. "Introduction," The Sphinx of the Ice-Fields, trans. unknown, in Edgar Allan Poe and Jules Verne, The Mystery of Arthur Gordon Pym, ed. Basil Ashmore. London, 1964.

Fabun, Don. The Dynamics of Change. Englewood Cliffs, New Jersey, 1967.

Fath, Robert. L'influence de la science sur la littérature française dans la seconde moitié du 19e siècle (le roman, la poésie, le théâtre, la critique). Diss. Lausanne, 1901.

Fiedler, Leslie A. Love and Death in the American Novel. New York, 1960.

Foreign Policy Association, eds. Toward the Year 2018. New York, 1968.

Friedman, Norman. "Forms of the Plot," pp. 223-258 in The Theory of the Novel, ed. Philip Stevick. New York, 1967.

Frye, Northrop. Anatomy of Criticism. Princeton, 1957.

Gaer, Joseph. The Legend of the Wandering Jew. New York, 1961.

Garçon, Maurice, and Vinchon, Jean. The Devil: An Historical, Critical and Medical Study, trans. Stephen Haden Guest. London, 1929.

Gardner, Martin. Fads and Fallacies in the Name of Science. New York, 1957.

Gerber, Richard. Utopian Fantasy. London, 1955.

Goncourt, Edmond and Jules de. The Goncourt Journals 1851-1870, ed. and trans. Lewis Galantière. Garden City, 1958.

Gove, Philip Babcock, ed. Webster's Third New International Dictionary. Springfield, Massachusetts, 1961.

Green, Martin. Science and the Shabby Curate of Poetry. New York, 1965.

Green, Roger Lancelyn. Into Other Worlds: Space-Flight in Fiction, from Lucian to Lewis. London, 1958.

Gurwitsch, Aron. The Field of Consciousness. Duquesne Studies, Psychological Series, 2. Pittsburgh, 1964.

Hansel, C. W. M. ESP: A Scientific Evaluation. New York, 1966.

Haycraft, Howard. Murder for Pleasure: The Life and Times of the Detective Story. New York and London, 1941.

Hayek, F. A. The Counter-Revolution of Science: Studies in the Abuse of Reason. Glencoe, Illinois, 1952.

Henkin, Leo J. Darwinism in the English Novel 1860-1910: The Impact of Evolution on Victorian Fiction. New York, 1940.

Herbrüggen, Hubertus Schulte. Utopie und Anti-Utopie: Von der Strukturanalyse zur Strukturtypologie. Beiträge zur Englischen Philologie, 43. Bochum-Langendreer, 1960.

Highet, Gilbert. "Perchance to Dream," pp. 3-10 in A Clerk of Oxenford. New York, 1954.

_____. "From World to World," pp. 130-137 in People, Places, and Books. New York, 1953.

Hillegas, Mark R. The Future as Nightmare: H. G. Wells and the Anti-Utopians. New York, 1967.

Holland, Norman N. The Dynamics of Literary Response. New York, 1968.

Hughes, Pennethorne. Witchcraft. Baltimore, 1967.

Isaacs, Alan. The Survival of God in the Scientific Age. Baltimore, 1966.

Jones, Ernest. Nightmare, Witches, and Devils. New York, [1931].

Jung, C. G. Flying Saucers: A Modern Myth of Things Seen in the Sky, trans. R. F. C. Hull. New York, 1959.

Kahn, Herman. On Thermonuclear War. Princeton, 1961.

Kahn, Herman. Thinking About the Unthinkable. New York, 1962.

_____, and Wiener, Anthony J. The Year 2000: A Framework for Speculation on the Next Thirty-Three Years. New York, 1967.

Knight, Damon. In Search of Wonder: Essays on Modern Science Fiction, 2nd ed. Chicago, 1967.

Koestler, Arthur. "The Boredom of Fantasy," pp. 142-147 in The Trail of the Dinosaur and Other Essays. New York, 1955.

Krysmanski, Hans-Jurgen. Die utopische Methode. Dortmunder Schriften zur Sozialforschung, 21. Köln and Opladen, 1963.

Lampa, Anton. Das naturwissenschaftliche Märchen. Reichenberg, 1919.

Lewis, C. S. An Experiment in Criticism. Cambridge, England, 1965.

_____. Of Other Worlds: Essays and Stories. New York, 1966.

Lindner, Robert. "The Jet-Propelled Couch," in The Fifty-Minute Hour: A Collection of True Psychoanalytic Tales. New York, 1961.

Martino, P. Le Naturalisme français (1870-1895). Paris, 1923.

Matthey, H[ubert]. Essai sur le merveilleux dans la littérature française depuis 1800: contribution à l'étude des genres. Diss. Lausanne, 1915.

Messac, Regis. La "detective novel" et l'influence de la pensée scientifique. Bibliothèque de la Revue de Littérature Comparée, 59. Paris, 1929.

Moore, Patrick A. Science and Fiction. London, 1957.

Moskowitz, Sam. Explorers of the Infinite: Shapers of Science Fiction. Cleveland and New York, 1963.

_____. The Immortal Storm: A History of Science Fiction Fandom. Atlanta, 1954.

_____. Seekers of Tomorrow: Masters of Modern Science Fiction. Cleveland and New York, 1966.

Murch, A[lma] E[lizabeth]. The Development of the Detective Novel. New York, 1958.

Nemecek, Zdenek. "Karel Capek," in Joseph Remenyi et al., World Literatures. Pittsburgh, 1956.

Nicolson, Marjorie Hope. Voyages to the Moon. New York, 1948.

O'Hara, Robert C. Media for the Millions: The Process of Mass Communications. New York, 1962.

Panshin, Alexei. Heinlein in Dimension: A Critical Analysis. Chicago, 1968.

Parrington, Vernon L., Jr. American Dreams, 2nd ed. Brown University Studies, 11. New York, 1964

Prehoda, Robert W. Designing the Future: The Role of Technological Forecasting. Philadelphia, 1967.

Read, Herbert. "Fantasy," pp. 136-151 in English Prose Style. Boston, 1952.

Robbins, Rossell Hope. The Encyclopedia of Witchcraft and Demonology. New York, 1959.

Rogers, Alva. A Requiem for "Astounding." Chicago, 1964.

Rosenberg, Bernard, and White, David Manning, eds. Mass Culture: The Popular Arts in America. Glencoe, Illinois, 1957.

Ruyer, Raymond. L'Utopie et les utopies. Paris, 1950.

Scarborough, Dorothy. The Supernatural in Modern English Fiction. New York and London, 1917.

Schlismann, Aloys Rob. Beiträge zur Geschichte und Kritik des Naturalismus. Kiel and Leipzig, 1903.

Schoeck, Helmut, and Wiggins, James W., eds. Scientism and Values. Princeton, 1960.

Scholes, Robert. The Fabulators. New York, 1967.

Schwonke, Martin. Vom Staatsroman zur Science Fiction: Eine Untersuchung über Geschichte und Funktion der naturwissenschaftlich-technischen Utopie. Göttinger Abhandlungen zur Soziologie, 2. Stuttgart, 1957.

Siclier, Jacques. Images de la science fiction. Paris, 1958.

Small, Miriam R. "Afterword," pp. 359-366, Signet Classic edition of Oliver Wendell Holmes, Elsie Venner. New York, 1961.

Snow, C. P. The Two Cultures and the Scientific Revolution. New York, 1959.

Sontag, Susan. "Imagination of Disaster," in Against Interpretation and Other Essays. New York, 1966.

Spender, Stephen. The Struggle of the Modern. Berkeley and Los Angeles, 1965.

Summers, Montague. The Gothic Quest: A History of the Gothic Novel. London, [1938].

Sypher, Wylie, ed. Comedy. Garden City, 1956.

Tolkien, J. R. R. "On Fairy-Stories," Tree and Leaf, London, 1964.

Wagar, W. Warren. H. G. Wells and the World State. New Haven, 1961.

Wheeler, Raymond Holder. The Science of Psychology: An Introductory Study. New York, 1929.

Yershov, Peter. Science Fiction and Utopian Fantasy in Soviet Literature. New York, 1954.

Zola, Emile. The Experimental Novel and Other Essays, trans. Belle M. Sherman. New York, 1893.

II. Magazine Articles

Alphabetical listing by authors, excluding book reviews specifically related to one of the six novels studied (see Bibliography B, section III), continuing book review columns and features in science fiction magazines (Bibliography B, section IV), introductions and essays in anthologies of science fiction stories (Bibliography A, section II), and essays in books (Bibliography B, section I).

Adams, J. Donald. "Speaking of Books," New York Times Book Review, July 12, 1953, p. 2; September 13, 1953, p. 2.

Aldiss, Brian. "British Science Fiction Now," S F Horizons, 2 (Winter, 1965), 13-37.

Amis, Kingsley. "Science Fiction: A Practical Nightmare," Holiday, February, 1965, pp. 8-15.

Anonymous. "Outpaced by Space," review of The Year's Best S-F, 7th Annual Edition, ed. Judith Merril, Time, January 4, 1963, pp. 71-72.

_____. "Overtaking the Future," Newsweek, October 8, 1962, p. 104.

_____. "Science Fiction Rockets into Big Time," Business Week, October 20, 1951, pp. 82-84, 89.

Asimov, Isaac. "Fact Catches Up with Fiction," New York Times Magazine, November 19, 1961, pp. 34, 39, 42, 44.

Ballard, J. G. "Which Way to Inner Space," guest editorial, New Worlds, May, 1962, pp. 2-3, 116-118.

Bernabev, Ednita P. "Science Fiction: A New Mythos," The Psychoanalytic Quarterly, XXVI, 4 (1957), 527-535.

Blish, James. "Theodore Sturgeon's Microcosm," F&SF, September, 1962, pp. 42-45.

Campbell, John W., Jr. "Portrait of You," Astounding, May, 1958, pp. 135-136.

_____. "Science Fact and Science Fiction," Writer, August, 1964, pp. 26-27.

_____. "Science-Fiction and the Opinion of the Universe," Saturday Review, May 12, 1956, pp. 9-10, 42-43.

_____. "The Science of Science Fiction," The Atlantic Monthly, May, 1948, pp. 97-98.

Clement, Hal. "Whirligig World," Astounding, June, 1953, pp. 102-114.

Frank, Stanley. "Out of This World," Nation's Business, March, 1952, pp. 41-42, 80-81.

Gardner, Martin. "Humorous Science Fiction," Writer, May, 1949, pp. 148-151.

Gibbs, Angelica. "Onward and Upward with the Arts: Inertrum, Neutronium, Chromaloy, P-P-P-Proot!" The New Yorker, February 13, 1943, pp. 42, 44, 47-48, 50, 52-53.

Harrison, Harry. "We Are Sitting on Our . . . ," S F Horizons, 1 (Spring, 1964), 39-42.

Häusermann, H. W. "Science Fiction, a New Kind of Mass Literature," Levende Talen (Brussels), CLXXXI (1955), 394-405.

Hillegas, Mark R. "A Draft of the Science-Fiction Canon to be Proposed at the 1961 MLA Conference on Science Fiction," Extrapolation, III (December, 1961), 26-30.

_____. "Dystopian Science Fiction: New Index to the Human Situation," New Mexico Quarterly, XXXI, 3 (Autumn, 1961), 238-249.

Hirsch, Walter. "The Image of the Scientist in Science Fiction: A Content Analysis," American Journal of Sociology, LXIII, 5 (March, 1958), 506-512.

Kostolefsky, Joseph. "Science, Yes--Fiction, Maybe," Antioch Review, XIII, 2 (June, 1953), 236-240.

Lear, John. "Let's Put Some Science into Science-Fiction," Popular Science Monthly, August, 1954, pp. 135-137, 244, 246, 248.

Mandel, Siegfried, and Fingesten, Peter. "The Myth of Science Fiction," Saturday Review, August 27, 1955, pp. 7-8, 24-25, 28.

McComas, J. Francis. "The Spaceman's Little Nova," New York Times Book Review, November 20, 1955, p. 53.

McDonnell, Thomas P. "The Cult of Science Fiction," Catholic World, October, 1953, pp. 15-18.

Merril, Judith. "Theodore Sturgeon," F&SF, September, 1962, pp. 46-55.

_____. "What Do You Mean--Science?/Fiction?" Extrapolation, VII (May, 1966), 30-46; VIII (December, 1966), 2-19.

Michaelson, L. W. "Science Fiction, Censorship, and Pie-in-the-Sky," Western Humanities Review, XIII, 4 (Autumn, 1959), 409-413.

Miller, Walter M., Jr. "Bobby and Jimmy," Nation, April 7, 1962, pp. 300-303.

Morse, C. Robert. "The Game of If," review of The Best from "Fantasy and Science Fiction," 7th Series, ed. Anthony Boucher, National Review, May 3, 1958, pp. 427-428.

Muller, Hermann J. "Science Fiction as an Escape," The Humanist, XVII, 6 (1957), 333-346.

Nathan, Paul S. "Books into Films," Publisher's Weekly, June 18, 1949, p. 2463.

O'Neil, P. "Barnum of the Space Age," Life, July 26, 1963, pp. 62-64.

Plank, Robert. "The Golem and the Robot," Literature and Psychology, XV, 1 (Winter, 1965), 12-28.

Pohl, Frederik. "Three in a Row," editorial, IF, December, 1968, p. 4.

Pratt, Fletcher. "Time, Space, and Literature," Saturday Review, July 28, 1951, pp. 16-17, 27-28.

Priestley, J. B. "Thoughts in the Wilderness: They Come from Inner Space," New Statesman and Nation, December 5, 1953, pp. 712, 714.

Smith, Godfrey. "Astounding Story! About a Science Fiction Writer," New York Times Magazine, March 6, 1966, pp. 28, 75-77.

Stine, G. Harry. "Science Fiction is Too Conservative," Analog, May, 1961, pp. 83-99.

Sturgeon, Theodore. "Most Personal," guest editorial, IF, November, 1962, p. 6.

Tunley, Roul. "Unbelievable But True," Saturday Evening Post, October 8, 1960, pp. 90-92.

Yaffe, James. "The Modern Trend Toward Meaningful Martians," review of Kingsley Amis, New Maps of Hell, and The Best from "Fantasy and Science Fiction," 9th Series, ed. Robert P. Mills, Saturday Review, April 23, 1960, pp. 22-23.

III. Book Reviews of Novels Studied

For each novel, the reviewers consulted are listed
alphabetically.

a. Childhood's End by Arthur C. Clarke (chapter III)

Boucher, Anthony, and McComas, J. Francis. F&SF, October,
    1953, p. 72.

Conklin, Groff. Galaxy, March, 1954, pp. 118-119.

Davenport, Basil. New York Times Book Review, August 23,
    1953, p. 19.

DuBois, William. New York Times, August 27, 1953, p. 23.

Holmes, H. H. New York Herald-Tribune Book Review, August
    23, 1953, p. 9.

Miller, P. Schuyler. Astounding, February, 1954, pp. 51-52.

Rollo, James J. The Atlantic Monthly, November, 1953,
    p. 112.

b. The Caves of Steel by Isaac Asimov (chapter IV)

Boucher, Anthony, and McComas, J. Francis. F&SF, May, 1954,
    p. 88.

Conklin, Groff. Galaxy, July, 1954, pp. 97-98.

Gerson, Villiers. New York Times, March 7, 1954, p. 16.

Holmes, H. H. New York Herald-Tribune Book Review,
    February 7, 1954, p. 10.

Miller, P. Schuyler. Astounding, November, 1954, p. 150.

Pratt, Fletcher. Saturday Review, August 7, 1954, p. 15.

c. <u>More than Human</u> by Theodore Sturgeon (chapter V)

Amis, Kingsley. <u>Spectator</u>, September 17, 1954, p. 350.

Boucher, Anthony, and McComas, J. Francis. <u>F&SF</u>, February, 1954, p. 93.

Conklin, Groff. <u>Galaxy</u>, January, 1954, pp. 128-129.

Gerson, Villiers. <u>New York Times Book Review</u>, November 22, 1953, p. 34.

Holmes, H. H. <u>New York Herald-Tribune Book Review</u>, November 22, 1953, p. 19.

Miller, P. Schuyler. <u>Astounding</u>, June, 1954, pp. 144-145.

Pratt, Fletcher. <u>Saturday Review</u>, August 7, 1954, pp. 14-15.

Richardson, Maurice. <u>New Statesman and Nation</u>. October 30, 1954, pp. 554-556.

d. <u>A Canticle for Leibowitz</u> by Walter M. Miller, Jr. (chapter VI)

Anonymous. <u>F&SF</u>, June, 1960, p. 87.

_____. <u>Time</u>, February 22, 1960, p. 110.

Balliett, Whitney. <u>The New Yorker</u>, April 2, 1960, p. 159.

Coleman, John. <u>Spectator</u>, March 25, 1960, pp. 444-445.

Fuller, Edmund. <u>Chicago Sunday Tribune</u>, March 6, 1960, p. 1.

Gale, Floyd C. <u>Galaxy</u>, February, 1961, p. 139.

Kennebeck, Edwin. <u>Commonweal</u>, March 4, 1960, pp. 632-634.

Klein, Marcus. <u>Nation</u>, November 19, 1960, pp. 398-402.

Levin, Martin. <u>New York Times Book Review</u>, March 27, 1960, pp. 42-43.

Miller, P. Schuyler. <u>Analog</u>, November, 1960, p. 87.

Perrott, Roy. Manchester Guardian Weekly, April 7, 1960,
    p. 13.

Phelps, Robert. New York Herald-Tribune Book Review,
    March 13, 1960, p. 4.

Prescott, Orville. San Francisco Chronicle, March 8, 1960,
    p. 27.

Richardson, Maurice. New Statesman, April 9, 1960, p. 533.

Rowland, Stanley J. Christian Century, May 25, 1960,
    pp. 640-641.

Yaffe, James. Saturday Review, June 4, 1960, p. 21.

      e. Rogue Moon by Algis Budrys (chapter VII)

Bester, Alfred. F&SF, June, 1961, pp. 104-105.

Blish, James. F&SF, June, 1961, pp. 105-109.

Gale, Floyd C. Galaxy, February, 1962, p. 194.

Miller, P. Schuyler. Analog, June, 1961, p. 164.

      f. The Crystal World by J. G. Ballard (chapter VIII)

Levin, Martin. New York Times Book Review, May 15, 1966,
    p. 41.

Merril, Judith. F&SF, August, 1966, pp. 57-69.

Young, B. A. Punch, June 1, 1966, p. 820.

IV. Continuing Magazine Features

Alphabetical listing by authors of book review
columns and such other recurrent features as have been
cited in the text.

Boucher, Anthony. "Recommended Reading," book review
    column, F&SF, September, 1954, through January, 1959.

Boucher, Anthony, and McComas, J. Francis. "Recommended Reading," book review column, F&SF, Winter-Spring, 1950, through August, 1954.

Budrys, Algis. "Galaxy Bookshelf," book review column, Galaxy, February, 1965, through January, 1969.

Campbell, John W., Jr. "The Analytical Laboratory," monthly feature with occasional absences, Astounding/Analog, January, 1950, through January, 1969.

Merril, Judith. "Books," book review column, F&SF, monthly with occasional lapses, March, 1955, through January, 1969.

Miller, P. Schuyler. "The Reference Library," Astounding/Analog, October, 1951, through January, 1969.

Sturgeon, Theodore. "On Hand . . . Off Hand: Books," book review column, Venture, July, 1957, through July, 1958.

_____. "Science Briefs," guest editorials, and miscellaneous articles, IF, July, 1961, through March, 1964.

_____. Science fiction book review column, National Review, irregularly, September 23, 1961, through May 30, 1967

V. Handbooks and Bibliographical Guides

Listing alphabetized by compiler.

A[simov], I[saac]. "Isaac Asimov: A Bibliography," F&SF, October, 1966.

Bingenheimer, Heinz. Transgalaxis Katalog der deutschsprachigen utopisch-phantastischen Literatur 1460-1960. Friedrichsdorf, 1960.

Clarke, I. F. The Tale of the Future: From the Beginning to the Present Day: A Checklist of Those Satires, Ideal States, Imaginary Wars and Invasions, Political Warnings and Forecasts, Interplanetary Voyages, and Scientific Romances--All Located in an Imaginary Future Period--That Have Been Published in the United Kingdom Between 1644 and 1960. London, 1961.

Cole, W. R. A Checklist of Science Fiction Anthologies.
[New York], 1964.

Day, Bradford M. The Checklist of Fantastic Literature in
Paperbound Books. Denver, New York, 1965.

_____. The Complete Checklist of Science-Fiction
Magazines. Woodhaven, New York, 1961.

_____. An Index on the Weird and Fantastica in
Magazines. New York, 1953.

Day, Donald Byrne. Index to the Science Fiction Magazines,
1926-1950. Portland, Oregon, 1952.

De Camp, L. Sprague. Science-Fiction Handbook: The Writing of Imaginative Fiction. New York, 1953.

Moskowitz, Sam. "Fantasy and Science Fiction by Theodore
Sturgeon," F&SF, September, 1962, pp. 56-61.

New England Science Fiction Association. Index to the
Science Fiction Magazines, 1966, 1967. Cambridge,
Massachusetts, 1967, 1968.

Nolan, William F. "A Theodore Sturgeon Science Fiction and
Fantasy Index," pp. 105-108, Three to the Highest
Power: Bradbury, Oliver, Sturgeon, ed. William F.
Nolan. New York, 1968.

Strauss, Erwin F. The MIT Science Fiction Society's Index
to the S-F Magazines, 1951-1965. Cambridge,
Massachusetts, 1966.

Tuck, Donald H. A Handbook of Science Fiction and Fantasy,
rev. ed. 2 vols. Hobart, Tasmania, 1959.

VI. Miscellaneous Published and Unpublished Materials

a. Biographical Periodicals

Contemporary Authors: The International Bio-Bibliographical
Guide to Current Authors and Their Works. Volumes II
(Asimov, Budrys), IV (Clarke), VII-VIII (Ballard),
1963.

Current Biography. Yearbook, 1953 (Asimov); October, 1966
(Clarke).

b. Annual Statements of Ownership, Management, and
Circulation. Including circulation figures,
required by law, for 1960 and the
years following.

<u>Astounding/Analog</u>. December issues, 1960-1968.

<u>F&SF</u>. January issues, 1961-1969.

<u>Galaxy</u>. February, 1961; April, 1962-1964; February, 1965;
April, 1966-1967; February, 1968; January 1969.

c. Booksellers' Catalogs

F&SF Book Co., P. O. Box 415, Staten Island, New York
10302. List No. 93, Fall, 1968.

Fantast (Medway) Ltd., 75 Norfolk Street, Wisbech, Cambs.,
England. Monthly catalogues, May through October,
1968.

d. Doctoral Dissertations

Clareson, Thomas Dean. "The Emergence of American Science
Fiction: 1880-1915: A Study of the Impact of Science
upon American Romanticism." Unpublished dissertation,
University of Pennsylvania, 1956.

Hirsch, Walter. "American Science Fiction, 1926-1950:
A Content Analysis." Unpublished dissertation,
Northwestern University, 1957.

Topik, Fred S. "Utopische Gedanken in modernen deutschen
Romanen, 1930 bis 1951." Unpublished dissertation,
University of Southern California, 1956.

e. Lectures

Friedrichs, Robert. Sociology course, "Introduction to
Cultural Anthropology," Drew University, Fall, 1958.

Herbert, Frank. "How to Make a World," 22nd World Science
Fiction Convention, September, 1964, Oakland,
California.

f. Correspondence

Moskowitz, Sam. Letter from Newark, New Jersey, February, 1963.

Scheidt, Jürgen von. Letters from Munich, West Germany, March, 1963; May, 1963; July, 1964.

Versins, Pierre. Letters from Lausanne, Switzerland, February, 1963; February, 1964.

g. Conversations

Ackermann, Forrest. Irregular, 1963-1966, Los Angeles, California.

Raguse, Siegfried. Three meetings, March through May, 1965, Berlin, Germany.

SCIENCE FICTION

An Arno Press Collection

FICTION

About, Edmond. **The Man with the Broken Ear.** 1872

Allen, Grant. **The British Barbarians:** A Hill-Top Novel. 1895

Arnold, Edwin L. **Lieut. Gullivar Jones:** His Vacation. 1905

Ash, Fenton. **A Trip to Mars.** 1909

Aubrey, Frank. **A Queen of Atlantis.** 1899

Bargone, Charles (Claude Farrere, pseud.). **Useless Hands.** [1926]

Beale, Charles Willing. **The Secret of the Earth.** 1899

Bell, Eric Temple (John Taine, pseud.). **Before the Dawn.** 1934

Benson, Robert Hugh. **Lord of the World.** 1908

Beresford, J. D. **The Hampdenshire Wonder.** 1911

Bradshaw, William R. **The Goddess of Atvatabar.** 1892

Capek, Karel. **Krakatit.** 1925

Chambers, Robert W. **The Gay Rebellion.** 1913

Colomb, P. et al. **The Great War of 189—.** 1893

Cook, William Wallace. **Adrift in the Unknown.** n.d.

Cummings, Ray. **The Man Who Mastered Time.** 1929

[DeMille, James]. **A Strange Manuscript Found in a Copper Cylinder.** 1888

Dixon, Thomas. **The Fall of a Nation:** A Sequel to the Birth of a Nation. 1916

England, George Allan. **The Golden Blight.** 1916

Fawcett, E. Douglas. **Hartmann the Anarchist.** 1893

Flammarion, Camille. **Omega:** The Last Days of the World. 1894

Grant, Robert et al. **The King's Men:** A Tale of To-Morrow. 1884

Grautoff, Ferdinand Heinrich (Parabellum, pseud.). **Banzai!** 1909

Graves, C. L. and E. V. Lucas. **The War of the Wenuses.** 1898

Greer, Tom. **A Modern Daedalus.** [1887]

Griffith, George. **A Honeymoon in Space.** 1901

Grousset, Paschal (A. Laurie, pseud.). **The Conquest of the Moon.** 1894

Haggard, H. Rider. **When the World Shook.** 1919

Hernaman-Johnson, F. **The Polyphemes.** 1906

Hyne, C. J. Cutcliffe. **Empire of the World.** [1910]

In The Future. [1875]

Jane, Fred T. **The Violet Flame.** 1899

Jefferies, Richard. **After London; Or, Wild England.** 1885

Le Queux, William. **The Great White Queen.** [1896]

London, Jack. **The Scarlet Plague.** 1915

Mitchell, John Ames. **Drowsy.** 1917

Morris, Ralph. **The Life and Astonishing Adventures of John Daniel.** 1751

Newcomb, Simon. **His Wisdom The Defender:** A Story. 1900

Paine, Albert Bigelow. **The Great White Way.** 1901

Pendray, Edward (Gawain Edwards, pseud.). **The Earth-Tube.** 1929

Reginald, R. and Douglas Menville. **Ancestral Voices:** An Anthology of Early Science Fiction. 1974

Russell, W. Clark. **The Frozen Pirate.** 2 vols. in 1. 1887

Shiel, M. P. **The Lord of the Sea.** 1901

Symmes, John Cleaves (Captain Adam Seaborn, pseud.). **Symzonia.** 1820

Train, Arthur and Robert W. Wood. **The Man Who Rocked the Earth.** 1915

Waterloo, Stanley. **The Story of Ab:** A Tale of the Time of the Cave Man. 1903

White, Stewart E. and Samuel H. Adams. **The Mystery.** 1907

Wicks, Mark. **To Mars Via the Moon.** 1911

Wright, Sydney Fowler. **Deluge: A Romance** *and* **Dawn.** 2 vols. in 1. 1928/1929

SCIENCE FICTION

NON-FICTION:
Including Bibliographies,
Checklists and Literary Criticism

Aldiss, Brian and Harry Harrison. **SF Horizons.** 2 vols. in 1. 1964/1965

Amis, Kingsley. **New Maps of Hell.** 1960

Barnes, Myra. **Linguistics and Languages in Science Fiction-Fantasy.** 1974

Cockcroft, T. G. L. **Index to the Weird Fiction Magazines.** 2 vols. in 1 1962/1964

Cole, W. R. **A Checklist of Science-Fiction Anthologies.** 1964

Crawford, Joseph H. et al. **"333": A Bibliography of the Science-Fantasy Novel.** 1953

Day, Bradford M. **The Checklist of Fantastic Literature in Paperbound Books.** 1965

Day, Bradford M. **The Supplemental Checklist of Fantastic Literature.** 1963

Gove, Philip Babcock. **The Imaginary Voyage in Prose Fiction.** 1941

Green, Roger Lancelyn. **Into Other Worlds:** Space-Flight in Fiction, From Lucian to Lewis. 1958

Menville, Douglas. **A Historical and Critical Survey of the Science Fiction Film.** 1974

Reginald, R. **Contemporary Science Fiction Authors,** First Edition. 1970

Samuelson, David. **Visions of Tomorow:** Six Journeys from Outer to Inner Space. 1974